Future Hum

Time For New Thinking

By Diane Tessman

Published by

FLYING DISK PRESS

4 St Michaels Avenue

Pontefract, West Yorkshire

England

WF8 4QX

To Kathleen, my star friend
Love, Peace,
Diane T.
6/14/2020

Copyright © 2020 by Diane Tessman. All rights reserved. Without limiting the rights under copyright reserved above, no part of this publication may be reproduced, stored in, or introduced into a retrieval system, or transmitted in any form by any means (electronics, mechanical, photocopying, recording or otherwise), without the prior written permission of both the copyright owner and the publisher of this book. Names and specific locations, when necessary, have been changed to protect the identity of individuals who are still living at the time of this publication. All stories are based on true events. Cover design is copyright © Sebastian Woszczyk.

CONTENTS

Introduction : Page 3

Prelude : Page 8

Chapter One: Time Travelers, Our Simultaneous Others : Page 10

Chapter Two: Tic-Tac Capsule UFOs : Page 24

Chapter Three: Future Humans Over Missile Silos, Nuclear Waste Deep in Future Earth : Page 40

Chapter Four: Sarfatti's Low Power Warp : Page 63

Chapter Five: There Are Always Possibilities : Page 72

Chapter Six: Jacques Vallee and The Others of Earth : Page 82

Chapter Seven: "The Singularity of Humanoid Life." : Page 95

Chapter Eight: Abductions in a New Light : Page 107

Chapter Nine: The Technology of Time Travelers : Page 144

Chapter Ten: ESP or Time Travelers' Nanochips? : Page 170

Chapter Eleven: Ancient Time Travelers : Page 180

Chapter Twelve: That's Just Us : Page 207

Chapter Thirteen: Consciousness Voyage : Page 210

Further Reading: Page 239

Introduction

I do not deny that there are probably thousands of advanced extraterrestrial races in the galaxy and that some may visit Earth. However, I think we have ignored what is right before our eyes; our children's children's children are the occupants in most or all unidentified flying objects!

The Golden Age of Science and Technology is upon us; at this moment in history, we are leaping forward in computer science, astronomy, physics, quantum physics, post-quantum physics, biomedicine, bioanthropology, neuroscience, genetic science, and more; Future Humans will use advanced forms of all that is now being laid as a foundation. Their society and who they are, will reflect this. We are their forefathers and foremothers who opened the windows on advanced knowledge and discovery.

I am not proposing spirituality based on Future Humans. I am not trying to replace extraterrestrials gods with Future Human gods. Of course, believe as you wish, but it is time for new thinking; it is time to set forth the very strong case for human time travelers as the source of UFOs. Incidentally, I am sure Future Humans are imperfect; it is unlikely that we humans will ever escape our flaws and become gods. Coincidentally, UFO occupants are not perfect, either.

Note: I capitalize "Future Humans" to illustrate a functioning, cohesive group.

Ironically, we current humans do not recognize evidence that we are being visited by ourselves (humans or post-humans traveling back from the future); the evidence is there, but it seems to be inconsequential to us. We have a mental block about believing our species has any worthy role in the future; instead, we figure the extraterrestrials have all that magic and have advanced incredibly far. We sell ourselves short.

Why did we assume in 1947 that Kenneth Arnold's "flying saucers" were piloted by aliens from a far-distant planet? It seems to have been partially a knee-jerk reaction due to human fascination and fear regarding alien life-forms, as reflected in Hollywood movies. Time travel is used in science fiction stories, but it simply doesn't pack that punch of fear and adrenaline that aliens do.

It is much easier to believe that extraterrestrials traverse unfathomable distances of interstellar space, than to believe that in the future, humans will find the key to traveling back in time. The suggestion that UFO occupants are humans or post-humans, is always greeted with, "But traveling back in time is impossible, so that ends that." Einstein never said traveling back in time is impossible.

What little confidence we have in ourselves and in our human curiosity and potential!

Incidentally, 500 light years, which is a relatively close distance from Earth compared to most of the universe, is 4,730,365,236,290,400,000 miles away. But many people believe beings from 500 light years away, have evolved to be identical to human beings with only tiny variations.

Occam's Razor states that the more assumptions we have to make, the more unlikely an explanation. There is only one assumption in the theory that Future Humans are the visitors in our skies; that assumption is that traveling back in time is possible and is being done. To assume we are visited by a variety of beings from far distant worlds, all are human or humanoid and some speak English, requires many more assumptions.

It is time for new thinking!

Science and technology are advancing exponentially. Quantum computers are here, and we can't yet imagine their full potential. What elusive, complicated, and speedy quantum equations will quantum computers offer? We'll have a look at quantum computers in our "Technology of Time Travelers" chapter.

Today, physicists research warping space, nullifying gravity, going back in time, and more. One promising theory by theoretical physicist Dr. Jack Sarfatti, uses quantum metamaterials to produce "low power warp," while staying true to Einstein's General and Special Theories of Relativity. In our interview herein, Dr. Sarfatti will explain it so that non-physicists like me, get the gist of it. He also gives us his equation for "low power warp," which creates a zero gravity bubble.

The Tic-Tac capsules with which the U.S. Navy interacts, demonstrate movements which do line up with Dr. Sarfatti's research. Here is the probable open door, not just to warping space, not just to zero-gravity, but the open door to traveling back in time. Of course, if the government(s) decide to build and test such a project, that would be the next step.

We will delve into exciting research offered exclusively for this book, with Dr. Michael Paul Masters, professor of biological anthropology, specializing in evolutionary anatomy, who offers expertise on reports of UFO occupants which describe basic human anatomy. It is very difficult to find an occupant report which is *not* humanoid or human. Dr. Masters offers the facts of genetic evolution which go in the direction of "us" becoming "them," in time.

We analyze the USS Nimitz and Roosevelt events of 2004 and 2014, 2015; we dive into theories on unidentified submerged objects (USOs), and the (future) human connection to oceans.

We examine how our missile defense system has been shut down on a variety of occasions by UFOs. Specifically, we look at Malmstrom, Minot, and Loring Air Force Bases and detail these events. Who would want their Earth *not* to be contaminated for centuries with radiation? Could the answer be humans in future time?

Chernobyl, Fukushima: Are they warnings of something even worse which will happen? There has been a preponderance of UFOs over nuclear power plants of all kinds since the 1960s and we offer case by case specifics.

Profiling UFO occupants is something which has seldom been done; in these chapters, we profile as the police do regarding suspects, and receive a clear picture of "them" and their reasons for being here, in this time. It is their planet too.

A respected pillar of UFO research and author of many intriguing books such as **Dimensions** and **Messengers of Deception,** Jacques Vallee offers a research paper which postulates "the hidden Others" and why they may well have an earthly origin. Jacques gives his approval and blessings on our efforts here and the use of his research paper.

Abductions hold many clues to the identity of UFO occupants; we take another look at well-documented, solid-case abductions to see if there are clues or indications that Future Humans were the abductors. I also offer little known facts on my own abductions. This chapter offers an open and different view on abductions.

Any book on Future Humans must include the possibility that the human race will become artificial intelligence, which carries enormous implications and questions. Is this what it means to be human in the future? If so, should we of the 21st Century, fear or embrace this future? These times are too critical to revert to knee-jerk reactions created by science fiction tales each time "AI" is mentioned.

If Future Humans can travel back to our moment in the 21st Century, they can travel back to any moment in Earth's history. Our chapter "Ancient Travelers" looks at indicators that time travelers have indeed done this over the millennia. It is their human history, too. Might they have posed as gods? Why would they have done that? Are there records of UFO occupant sightings throughout history which might offer evidence that it was humans in incredible flying machines?

The final chapter "Consciousness Calling," explores the connection which ties us to our ancestors and to our descendants. I feel that this link, this DNA/consciousness connection, is a major reason why Future Humans travel back into their own history and it is therefore one of the main reasons for the UFO phenomenon. The other reason is probably something more self-serving on the part of Future Humans. We can be a selfish species.

Is there contact with Future Humans in ways other than UFO encounters? Is this contact "psychic" or do the time travelers use advanced technology to upload information into our collective consciousness?

The Focus of This Book: I am featuring important UFO events (the classic, proven events, if you will), which have been thoroughly investigated, rather than highlighting recent/current UFO events and images.

My reason: There was less fake photography and possibly fewer fake stories in the earlier days – and no fake videos. Both investigators and witnesses were more likely to be honest and truthful before we became (subconsciously) influenced by all sorts of commercial UFO story-telling such as Hollywood films and social media.

The second reason is that I am building the case for Future Humans as the primary answer regarding UFOs, by re-examining iconic cases and concepts which point toward, "UFOs are real" but which then assume the UFO occupants are extraterrestrial. I am offering the strong evidence that UFOs are indeed real, but I offer a new perspective which points to human time travelers.

***

Prelude

"There are places to go beyond belief." – Neil Armstrong

Neil Armstrong gave us this promise: At this very moment in the Eternal Now, there are places we are going beyond belief. Did he have knowledge of time travelers from our future? Perhaps not, but this quotation hints at his "knowingness," which proclaimed that we as a species will make it through these dark times. We will rejuvenate our beautiful planet, we will travel space/time, and we will succeed as a worthy species. In doubting our own future as we do, we kill not only hope for the future, but our own worth.

If there were certain knowledge that we did make it into the future, and that we possess incredible scientific abilities - and that we as a species are of good intent - wouldn't this send shockwaves of hope, inspiration, and heightened awareness, throughout all of Earth's human tribes? Consider how the entire world thrilled to Apollo 11's moon walk! That would pale compared to the truth becoming known that it is Future Humans – we ourselves – who have been inside those UFOs all these years!

Certainly, it is worth looking at the evidence and research.

Have you ever stretched out under the stars on a summer night and had a deep conversation with yourself, your offspring, your friend, or even your dog, on how weird "time" is? Perhaps this was something you did when very young or in college, because you've been too busy for the past 40 years earning money for the family. However, the question is a profound one.

A few thoughts under the starry summer sky: Humans are all over the surface of Mother Earth in every layer of time which is laid down. The prehistoric time-layer is still right here, in the same exact spot as we now live. To the cave men, it is the Eternal Now, just as it is for us, today. We never are in the past, we never are in the future, and we only are in "the Now."

So, the Eternal Now is a crowded place! The next layer which is laid down upon this infinite moment in time, is the layer of "ancient times" as humankind begins to expand and invent; survival and curiosity drive humans, the same as they do today.

Layer upon layer is laid upon the same spot, Planet Earth, and by the same race of beings: Homo sapiens. Light years of space do not separate us, only "time."

What if, with advanced science and technology, humans in the future find a way to drill through those layers of time? They might have found the shortcut, folding that inscrutable commodity called "time," which Einstein and all physicists have said, is relative and simultaneous. "All time happens at once" becomes discernible truth, not just the ranting of a genius.

* * *

Chapter One: Time Travelers, Our Simultaneous Others

"Ultimately, all moments are really one, therefore now is an eternity." - David Bohm, theoretical physicist

No wonder current governments and militaries have tried so hard to keep the common people from knowing that our visitors are human time travelers! After the initial shock, many people would feel secure in offering friendship to alternate humans who are not scary aliens after all. Future Humans are familiar to our collective psyche.

We often say that the powers-that-be fear Disclosure (of extraterrestrials) will threaten their grip on the populace; then what about another group of humans with advanced science to cure cancer, eliminate hunger, and create a whole new paradigm of planetary civilization? Talk about a threat to the powers-that-be!

I suspect the time travelers' laws and policies would not allow them to woo away the current population from the powers-that-be, at least not overtly. They may place their efforts on covertly nudging us to "wake up!" If so, this would happen normally within the timeline, anyway, per the Novikov Self-Consistency Theory (details in later chapter).

The Future Humans must have a non-interference directive. The "Prime Directive" is a good place to begin:

Seven Logical Reasons Why UFO Occupants Are Future Humans:

Reason 1: Who Needs a Prime Directive? It does seem that extraterrestrials from far distant planets, should have said "Hello!" by now to the people of Earth. Or if you look at the dark side, it seems they should have conquered Earth by now and taken our beautiful world for their own. Neither of these have happened.

Yes, perhaps aliens just want to observe, but the modern UFO era is commonly believed to have begun in 1947, and UFO occupants still seem to be doing what they did in the first place. "Still just observing" doesn't make sense. It's a big galaxy and you'd think extraterrestrials would want to move on. They would be enthusiastic, tenacious explorers to have found Earth in the first place in the vast universe, and thus would have insatiable curiosity to explore more worlds.

If we are such a violent race that extraterrestrials don't feel safe meeting us in person, there is always SETI (Search for Extraterrestrial Intelligence), television, the Internet. Hello? Hello? At any rate, it seems they would move on at some point or else put some sweeping plan for Earth into action.

There may well be a non-interference directive which makes the most sense if it is the policy of time traveling Future Humans, not extraterrestrials. "We sure don't want to negate our own future or mess up the rightful timeline, and our ancestors are not yet ready to know of us!" does make sense.

It is probable that Future Humans are not allowed to make their identity known to unknowing 21st Century primitive folk. The presence of advanced human time travelers throughout human history opens a Pandora's Box which would shake religions to their core. The history and foundation of all Earth cultures would be called into question. We would have to wonder if some heroes and villains of religion and history, were Future Humans. And that is the tip of this iceberg!

They do abduct current humans, but they must remain aloof, dominate the event with a degree of fear, not communicate honestly, and if need be, say they are from a distant star system.

The non-interference policy has probably been in force throughout human history, but It may have been broken a few times because, let's face it, humans usually break the rules eventually. Also, there may be planned interference from whoever is in charge of the Future Human crew; such ideas give rise to science fiction stories but, at this point, we simply do not know the loops, complications, the rights and the wrongs, of traveling back in time.

The Greek gods and the "ancient astronauts" who might have had a hand in creating the stone monolithic structures found around the globe, were possibly Future Humans. In ancient times, they mingled, influenced, and even dictated certain events and advancements. At the least, they may have begun the myths and legends of culture and civilization around the planet. It is believed by some that it was extraterrestrials who interacted with ancient humans; I believe that if interaction happened at all, it is more likely it was with Future Humans. We will take a closer look at this topic in another chapter.

From the Future Human point of view, not testing that old "I killed my grandfather" paradox is highly preferable, so time traveling back into your own roots is probably not advised, but being human, they have done so anyway. Even if this paradoxical grandfather question is not the insurmountable time travel problem it is said to be, but no use of giving one's great, great, great grandfather, a heart attack. Our chapter with the Novikov Principle goes into the "Grandfather Paradox" and shows how the time traveler cannot kill his grandfather according to physics – an impossibility. We'll attempt to explain some other "fun" physics/time oddities too.

I believe that when the people of 21st Century Earth discover the secret of the UFO puzzle; we will have done so on our own except for covert nudges. This is probably the best option.

After that first excitement and possible chaos of discovering "It is us!" we will cross an evolutionary threshold. Our step upward on the awareness ladder may mean that not only Future Humans will then share knowledge with us, but also perhaps real extraterrestrials will say hello. Perhaps these "Others" (Future Humans and a variety of extraterrestrials), will offer us only limited information at first, but we will have broken out of the darkness at long last. We will no longer be chained to time and ignorance. Even if none of them then share with us, we will have reinvigorated ourselves as a species.

I do feel there is a huge distinction among universal entities, which is: "Those who are not chained by "time" and those who are still in the dark as time's prisoners.

I feel the evidence shows, Future Humans are not angels in terms of behavior and motivation, but I believe they (we) have evolved over the years to be better as a species than we are now.

I believe the Future Human component is a major part of UFO Disclosure, which is being given even now in tiny droplets like a leaky faucet.

It has been said that current authorities fear they will lose their power when Earth's people finally have complete Disclosure. The power held over us by governments and religions is a tenuous one even if it seems insurmountable.

How empowered we will be to learn that we made it into the future and are a worthy species of the future! Therefore, we are worthy *now,* because present and future are simultaneous, or put more simply, "they" are not the "great unknown," but are connected to us beyond any undoing. This is, I feel, the most important human milestone of all.

Reason 2: Who Needs Human DNA? During abductions, UFO occupants sometimes take a tissue sample of their "catch and release" human subject, or a medical procedure is performed. For instance, during one of my abductions, a membrane was removed from my mouth. It has always seemed to me that a race of aliens from many light years away, would not benefit from our unique DNA. It is likely that human DNA and an earthworm's DNA have more in common than do human DNA and extraterrestrial DNA.

It is established that tissue samples have been taken from abductees, and so I ask, who would most likely benefit from human DNA? Who, for instance, would want to remove the likelihood of developing cancer from human DNA so that we do not get this dreaded condition in the future? Who would want most to eliminate birth defects in human genes?

Yet, perhaps Future Humans must not interfere with the present so are forbidden by policy to help cancer patients of the present. Or being skeptical, perhaps they don't care "enough," or perhaps they simply cannot heal the entire current world, similar to someone not being able to save every dog and cat at a shelter. In any of these examples, we as humans know similar feelings when we are asked to help a number of complex, tragic, situations all at once.

That said, there are many instances of UFO occupants apparently healing humans of the 20th/21st Century who are ill.

Footnote 1: UFO Healings, by Preston Dennett, Wild Flower Press, October 1996

I suffered from what was probably the beginning stages of childhood leukemia before I was abducted twice at age four; less than half a year later, I was bouncing off the ceiling, doing cartwheels around the house and climbing tall trees – after 2 abductions wherein at least one medical procedure was done.

Perhaps a non-interference directive prohibits "mass healing," such as correcting the genes in everyone which allow cancer to form. That step forward on the evolutionary ladder is something the current human race must do for ourselves. "The gods" cannot come down and tie our shoes for us; also, there may be a set progression of our accomplishments as a species, which can be viewed from a vantage point in the future.

We simply do not know the specific answers to such questions, but logical clues remain that a lot of evidence points to Future Humans. The behavior of UFO occupants regarding human health crises like cancer, could be extraterrestrial behavior, but our descendants have a bigger stake in our genes than aliens do.

A possibility: Future Humans may conduct genetic research having encountered species-wide sterility following nuclear war, or because their DNA is damaged from extreme environmental contamination on Earth. Humans of the current era have allowed this environmental contamination and over-development, but it is our great grandchildren who will pay the highest price. What undesirable gene mutations will have occurred?

Another possibility: Perhaps centuries of deep space flight has exposed Future Humans to radiation which has damaged their DNA. Our species may have had to go to deep space, looking for a new planet as Earth became uninhabitable.

These are speculations. One thing is clear, what we do today, matters tomorrow.

Our species' sperm count is falling. "Sperm counts in men from America, Europe, Australia and New Zealand have dropped by more than 50 percent in less than 40 years," says Hagai Levine, who co-led research at the Hebrew University-Hadassah Braun School of Public Health and Community Medicine in Jerusalem.

This analysis did not explore reasons for the decline but falling sperm counts have previously been linked to various factors such as exposure to certain chemicals and pesticides, smoking, stress and obesity.

Footnote 2: Newsweek, article by Brian Walsh, "Male Infertility Crisis Has U.S. Experts Baffled," September 12, 2017

Future Humans might want to research and somehow use (or need) human DNA from before the time of the human race's sterility. My own abductions were in 1952; many abductions took place in the 1950's, 1960's, and 1970's.

Perhaps time travelers are researching what year Chernobyl or Fukushima's radioactivity begin to show real damage to human DNA. Were there fewer damaged genes in a child who lived in 1898 than 2020? These are the kind of questions our time traveling descendants may be researching.

Even if Future Humans have no pressing reason to be researching DNA from the past, it seems they would have a keener interest in studying human DNA and health throughout the centuries and millennia than extraterrestrials would. There must be intense interest in early human history, of which we today are a part.

Reason 3: UFO Occupants: Almost Always Humanoid

The vast majority of UFO abductions and encounters involve humanoids. Even the bizarre creatures Calvin Parker encountered on the west bank of the Pascagoula River in Mississippi, had a head, a torso, two arms and two legs.

The bizarre Falcon Lake, Ontario, UFO incident of May 20, 1967, in which Stephen Michalak received serious burn marks on his chest in a distinct pattern, has a human component. Michalak stated that when he carefully approached the strange craft, which looked like a bowl with a dome on top, it was emitting a humming sound and a Sulphur-like odor. On the bottom half was an opening from which muffled voices emanated. "They sounded like humans," Michalak reported. "I was able to make out two distinct voices, one with a higher pitch than the other."

Footnote 3: CBC News: "Manitoba Falcon Lake incident 'Canada's 'Best-Documented UFO Case,' Even After 50 Years," by Darren Berhardt, May 19, 2017

It might have been a 1967 military experiment but if it were the elusive, unknown UFO occupants, it is unlikely they were extraterrestrials since ETs probably don't sound like humans.

Betty Hill reported that the leader of the grey-colored little men who abducted her and husband Barney, spoke English. This would mean the leader's voice box and tongue (his speech apparatus), were the same as the human design. More on the Betty and Barney Hill in our abduction chapter.

Footnote 4: Armagh Planet.com "The Truth About Betty and Barney Hill's Star Map," By Colin Johnson, August 19, 2011

If you walk through abduction accounts and profile the abductors, it seems the "aliens" are more likely humans from a different timeframe, than they are extraterrestrials who would be "alien beyond alien." ETs are not humans from an isolated Pacific island who are not of the modern world and have strange customs and behavior; ETs would be far more "alien" than that! The humans or humanoids who abduct people, seem to be an unknown branch of humanity or at least humanoid.

It is not just the grey little men who seem to be a branch of "human." There are "golden humans" like Travis Walton encountered and "tall Nordics" who are extra tall instead of extra short (by our standards). Perhaps there are actual aliens among the long list of various UFO occupant "suspects," but certainly the majority are of human or humanoid origin. In looking through hundreds of UFO sightings and abductions, I have not found one description of the occupant(s) which is not basically "humanoid."

Human actors play aliens in movies and on television, so they may have pointy ears, have a green shade of skin, or have a big bulbous forehead, but they quite recognizably human. Yet, in the UFO field, we assume that real aliens are as human-looking as those movie and television actors - in other words, not very alien. Alas, we have only human actors to take the roles of aliens.

Kevin James Anderson is an American science-fiction author. He has written spin-off novels for **Star Wars,** and **The X-Files**. Here are is thoughts on what extraterrestrials might look:

"Look at the incredible diversity of biotypes here on Earth, all of which evolved under the same planetary environment. I don't believe an alien species from an entirely different biochemical foundation would happen to turn out with two arms, two legs, two eyes, ears, nostrils . . . two genders, warm-blooded, and so on. But, for intelligence one would assume brain capacity, and therefore the body would need some sort of protective mechanism for the vital brain—an exoskeleton, a skull, something like that."

"To build tools they would need manipulative digits, like fingers (not necessarily an opposable thumb, maybe prehensile tentacles). There would have to be a reproductive system, but it could be budding, seeding, fission, egg laying—not necessarily live, warm-blooded birth. They would require some sort of sensory

systems, the analogs of eyes, ears, smelling apparatuses. But their "eyes" would have evolved for the peak spectrum of their own sun, not necessarily ours."

"Do they live in a sea? In the clouds of a gas giant? On land? In a desert? In a jungle? They would need a way to eat or consume energy, and they would need to excrete waste. For intelligence, they'd need to communicate—by voice? Pheromones? Blinking phosphorescent patches?"

Footnote 5: Popular Mechanics: "What Would Aliens Actually Look Like? We Asked 7 Experts," By John Brandon, August 6, 2014

Aaron Rosenberg is an award-winning, bestselling novelist, children's book author, game designer and science fiction author. Here are his ideas of sentient alien life:

"Never mind the gaunt, nearly skeletal figure with the long talons and the scorpion-like tail and the mouth full of razor teeth. Never mind the little green or gray men with oversize craniums and oversize eyes and tiny mouths. Never mind the cat-men or lizard-men or dog-men or people with blue skin and strange, tattoo-like markings or odd brow ridges or pointier ears. Why would an alien look that similar to us?"

"Bilateral symmetry is actually a pretty crappy design, when you think about it. Yes, it looks nice and even but what's the point? Why have two sides exactly the same when you could have something completely different on the other side? Even the Daleks of **Dr. Who** figured this one out—they had a sucker arm on one side and a laser on the other. And bipedal? Ridiculous—one good push and we fall over. Why would another world's race evolve with that exact same design flaw? Why would another world's race grow eyes and a nose and a tongue and all the other fiddly bits we have? They wouldn't."

"Living beings evolve in response to their environment. We grew opposable thumbs so we could better grasp objects. Monkeys developed prehensile tails for the same reason. We have eyes because light breaks down into the visible end of the electromagnetic spectrum here."

"But if we had occurred on a completely different world, with different temperatures and topography and flora and fauna, we would have evolved differently. And if that other world had a completely different chemical composition, so would we. All life on Earth is carbon-based, but that wouldn't be the case *elsewhere. Life forms could be silicon-based or iron-based or anything else at all. They could have any number of arms and legs—or none at all..."*

Footnote #6, same source as Footnote #5

We must consider that we have not grasped how physically different actual aliens would likely be from humans! It would seem that the truth is staring us in the face, but we choose to ignore it.

Reason 4: Grey Aliens or Grey Humans?

What year are these Future Humans from? Once we travel time, escaping its rule over us, we are chained to no particular time or year. That is something difficult to imagine for us back in these primitive days. It is probably as easy to go back to the Year 10,000 B.C. as it is to travel to 1930 A.D. or 2020 A.D.

Traveling forward in time is, of course, already an option. For many years, forward time travel has been accepted as fact. The classic example of this is the twin scenario. One twin blasts off in a spaceship traveling close to the speed of light, and one twin stays behind on Earth. When the space-traveling twin returns to Earth, she's only aged a couple years, but finds that her Earth-bound sister has aged over the two decades of time on Earth.

Time moves slower when in the gravity-well of a massive object. The fabric of Space/Time sags like a trampoline with a bowling ball in the middle of it. The phenomenon is called "gravitational time dilation," meaning time moves slower as gravity increases. Therefore, the twin who stayed on Earth experienced a longer span of time, thus got older, than the space-going twin.

Time is indeed relative. A minute on Earth is different than a minute on Pluto. A minute on Pluto is different than a minute on Ceti Alpha 6. In the same way, a human from 2020 A.D. is different from a human in 2350 A.D. who, in turn, is different from a human in the Year 42,000 A.D.

Time will change our species as the future unfolds, but we will still have human origin and probably a human core in terms of consciousness. By "core," we mean, the core of a cat is cat-like. The core of a parrot is parrot-like, and so forth. A wolf thinks, feels, and behaves like a wolf.

One way or the other, we will change; evolution will see to that. However, it seems likely that even in the future, we will keep the basic human design and core, as our own.

It has been theorized that the Grey Aliens (capitalized to specify a cohesive group), may not be aliens at all, but humans whose genetics have been greatly altered over time naturally or possibly by the radiation and contamination of Earth in their ancestors' days (that's us). Genes mutated. Grey Aliens (humanoids) may be a group of Grey Humans (humanoids). Perhaps they are from a specific phase of the future.

Throughout the years, accounts, rumors, and tall stories of the Greys have assumed they are extraterrestrial, perhaps from Zeta Reticuli or EBEs (extraterrestrial biological entities) from somewhere far away. Perhaps they are.

However, these entities may be of human origin; they are usually shorter than current humans, are said to have large heads, atrophied digestive tracts and genitals, no hair, and non-muscular bodies, but the human design is there. The large slanted dark eyes might be an artificial intelligence sensing mechanism, giving them more information about an object than our eyes give us.

Or those huge eyes might be a protective covering, similar to goggles, possibly due to a difference in their comfort level with the sun's light as opposed to ours. Or, if they spend much of their life in artificial light, actual sunlight might cause them difficulty on their assignment, whatever that might be, on Earth, 2020.

We have an upcoming chapter with Professor Michael P. Masters, who teaches biological anthropology specializing in human evolutionary anatomy, discussing the humanoid reality in virtually all UFO occupant sightings.

And, we feature several of researcher Leonard Stringfield's cases which detailed Grey Alien corpses and what our government did with them.

Reason 5: How Far Is Far? Science fiction and some stories in Ufology, postulate that there is an ancient alien race some people call "The Preservers," who spread the humanoid seed on many planets. This is why so many extraterrestrials have human form, so the theory goes.

The "Preserver approach" first assumes there were extraterrestrials who once traveled across the unfathomable distances of the universe; second, it assumes they were so smitten with the human design that they interfered with natural evolution on countless planets to create or plant sentient humanoids, including Earth humans. Finally, it assumes these humanoids who were planted on a variety of distant worlds long ago by the Preservers, have now found Earth and decided to stay around since at least 1947, and perhaps for millennia.

The Preserver theory requires many assumptions which have no evidence or basis in truth. Like other ideas in ufology, not only is it illogical, it is also humancentric. We are a self-engrossed, egotistical species; in a sense, we still think the sun, moon, and universe revolves around us. We cannot begin to imagine how vast the universe truly is!

It is a wonder if Earth is even noticed by sentient aliens out of the 100 billion planets estimated to fill our Milky Way. As with the number of stars and galaxies, the number of exo-planets keeps growing each year as we search the galaxy with telescopes. When we look up at the stars, we are looking back in time. If a star is 100 light years away, we are seeing that star as it was 100 years ago. We gaze up at stars which aren't even in existence now.

One light year is 5.88 trillion miles. We are told that the aliens from the Pleiades Cluster visit us; that star cluster is 444.2 light years away. In answer to the incomprehensible distance involved as we multiply 5.88 trillion times 444.2, there is the assumption that the Pleiadeans have warp drive or something similar.

Aliens have all sorts of credit for their space/time travel accomplishments. And yet we don't consider that in the future, Earthers (that's us), will learn how to travel forward and backward in time within Earth's domain. Probably, we also travel deep space.

We conceitedly think that aliens come to visit us and find us so interesting that they stay year after year, millennia after millennia, and yet we lack confidence in our own future accomplishments.

There is only one assumption in the concept that Future Humans travel back in time, and that assumption is that traveling back in time is possible. To delve into the likelihood of extraterrestrials being the UFO occupants, requires many assumptions.

"No time travel back" has been our level of knowledge in the 20th and 21st Centuries, but our level of scientific knowledge is now entering a new, higher phase; physicists are opening the door to the probable scientific fact that traveling back in time is possible.

It is indeed time for new thinking!

Reason 6: Researchers of Grandparents, Internet, Flora and Fauna:

Our great, great, great grandchildren may be conducting scientific research of water, air, animals, plants, and ancestors. Perhaps they hope to discover specifically how insecticides, herbicides, plastics, and other contaminants, hurt the vigor of Earth. For instance, a child in 1952 might have less plastic in her system and less herbicide, than a child in 1980, following the wide use plastics and defoliants like Agent Orange, used in the Vietnam War.

The Internet gives a sometimes wonderful, sometimes frightening, look into the collective human consciousness of the 21st Century. Perhaps abductions, whether by aliens or Future Humans, have lessened in number, because the collective consciousness of today's humans is in full view, online. Do our visitors surf the net disguised as us? It is likely.

Extraterrestrials might perform Earth studies too, but certainly scientists of the human future, would. This is their planet. Perhaps there are university courses offering time travel as field research, going back to the days of the ancestors; this would be "Anthropology 101, Observe the Ancestors." Or, perhaps traveling back in time has more urgent and serious reasons.

It seems reasonable that extraterrestrials might have moved on to other challenges because they do not have the stake in us and our Earth as our descendants do.

Future Humans presumably have Future Earth as their home planet, and they travel to other moments in their species' history. Since many different levels of future time may be represented by Future Humans, we assume that those from "2350," have their home base at that time, and those from "42,000" consider that time period to be home. Perhaps the word "time" should not even be used beyond a certain point of our advancement.

We can only hope that the Earth which Future Humans know and probably love, is rejuvenated, honored, and protected and that they now know enough not to contaminate and cripple their own planet as we have tended to do.

What of the damage and threats we have left them? Can the climate crises be somehow corrected or rebalanced? Is there any fresh water left? How much nuclear waste have we left them deep underground and/or leaking into the ground and water? The list is long.

Reason 7: A Great Interest in All Things Nuclear

It is fact that UFO occupants have tampered with United States launch codes on nuclear warheads atop missiles in secret silos; they obviously do care about Earth. If they tampered but did not care about Earth, armed missiles might have flown or a similar catastrophic scenario might have happened.

Would ETs care about Earth as much as Future Humans do?

The entities who bother our nuclear installations seem to have a message which they must get across to us. It seems that message could be to warn us of the devastating doomsday reality of widespread nuclear radiation.

We go into dramatic detail on the "nuclear question" in upcoming chapters.

Question 8: Today, We Move Toward Artificial Intelligence; Will "AI" Be a Positive or a Negative in the Future?

It seems logical considering the lightning speed with which technology is moving, that Future Humans probably have artificial intelligence components. There are theories which state that in the not-distant future, a "quantum nanochip" can be inserted to create consciousness in artificial intelligence. AI will become fully aware (conscious), with a subjective side to its nature which contains humor, empathy, anger and general emotional complexity.

There may well be advanced post-human (AI) beings who pilot those unidentifiable craft which do incredible maneuvers and reach incredible speeds which would kill an organic (flesh and blood) human. They likely would kill an organic alien as well.

We are almost ready to embark on long distant space voyages to Mars and beyond, but organic human flesh is fragile. Natural humans cannot withstand prolonged exposure to the deadly space radiation on long voyages. Space/time is a tough place for organic humans, but not so for artificial intelligence humans (post-humans).

There is also a mental component to artificial intelligence being necessary for space exploration. Astronauts in deep space exploring strange new worlds, would be confronted with a bombardment of incoming, strange, unknown data which would require complicated but quick decisions for the welfare of the crew and ship. Having a quantum computer aspect to Captain Kirk's magnificent organic brain, would be handy.

Yes, UFO occupants might be extraterrestrial artificial intelligence but the simpler, more logical answer is, they are artificial intelligence which is rooted in AI development in our own future; that AI development is leaping ahead toward that future, even at this moment.

Do we think so little of ourselves as a species that we just don't have a future at all? Must we assume it is ETs who are the sky lords? The answer with the least complications and extended explanations: It is us!

***

Chapter Two: Tic-Tac Capsule UFOs

The Greatest Danger Facing Us Is Ourselves, an Irrational Fear of the Unknown. -- James T. Kirk

Retired Cmdr. David Fravor, who has spent 18 years as a Navy pilot, explains that nothing prepared him for the morning of November 14, 2004, as he flew his F-18 fighter jet over the Pacific Ocean near San Diego and 90 miles off Mexico. The U.S. Navy was on regular training maneuvers.

Commander Fravor witnessed something which was impossible, and yet it happened! Six Navy pilots and several ground personnel were ordered to stay quiet about these events, and they did for thirteen years. Then, the lid blew off!

Retired Navy Commander David Fravor

Here is Commander Fravor's interview with ABC News, from 2017:

Fravor says, "I can tell you; I think it was not from this world. "I'm not crazy, haven't been drinking. It was — after 18 years of flying, I've seen pretty much about everything that I can see in that realm, and this was nothing close."

"I have never seen anything in my life, in my history of flying, that has the performance, the acceleration — keep in mind this thing had no wings," Fravor said.

He recalled flying his F/A-18 fighter on a training mission on a beautiful Southern California day 13 years ago when things started to get strange. Controllers on one of the Navy ships in the water below, reported objects that were dropping out of the sky from 80,000 feet and going "straight back up," Fravor said.

"So we're thinking, OK, this is going to be interesting," he said.

As they were looking around for the object that appeared on the radar, another aviator spotted something. "I was like, 'Dude, do you see that?'" Fravor recalled saying.

"We look down, we see a white disturbance in the water, like something's under the surface, and the waves are breaking over, but we see next to it, and it's flying around, and it's this little white Tic Tac, and it's moving around — left, right, forward, back, just random," he said.

The object didn't display the rotor wash typical of a helicopter or jet wash from a plane, he said.

The planes flew lower to investigate the object, which started to mirror their movements before disappearing, Fravor said. "As we start to cut across, it rapidly accelerates, climbs past our altitude and disappears," Fravor recalled.

"When it started to get near us, as we started to descend towards it coming up, it was flying in the elongated way, so it's [like] a Tic Tac, with the roundish end going in the forward direction ... I don't know what it is. I don't know what I saw. I just know it was really impressive, really fast, and I would like to fly it," he said.

The disturbance in the water also vanished with object, he remembered.

"So we turned around — we couldn't have been more than about a couple miles away — and there's no white water at all in the ocean," Fravor said. "It's just blue."

At that point, they decided to return to complete the training exercise when they were told the object or something similar reappeared.

"And the controller comes up and says, 'Sir, you're not going to believe this. That thing is at your half point,' which is our hold point," Fravor added. "And I'm like, 'Oh, great.'"

Another plane that launched from the aircraft carrier USS Nimitz around the same time had its radar jammed but was able to pick up the object on an infrared channel.

"He gets close enough to see a couple of objects come out of the bottom, and then all of a sudden it takes off and goes right off the side of the screen and, like, takes off," Fravor said.

He recalled that the speed of the object, which he said had no exhaust trail in infrared scanning, was stunning. There were not plumes, wings, or rotors and outran out F-18s, but "I want to fly one," exclaimed Flavor.

"No aircraft that we know of can fly at those speeds, maneuver like that and looks like that," ABC News contributor and former Marine Col. Stephen Ganyard said.

Fravor said there is no rational explanation for what they saw that day.

"I don't know if it was alien life, but I will say that in an infinite universe, with multiple galaxies that we know of, that if we're the only planet with life, it's a pretty lonely universe."

There was no further investigation into the incident, he said.

"You know, you see a lot of interesting things," Fravor said. "But to show up on something that's a 40-foot-long white Tic Tac with no wings that can move, really, in any random direction that it wants and go from hovering over the ocean to mirroring us to accelerating to the point where it just disappears — like, poof, then it was gone."

Footnote 7: ABC News, "Navy Pilot Recalls Encounter with UFO: 'I Think It Was Not From This World'" by Kelly McCarthy, December 18, 2017

Profiling the Tic-Tac Pilots:

"Loose formations of five to ten strange craft (shaped like Tic-Tacs, the breath mint), had showed up on the U.S.S. Princeton's radar repeatedly before the Navy's Super Hornet F-18 jets took to the sky to investigate; Tic-Tacs had been seen on radar on previous days. Did the pilots of the Tic-Tac capsules not care that they showed up on radar?

UFO Occupant Profile: Either the Tic-Tac pilots did not know about "radar" or they didn't care if they were on the Navy's radar; perhaps they even wanted to register on it. It makes little sense that either extraterrestrials or Future Humans would not know about 21st Century radar, and so it seems obvious, the unknown visitors wanted to be seen and documented or at least did not care.

Why did the Tic-Tacs want to be seen and documented, if this is the case?

Either they enjoy thumbing their noses at our military in this cat and mouse game which has gone on for many years between the military and UFO occupants, or whoever controls the Tic-Tacs is working toward UFO Disclosure in this, the early

21st Century. This passing acknowledgement by "it," that it exists, could be its way of saying a friendly hello, or it could be a policy or game plan which documents that it is time the 21st Century humans wake up.

There was no aggressive action on either side. These encounters probably would have ended in the destruction of the Navy F-18 jets if the Tic-Tacs had wanted this to be the outcome. They could make a clean getaway considering how fast they go.

This profiling of Tic-Tac behavior could indicate either extraterrestrials or Future Humans are behind the Tic-Tacs. However, the competitive attitude of the Tic-Tacs, dramatically illustrating their craft to be superior, is very similar to the Navy pilots' pride and even arrogance regarding their Super Hornet F-18 fighter jets. This seems human-like. The Tic-Tac pilots seem like skilled, hot shot military pilots.

It would be a huge coincidence if extraterrestrials from say, 500 light years away, just happen to be arrogant hot shots too, right out of **Top Gun.** Instead, extraterrestrial behavior might be to shoot the Navy jets out of the sky, or on the other extreme, ETs might get out of the area, upset at the rudeness and aggression of humans.

What purpose or mission did the Tic-Tacs have that day? Why did they not get out of the way of the F-18's? It would have been easy for the strange craft to simply get out of the way and not have been seen by the Navy pilots, thus no video taken, secrecy kept.

Just as with radar, we can assume the Tic-Tac pilots, those entities with such fantastic craft, would have information on Navy maneuvers in that area which take place on a regular basis. And that is where the Tic-Tacs chose to be that day.

Thus, either the Tic-Tacs were there to annoy the Navy and illustrate the superiority of their craft (and possibly nudge along Disclosure), or the Tic-Tacs had a purpose or mission which could not be postponed, regardless of the Navy.

If they had a mission of their own, it may have been underwater with a larger craft or vessel which made the ocean water fizz and churn.

Controllers on the U.S.S. Nimitz state that the objects were dropping out of the sky at 80,000 feet, stopping abruptly (a full stop), at 20,000 feet, then shooting off at

3,600 mph after a right angle change of direction, then zoomed straight back up, still at incredible speed many times faster than the F-18's were capable of.

(3,600 to 3,900 mph according to radar operators on the USS Princeton, part of the Nimitz carrier group).

Any portion of these Tic-tac maneuvers would have killed a human pilot unless he or she were in a zero-gravity bubble. We will get to this advanced technology in Chapter Four.

The other option is that the pilot or guidance system of the Tic-Tacs is artificial intelligence, thus no flesh and blood humans or aliens to be killed by the g-forces.

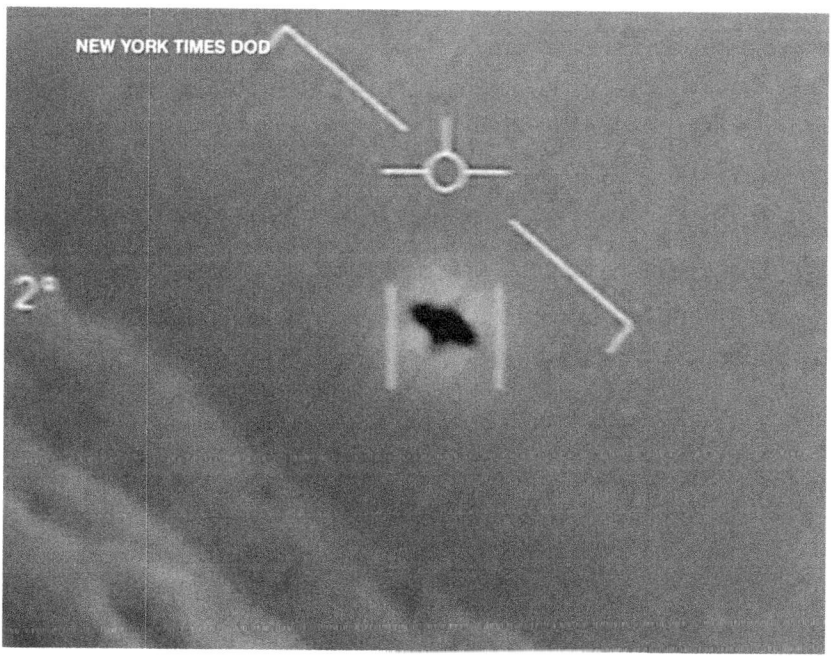

An unidentified flying object shown in a photo first obtained by the New York Times. This photo is likely from the U.S.S. Roosevelt fighter jets' Gimbal footage.

Upon the return of the first two F-18's to the Nimitz in 2004, a second team of pilots took off with advanced infrared equipment. The camera recorded an "evasive unidentified aerial system" on video, publicly released by the Pentagon on December 16, 2017.

A second infrared footage known as the "Gimbal video" was been released with the 2004 footage, but the Gimbal footage was taken over the Atlantic on the east coast; it is not related to the Nimitz encounter.

The Washington Post says that the Gimbal video was released by former intelligence officer Luis Elizondo to shed light on the secrecy with which the Department of Defense holds military interactions with UFOs, keeping it from the public. There were also Freedom of Information requests.

The Navy has now updated their protocols for pilots to report UFO sightings. Presumably we can gather that it is the U.S. military keeping the truth about UFOs under wraps, not the Future Humans and/or the extraterrestrials. The Tic-Tacs seemed happy to come say hello.

It is fortunate that whatever or whoever it is, seems not aggressive because they obviously have highly superior technology; we assume they have weapons, and we assume their weapons match the rest of their technology.

The USS Roosevelt's Encounters from Whence the Gimbal Footage Comes

In 2014 and 2015, experienced Navy pilots had several astounding experiences with UFOs during training maneuvers over U.S. waters. The jets' cameras and radar indicated objects that had no wings, no exhaust trail, non-aerodynamic shapes, and no visible means of propulsion, flying at hypersonic speeds.

Six seasoned Navy pilots stationed on the U.S.S. Roosevelt told the New York Times about seeing UFOs along the southeastern coast from Virginia to Florida. We note here that the UFOs were again over an ocean, not dry land where so many humans live.

Video of two aerial encounters appears in the series, showing clips of UFOs: one tiny white speck and one large, dark blob. These UFOs later came to be known respectively as "Go Fast" and "Gimbal."

"They had no distinct wing, no distinct tail, no distinct exhaust plume," Lt. Danny Accoin, one of the Navy pilots who reported UFO sightings beginning in 2014. "It seemed like they were aware of our presence, because they would actively move around us," Lt. Accoin said.

According to the lieutenant, when a strange reading shows up on radar for the first time, it's possible to interpret it as a false alarm, "but then when you start to get multiple sensors reading the exact same thing, and then you get to see a display, that solidifies it for me."

Accoin told The Times that he encountered UFOs twice, during flights that were a few days apart. He also said that though tracking equipment (radar and infrared cameras on his aircraft), detected the objects, he was unable to capture them on his helmet camera.

Lt. Ryan Graves, an F-18 pilot, said that a squadron of UFOs followed his Navy strike group up and down the eastern coast of the U.S. for months. And in March, 2015, after the Roosevelt was deployed to the Arabian Gulf, Graves said the UFOs reappeared.

"These things would be out there all day," Graves told the Times. "Keeping an aircraft in the air requires a significant amount of energy. With the speeds we observed, 12 hours in the air is 11 hours longer than we'd expect."

"We did have issues with them when we went out to the Middle East," Lt. Graves said.

Pilots who spotted the UFOs speculated among themselves that the unnerving objects may have belonged to a highly classified drone program using unknown technology, and they did not consider them to be extraterrestrial in origin, The New York Times reported.

Lt. Graves and others are speaking out now because what they saw raised concerns for their comrades and national security. They say there was not one or two, but an entire fleet of them.

Footnote 8: Live Science.com, "Fleet of UFOs Followed US Aircraft, Navy Pilot Says," by Mindy Weisberger, May 2019

Sean Cahill was Chief Master-At-Arms on the USS Princeton in 2004 during the "Tic-Tac" encounters which lasted multiple days. In 2004, the Princeton was a part of the Nimitz Carrier group.

Today, Sean Cahill is an independent film maker. He appears in **To the Stars Academy's** new television show entitled "Unidentified," he teaches meditation, and explores consciousness.

Sean's interview on the **Silva Record** website is compelling and inspiring; needless to say, his reference to the UFO phenomenon controlling "perhaps the arrow of time" caught my attention. In Chapter Five, we discuss the arrow of time and recent discoveries which may negate the previous belief that "the arrow" only travels forward.

If the source of UFOs is Future Humans, obviously they do have control of time; granted, extraterrestrials or some other source could also have control of time, but it is a "given," that once technology gives humans control of time, we would travel back to the days of various ancestors. As well, this is a crucial moment in time historically and in terms of evolution.

In the Silva Record's interview, here is Sean Cahill's reference to possible control of the Arrow of Time by the UFO source: *"Opportunity, Capability, and Intent, is the golden triangle. For those of us acquainted with the history of UFO encounters by our military we know that to say they have harassed our forces before is a no-brainer. The proximity to our forces gives the obvious opportunity. They exhibit the ability to out-maneuver us to an impressive degree and though I cannot confirm the veracity of any reports, it is said that their ability to destroy matter is as equally impressive as their acceleration."*

"Though it covers Opportunity and Capability, it leaves us so far with a pretty empty page on Intent. Again, I am talking what we can prove, and what we can prove about this phenomenon is not agreed upon by many but the non-threatening cases do seem to outweigh the threatening ones, in my mind because of lack of intent."

"That said, the phenomenon operates with the intent to deprive us of direct vision, knowledge, and communication on a public scale. It seems to completely control the environment and if the technology is understood, **perhaps the arrow of time**.*"*

Footnote 9: Silva Record, "Interview with Sean Cahill from TTSA's 'Unidentified'" April 27, 2019

New, Additional Information on the Tic-Tacs as of September 18, 2019: Navy Says They are Real Videos

The U.S. Navy has confirmed that three UFO videos released by **To the Stars Academy of Arts and Sciences,** a UFO research group headed by Tom DeLonge are authentic U.S. Navy videos of "unexplained aerial phenomena."

Two of the videos, both from 2015, contain audio from US fighter pilots attempting to make sense of what they're seeing.

"It's a f****g drone, bro," a pilot says to his colleague in the first clip.

"My gosh! They're all going against the wind."

"Look at that thing, dude!"

The UFOs were detected by a variety of means, including the human eye, infrared, and radar.

There are at least two, maybe three types of craft, including one that was spotted underwater. These are what the Navy calls "unexplained aerial phenomena (UAP).

First, there were at least two different UFOs/UAPs involved in the Navy sightings. In a **New York Times** interview, retired U.S. Navy Commander David Fravor said the flying object that he observed from the cockpit of his F/A-18F Super Hornet in 2004 was "around 40 feet long and oval in shape," and described it as similar to a Tic Tac.

Lieutenant Ryan Graves, another Super Hornet pilot, told the **NY Times** that the objects he saw in 2014 and 2015 looked like **a "sphere encasing a cube."** These sightings could be of two separate objects or a single object viewed from different perspectives.

Fravor also reported seeing a second object during his encounter that was the size of a Boeing 737 sitting just below the wavetops, with waves breaking over the top. Fravor spotted the Tic Tac-like object hovering over the larger UAP.

How Were the UFOs Spotted?

The objects were detected with a variety of means. Fravor and other pilots saw the UAPs with their own eyes, while the radar operators aboard the nearby guided missile cruiser USS *Princeton* observed the objects for "several weeks" with their SPY-1 radar system.

Fravor couldn't detect the craft with his APG-73 radar, but Graves was able to do so in 2015 with his new APG-79 active electronically scanned radar array. The APG-79 has increased sensitivity and processing power over the older radar system.

The three publicly released videos, nicknamed "FLIR1," "Gimbal," and "GoFast," were all taken using the AN/ASQ-228 Advanced Targeting Forward-Looking Infrared (ATFLIR) pod. In "Gimbal," the infrared pod clearly sees a "hot," whistle-shaped object that pilots say is going against a 120 knot wind. Graves told the **Times** that the infrared sensor on his CATM-9 training missile also picked up the object.

All in all, the objects were observed by multiple sensors per sighting: the naked eye, radar, and infrared, ruling out a sensor malfunction as the cause of the sightings. Fravor saw the objects with his own eyes, and they were also seen by the *Princeton* and the ATFLIR pods.

It may be possible that the ATFLIR pods malfunctioned and depicted objects that weren't really there, but that makes less sense considering the objects were only detected in these three instances (that we know of) and are otherwise used on a daily basis. If there *was* a malfunction, why was it only when objects had already been detected by the human eye, radar, and other infrared detection systems?

What Do UFOs Do?

The mystery craft pull off aerial maneuvers that are impossible for current, state-of-the-art aircraft to perform. According to Fravor, the USS *Princeton* told him it had been tracking objects for weeks that "appeared suddenly at 80,000 feet, and then hurtled toward the sea, eventually stopping at 20,000 feet and hovering. Then they either dropped out of radar range or shot straight back up."

Graves, in describing his 2014-15 incidents, said the objects were known for "showing up at 30,000 feet, 20,000 feet, even sea level. They could accelerate, slow down and then hit hypersonic speeds."

Graves also mentioned another feature the UAPs seemed to have that his own fighter jet did not: **much more energy than one would expect for a small craft. (This would indicate something like Dr. Jack Sarfatti's "low power warp," explanation in upcoming chapter).**

"These things would be out there all day," Graves said. "Keeping an aircraft in the air requires a significant amount of energy. With the speeds we observed, 12 hours in the air is 11 hours longer than we'd expect."

Finally, according to pilots in the "Gimbal" video, there were **a "whole fleet" of whistle-shaped objects in the distance**, not just the one in the ATFLIR video. The objects were apparently being picked up by their Super Hornet's APG-79 radar system.

It's important to stress that the Navy refers to the objects as "unidentified aerial phenomena." That does *not* automatically mean they are spacecraft from another planet, or even some form of classified aircraft. These objects could be birds, drones, the result of equipment malfunctions, or any one of dozen or more things.

However, if we take what the men and equipment tell us at face value, the objects—whatever they are—are quite extraordinary.

Footnote 10: Popular Mechanics, "The Navy Says Those UFO Videos Are Real," by Kyle Mizokami, September 16, 2019

Footnote 11: The Black Vault.com, "U.S. Navy Confirms Videos Depict UAP"

Footnote 12: Jack Sarfatti, on researching low power warp

Underwater Submerged (or Swimming) Objects, "USOs:"

Now for a dive into underwater submerged objects (USOs) which are a part of the Nimitz encounters.

Eight Navy pilots indicated there may have been something in the water as well that day in November 2004. One pilot detailed a disturbance up to the size of a football field. Were the Tic-Tac UFOs trying to rendezvous with the mysterious large object underwater? The account by Lt. Colonel "Cheeks" Kurth, "continues:

"The disturbance appeared to be 50 to 100 meters in diameter and close to round. It was the only area and type of whitewater activity that could be seen and reminded me of images of something rapidly submerging from the surface like a submarine or a ship sinking."

The disturbed area also resembled shoal water around "a barely submerged reef or island," but as the pilot flew away, he could see that the disturbance had cleared and seas calmed. Although he never made visual contact with whatever caused the disturbance, the report stated that it may have been caused by an AAV, which was unseen due to cloaking "or invisible to the human eye."

Another pilot described a disturbance beneath the water of an AAV that "looked like frothy waves and foam almost as if the water was boiling."

A submarine in the vicinity did not detect anything unusual underwater. If an object was indeed in the Pacific Ocean. "it would represent a highly advanced capability given the advanced capability of our sensors."

One aircrew reporting on the events received "a high level of ridicule" about the incident, the report noted.

The military did not confirm nor deny any of the details in the report and had little to say about other recent footage, including a video released in March of a 2015 encounter.

The videos of the "Tic Tac" UFO caused a sensation when they were first released last year as the New York Times reported on a secret Pentagon UFO program that has now concluded with no evidence of alien life visiting the Earth. However, Luis Elizondo, the former military intelligence official who led the program, indicated that there was more information the public had not yet seen.

"My personal belief is that there is very compelling evidence that we may not be alone," he told CNN last December.

Other possible explanations include advanced capabilities by the U.S. military or foreign governments that have not yet been made public.

Footnote 13: Huffington Post, "Military Report: UFOs May Have Attempted Rendezvous with Giant Undersea Object," by Ed Mazza, May 29, 2018

The underwater turbulence was also described as similar to what a downed airliner would look like and it was much larger than a submarine.

As Commander Flavor gazed at the churning water, that was the moment a capsule (Tic-Tac) showed up and buzzed around over the turbulent water. Flavor pursued this Tic-Tac and at one point, he wondered where it had gone only to find it had hopped behind him.

The Past, Present, and Future Human Relationship with the Ocean: Are there indications that Future Human have something going on in Earth's oceans? There is a long history of USO (unidentified submerged object) sightings wherein witnesses report that UFOs dive their craft into oceans and lakes with apparently no impact when they hit the water. Again, in Chapter Four, we offer an explanation as to how this can happen through zero gravity.

We simply do not know what "water" means to a variety of possible extraterrestrial races which are said to visit Earth. We do know that human beings are water dependent and that we sprang from the oceans. We do know that today Earth's oceans are considered the final frontier of Earth; we explore them with advanced equipment more than we dreamed possible in the past.

In the future, some of our Earth populace might live in ocean cities. This is an idea being actively pursued today by several research organizations in different parts of the planet. Humans are already overpopulating Earth, there are too many of us for the good of the planet, its other life-forms, and ourselves.

Earth's largest cities will have 60% of the world's population living in them by 2030. The metropolises will be strained as they deal with huge populations and also with climate change. 90% of Earth's largest cities are on the waterfront, thus they are especially vulnerable to rising sea levels.

Therefore, engineers and researchers are saying, "It's time to do something totally different. Instead of building on land, let's build cities which will float on the ocean."

In the future, from whence Future Humans come, there may well be cities which float on oceans and even large lakes. With planning, the ocean environment might not be damaged, and might be healed and enhanced.

It seems likely that people who grew up on a world which has large floating ocean cities, would also explore the ocean depths and be generally "ocean" minded. If Future Humans travel back in time to the pre-ocean city days, they would consider Earth's oceans the perfect sanctuary to keep themselves safe and to not allow their existence to be known.

But, is it foolish to think there will be ocean cities in the future? Here are two examples of innovators who are working actively on the reality of ocean cities.

Aquapreneurs from Water Studio: It's worth remembering that cities have long been encroaching upon the sea as they have searched for space to house their growing populations. In Singapore, for example, 25% of the city is built on reclaimed land while 20% of Tokyo is built on artificial islands which jut out into the sea. Dubai has artificial islands with luxury homes. And famously, huge tracts of The Netherlands were reclaimed from the North Sea with complex dykes and levees which protect urban areas from flooding.

But rather than trying to hold back the sea from the land, there are some who believe it is time to stop fighting the oceans and to work with them instead. These "aquapreneurs" say the solution to the housing shortages and social problems that exist in many of the world's cramped, rapidly growing cities can be found by spreading out across the water.

"We have to start living with the water as a friend and not always as an enemy," says Koen Olthuis, founder of the Dutch architect firm "Water Studio." They are designing and building floating platforms that can act as the foundations to support buildings. Initially they have focused on building single villas or offices, but Olthuis believes it may be possible to construct entire cities in this way.

Floating cities could be repeatedly remodeled according to the seasons or population changes; Olthuis points to the natural cooling effect of water as an example – by moving the floating foundations further apart during the hot summer months, a city could be opened up to create channels of water that will cool the air, while closing these gaps in the winter could help to keep the heat in. Or imagine if the city could be temporarily expanded to allow for sporadic population increases from tourism or refugees, shrinking back down again when they leave.

Footnote 14: BBC, "The Future of Floating Cities and Their Reality," by Ellie Cosgrave, November 29, 2017

Aquapreneurs from Shimizu Corporation offer the second example of a city capable of being on the ocean or under it. Their audacious idea: a domed city on the surface of the ocean, powered by bio-gas from microorganisms and thermal heating from the ocean floor. **Up to 5,000 people could live there, with the ability for the city to submerge itself underwater when the surface of the ocean is rocked with storms.**

It sounds like the stuff of science fiction, which is par for the course for Shimuzu, which has also envisioned moon bases and space elevators. The firm claims the floating city is about 15 years from becoming reality; comes with a price tag of $25 billion across five years of construction.

Shimizu's Domed City, Fully Submersible, like a USO?

Footnote 15: Popular Mechanics, This Japanese Company Wants to Build a Submersible City on the High Seas," by John Wenz, November 25, 2014

***

Chapter Three: Future Humans Over Missile Silos, Nuclear Waste Deep in Future Earth

All the waste in a year from a nuclear power plant can be stored under your desk. – Ronald Reagan

Even if true, do you want to store it under your desk?

Let's start with our spent nuclear fuel:

75 years in the future, Future Humans will still be dealing with our buried radioactive waste which leaks sometimes even today. In fact, we will still be dealing with our nuclear waste in 100,000 years. Future Humans will have to deal constantly with the radioactive mess we left behind in the 20th and 21st Centuries.

Danish director Michael Madsen has made a haunting, award-winning feature documentary entitled **Into Eternity**. It follows the construction of the Onkalo waste repository at a nuclear power plant on the island of Olkiluoto, Finland. The film questions the intended **eternal existence** of nuclear waste storage.

This site cannot be safely disturbed for 100,000 years. No structure in human history has lasted 100,000 years, far from it; the Egyptian pyramids are around 5,000 years old. But this is Finland's best effort and it is a better effort than most efforts at nuclear waste storage.

Every day, all over the planet, nuclear power plants create nuclear waste which is placed in often temporary storage because "permanent" storage (not as secure as Finland has created), is full. Once full, it is sealed off, but what of the next day's batch of radioactive waste which lasts 100,000 years?

Michael Madsen asks, "And how is it possible to warn our descendants of the deadly waste we left behind? How do we prevent them from thinking they have found the Giza Pyramids from our time, mystical burial grounds, hidden treasures?

Which languages, symbols and signs will they understand? I doubt they will still speak English or any of our current languages. And if they understand, will they respect our instructions?"

"What do we say about ourselves when we create something that will outlast everything we understand, that which may be the last thing that remains of our society?"

And what of earthquakes, floods, and what if the next ice age covers Finland for a time? Some indicators do predict that climate chaos could have a "flip" effect of Earth's currents causing another ice age to occur.

Here is information on one nuclear plant's waste problems in the United States: Congress is once again debating how to dispose of the country's growing inventory of nuclear waste. And in the meantime, nuclear plants are running out of room to store spent fuel.

Running out of room: The Peach Bottom Nuclear Station in south-central Pennsylvania, illustrates the problem. It's one of 80 sites across dozens of states, where nearly 80,000 metric tons of waste from power plants is stored where it was generated, at taxpayer expense. Spent fuel removed from the Peach Bottom reactor is first stored in racks in a big pool. It's surrounded by a bright yellow plastic barrier and signs that read "Caution: Radiation Area." "They are under about 22 feet of water," says reactor engineering manager Mark Parrish. "They are continuously being cooled, as they still have some amount of decay heat even after they've operated in the reactor."

The spent fuel stays here for seven to 10 years while it cools. Once it's safe to remove the spent fuel from the pool, it's stored outside in white metal casks that look like big hot water heaters. They are lined up on a concrete base behind razor wire and against a hillside near the power plant.

Currently there are 89 casks at Peach Bottom with room for three more, says Pat Navin, site vice president for Exelon, the company that partially owns and operates the power plant. "That is 40 years' worth of spent fuel stored over there currently and it's less than the size of a football field," says Navin, "probably half a football field." It's a surprisingly small amount of waste when you consider that's enough spent fuel to produce about 10 percent of Pennsylvania's electricity over four decades.

But without a permanent disposal site, Navin says they're going to run out of room. **So, they're expanding the temporary storage to hold all the waste generated through the 60 years the plant is licensed to operate.**

Footnote 16: NPR, "As Nuclear Waste Builds Up, Private Companies Pitch New Ways to Store It", by Jeff Brady, April 2019

So, the *temporary storage* will have to hold all the waste generated through the next 60 years -- and, in fact, through the next 100,000 years. And here come the Future Humans, looking down at a leaking temporary storage facility which, of course, began leaking years before.

This is but one scenario, but it can be multiplied into similar scenarios, just look at all the nuclear waste storage that has nowhere to go, and it awaits our grandchildren's children.

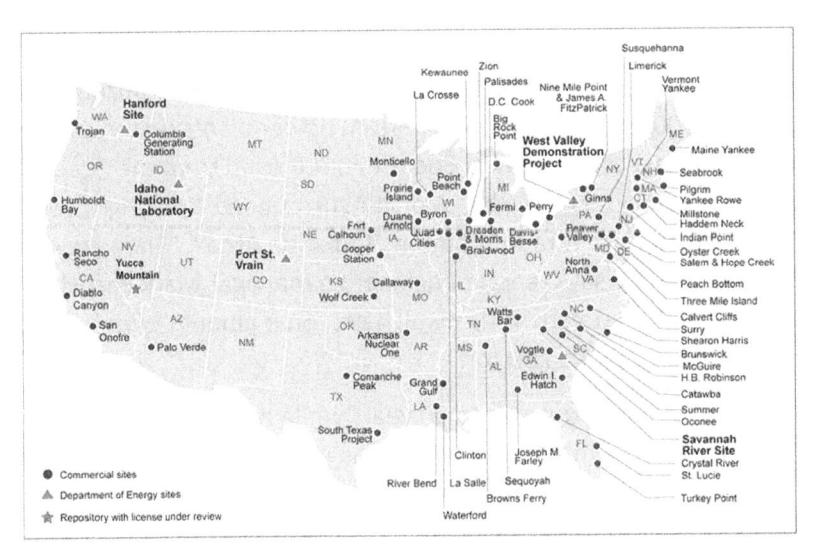

Is it any wonder, UFOs hang around nuclear power plants? Their ancestors' lack of care, lack of understanding, about nuclear perils, must be one of the future's biggest problems!

"Los Alamos, Livermore, Sandia, Savannah River, have all had dramatic incidents where these unknown craft appeared over the facilities and nobody knew where they were from or what they were doing there," says investigative journalist George Knapp, who has studied the UAP-nuclear connection for more than 30 years. Knapp has gathered documentation by filing Freedom of Information Act requests to the Departments of Defense and Energy.

Footnote 17: History.com, "Why Have There Been So Many UAVs Near Nuclear Facilities?" by Adam Janos, June 21, 2019

Los Alamos, Livermore, Sandia, and Savannah River are highly secure, secretive U.S. government facilities involved in nuclear research and development. For instance, Sandia's main mission is to maintain the reliability and surety of nuclear weapon systems. Alamos is better known than Sandia as the U.S. nuclear research and development mecca.

1949 through 1953, the United States government was very concerned about "great balls of green fire" concentrated around the Los Alamos and Sandia atomic-weapons laboratories. Other highly sensitive military installations, including radar stations and fighter-interceptor bases, are in the same area, which was another concern. This meant the sightings were reported by typically cool-headed pilots, weather observers, scientists, intelligence officers and other defense personnel, and led some to suspect the fireballs were Soviet spy devices.

In February 1949, the Los Alamos, New Mexico *Skyliner* **newspaper** wrote an article on "green light flying saucers:"

"Los Alamos now has flying green lights. These will 'o wisps seen generally about 2 a.m., have alerted the local constabulary and their presence is being talked about in Santa Fe bars. But local wheels deny any official knowledge of the sky phenomena. Each one passes the buck to another." The story ended with, *"Have you seen a green light lately?"*

Footnote 18: Skyliner newspaper, Los Alamos, New Mexico, February, 1949

Who Is Lue Elizondo? Lue Elizondo, served from 2007 to 2012 as director of a covert team of UAP researchers operating inside the Department of Defense. The Advanced Aerospace Threat Identification Program (AATIP), which Elizondo headed, received $22 million of the Pentagon's $600 billion budget in 2012, *The New York Times* reported. Elizondo now helps lead **To the Stars Academy** investigations and is otherwise involved in working toward disclosing truth about UFOs to the people of the U.S. and the world.

Why Are UFOs and UAVs Interested in Nuclear Sites? Lue Elizondo states that UAVs and UFOs are legitimate unknowns which have been here a long time, do incredible maneuvers, and which may be (he feels) a threat to us.

That idea of "threat" is thrown into the mix by many officials but there is no evidence that UFOs have done actual harm to military and/or nuclear installations and weaponry in the past 75 years. Of course, a way to maintain funding is to indicate a potential threat.

A Minuteman missile at Malmstrom Air Force Base in the 1960s Photo: AP/USAF

Here is an overview of UFO occupants' continued activity around military bases with nuclear weapons in both the United States and Britain from **CBS News:**

Whatever the mysterious lights in the sky were, they seemed to have an interest in our nukes.

One of the more out-of-the-ordinary press conferences held in Washington this week consisted of former Air Force personnel testifying to the existence of UFOs and their ability to neutralize American and Russian nuclear missiles.

UFO researcher Robert Hastings of Albuquerque, N.M., *who organized the* **National Press Club** *briefing, said more than 120 former service members had told*

him they'd seen unidentified flying objects near nuclear weapon storage and testing grounds.

Star & Stripes quoted **former Air Force Capt. Robert Salas**, who was at **Malmstrom Air Force Base** in Montana in 1967 when 10 ICMs he was overseeing suddenly became inoperative - at the same time base security informed him of a mysterious red glowing object in the sky.

Similar sightings at nuclear sites in the former Soviet Union and in Britain were related.

CBS Affiliate KSWT describes "Britain's Roswell," a case of unidentified phenomena in December 1980 incident near **two Royal Air Force Bases** in Suffolk, England.

Several U.S. Air Force personnel reported seeing a strange metallic object hovering in **Rendlesham Forest near RAF Woodbridge**, and found three depressions in the ground.

Speaking at Monday's press briefing, retired USAF **Col. Charles Halt** said that in December 1980, when he was Deputy Base Commander at **RAF Bentwaters**, strange lights in the forest were investigated by three patrolmen.

Halt said they reported approaching a triangular craft, "approximately three meters on a side, dark metallic in appearance with strange markings. They were observing it for a period of time, and then it very quickly and silently vanished at high speed."

Two nights later, Halt investigated another sighting near the base when he was told by the base commander, "It's back."

Halt found indentations in the ground, broken branches, and low-level background radiation. He and his team also witnessed various lights moving silently in the sky, of one which was "shedding something like molten metal." Another shined a beam of light down towards them.

The incidents were never officially explained.

Several of the ex-servicemembers speaking Monday said when they'd brought their concern of such appearances to superiors, they'd been told it was "top secret" or that it "didn't happen."

Hastings suggested the presence of such phenomena meant that aliens were monitoring our weapons, and perhaps warning us - "a sign to Washington and Moscow that we are playing with fire," as he was quoted in the **Telegraph.**

Hastings predicted a "paradigm shift" in the mindset of humanity owing to the existence of alien life.

"Traditional institutions such as religions, governments, other social institutions may be threatened by what is coming. That is just the logical consequence of what is about to occur."

The U.S. Air Force ended its 22-year-long **Project Blue Book** *investigation of UFO sightings after investigating 12,618 sightings; all but 701 were explained, and the reminder categorized as "unidentified" due to sketchy reports, a Pentagon spokesman said in 1997.*

"We cannot substantiate the existence of UFOs, and we are not harboring the remains of UFOs," said Pentagon spokesperson Kenneth Bacon in 1997. "I can't be clearer about it than that."

Footnote 19: CBS News, "Ex-Air Force Personnel: UFOs Deactivated Nukes," September 28, 2010

RAF Woodbridge: The RAF Woodbridge case near Rendlesham Forest has been covered extensively; it is a landmark event. There were nuclear warheads at RAF Woodbridge, and it is believed by most of the people there, that the UFO(s) "tampered with the nukes." There are no details on what tampering took place.

It has been postulated by some involved that it was time traveling humans in that strange craft, not extraterrestrials; this has always been a part of Rendlesham theories.

There is much conflicting information on "Rendlesham" and so I prefer to feature other "nuke tampering" instances at military bases. There are many sources of literature on "Rendlesham" from various points of view.

Malmstrom Air Force Base, Nuclear Codes Inoperative

Captain Robert L. Salas, relates the following:

"On March 16, 1967, sixteen nuclear missiles became non-operational at two different launch facilities immediately after guards saw UFOs hovering above. The guards could not identify these objects even though they were only about 30 feet away."

"I was on duty along with my commander Fred Mywald. We were both on duty at Oscar Flight as part of the 490th strategic missile squad and there are five launch control facilities assigned to that particular squadron. It was still dark out and we were sixty feet underground at the ICBM launch control facility."

"It was early in the morning and I received a call from my topside security guard who's the flight security controller. He said that he and some of the guards had been observing some strange lights flying around the site around the launch control facility. He said they were acting very unusual just flying around, and I said, "You mean UFOS?" He said, well, he didn't know what they were, but they were lights and were flying around. They were not airplanes; they weren't making any noise. They were not helicopters; they were making some very strange maneuvers and he couldn't explain it."

"It wasn't more than a few minutes — maybe a half hour later — and he calls back. This time he's very frightened. I can tell by the tone of his voice he's very shook up. He says, "Sir, there's a glowing red object hovering right outside the front gate. I'm looking at it right now. I've got all the men out here with their weapons drawn.""

"....our missiles started shutting down one by one. By shutting down, I mean they went into a "no-go" condition meaning they could not be launched. So we get bells and whistles — a red light no-go condition."

"These weapons were Minuteman One missiles, and were of course nuclear-tipped warhead missiles...As I recall, most of them were guidance and control system failures... the guard said, well, the object has left — it just left at high speed."

"The Air Force did an extensive investigation of the entire incident and was not able to come up with a probable cause for the shutdowns..."

"Each missile is basically self-supporting. Most of them are powered by commercial power but each missile has its own power generator. At our site anywhere from six to eight went down, but they went down in rapid succession, which again is an extremely rare happening. We rarely had more than one missile go down for any reason at all."

"My commander turned to me and said, 'The same thing occurred at ECHO Flight.' ECHO Flight is another squadron, I'd say probably 50 - 60 miles away from our location, but they had the same sort of thing happen. They had UFOs that were hovering, not at the launch control facility, but at the actual launch facilities where the missiles are located. They had some maintenance and security people out there at the time and they observed the UFOs at those sites. Now they lost all ten of their weapons – all ten."

"So ... we lost anywhere from between 16 to 18 ICBMs at the same time UFOs were in the area and were observed by airmen. Those missiles were down the entire day..."

"...we had to report to our squadron commander right away. And in that room with my squadron commander was a fellow from the Air Force Office of Special Investigations... He asked for my logs, and he wanted a quick briefing, although it seemed to me he knew pretty much what had happened already..."

"Then he asked us both to sign a non-disclosure agreement saying this was classified information. We were not to release this to anybody, and that was it. We couldn't talk. He told us we could not talk about this to anyone, including any of the other crews, our spouses, our family, even amongst each other."

"We did get the security incursion alarms at those sites when the missile went down. That is unusual because usually when a missile went down for something like guidance failure, we wouldn't get security incursion alarms, which means a perimeter is breached, an object crossed the fence, or something broke the security alarm system that we had on the perimeter of the launch facility. I did send out guards to a couple of those facilities to investigate that."

*"The reason I think this story is very significant is because, going back to August of 1966 at Minot, ND, a very similar thing happened at one of the launch control facilities at **Minot Air Force Base**. They had the same kind of weapon system that we had. They had M-1 missiles. This [UFO] was observed on radar, there was some*

communication failure, and the object was observed over the launch control facility. That happened in August 1966 and that's a well-documented incident."

"About a week prior to my incident, in March 1967, I've got a record of a call from one of the security guards who was out roaming looking at the launch facilities and saw an object very similar to what I just described over the launch facility."

Footnote 20: Spiral Galaxy, Robert Salas website: "My Evidence,"

Minot Air Force Base, Nuclear-Tipped ICBMs Turned Off:

On December 6, 1966, the **Minot Daily News in Minot, North Dakota**, carried a front page story about UFO sightings in the area, especially around the Minot Air Force Base, home of a number of nuclear missiles poised to be launched if the Cold War turned hot.

In a tell the truth memoir in his later years, Captain David D. Schindele, who was the Minuteman intercontinental ballistic missile launch crew commander at the base that day, says that nothing more was reported about the UFO sightings because the Air Force ordered everyone there to never speak about what happened next.

What happened next as the UFOs buzzed the area? There was an unexplained change in status of 10 ICBMs, suddenly switched to the "off-alert," meaning that they could not be launched.

Schindele: *"I remember that when we were relieved the next morning, I attempted to query the Flight Security Controller, who told me he could not speak about the incident. It was then that my commander also informed me that he had received word that we were to never speak about the incident."*

Schindele kept silent until 2010, when he first told his experiences to Robert Hastings, author of **UFOs & Nukes: Extraordinary Encounters at Nuclear Weapons Sites.** Why did Schindele finally disobey that order?

Schindele: *"During that time in Minot, many of us experienced unworldly incidents at Minuteman facilities but we were all individually instructed to keep silent. We* never realized at the time that others among us were also experiencing incidents, but now the truth is becoming known. About 35 years after my Minot incident and learning about an identical incident experienced by another missileer, Captain Robert Salas, connected to Malmstrom AFB in Montana, which was during the same general timeframe as my incident, I then contemplated coming forth with the 'truth'."

"From the beginning, I've been conflicted with the goal of bringing truth to as many people as possible, while having no appetite for bringing attention to myself or receiving monetary benefit. But I also realize the fallacy in that."

There have been many reports of UFOs at nuclear missile sights and nuclear plants around the world, ranging from UFO activity at the plant where plutonium was processed for the first atomic bomb to UFO sightings at nuclear plants in France to documents from Russia indicating similar unexplained missile shutdowns in the Soviet Union after UFO sightings.

Footnote 21: Mysterious Universe.com, "Air Force Captain Claims UFOs Deactivated 10 Nukes in Silos," by Paul Seaburn, June 2017

Loring Air Force Base, Northern Maine: On October 27 and 28, 1975, strange events occurred in the northern part of the State of Maine that remain unexplained; however, other Air Force bases (Minot, Malmstrom and others) had experienced the same kind of event. The media at the time chalked it up to "a black helicopter from Canada."

Loring (now closed) was one of the largest nuclear weapons storage facilities in the continental United States. It was also one of the world's largest Strategic Air Command bases. Perhaps one of its greatest strengths was its great isolation at the northern tip of the country also giving it the closest approach directly over the pole to our enemy, the Soviet Union. The base hosted the 42nd Bombardment Wing with a capacity of nearly 100 B-52 intercontinental bombers capable of flying very great distances to deliver their payloads.

Then, a bizarre breech of Loring security by someone or something, occurred for two strange days in October, 1975. The writer of the report I am quoting here is from a military family. His father spent ten years in the Air Force and was stationed at Loring AFB when these events happened. His brother was an enlisted AF man and spent time at Loring with friends. The events of that October still cause these men confusion but a sense of wonder as well. The U.S. military ended up on high alert due to the Loring events.

These events began on October 27, shortly before 8 PM. It was a fairly clear, cold night when an air policeman patrolling the nuclear weapons storage site first saw an unidentified aircraft approaching the edge of the base at a very low level, no more than three hundred feet. It had a red light and white strobe light.

At nearly the same moment, the tower made radar contact with an unknown aircraft north of the base. For the next forty minutes, the UFO "explored" the base, moving in ways that were "helicopter-like." Try as they might, the military could never get a fix on the aircraft before it moved quickly away. Then, after about forty minutes, it quickly departed in the direction of Grand Falls, New Brunswick, about twelve miles away.

Somehow, a UFO had successfully buzzed one of the world's most heavily-guarded nuclear weapons storage areas and escaped successfully. The only guess to be made, "It must have been a Canadian black helicopter."

That was "it" for the first visit. What happened next has only recently come to light and deserves to be added to the few sources of information to surface from these events. Captain Michael Wallace was a pilot and Aircraft Commander of a KC-135 assigned to the 407 Refueling Squadron assigned to Loring AFB. In a video that he posted on **YouTube** in the interest of disclosure, he outlines his memories of what happened at the base on the night of the second visitation.

Direct quote from "UFOs Over Northern Maine" article by Tom Burby:

On the day after the events of the first night, Captain Wallace and all other flight crew members were summoned to a briefing. By his estimates, between 200 and 250 people attended and each one of them had a security clearance of secret. He had never attended such a large briefing before. The topic, he relates, was that a UFO had been sighted at the base around the nuclear weapons storage facility.

The uniformed staff officer from the Wing Staff in charge of the briefing referred to the object as a UFO and described to the assembled flight crews the flight characteristics that had been observed the prior evening. Whatever it was, it could hover silently, move erratically and fast and make an almost instantaneous jump from place to place at the base. The Wing Staff was concerned that already things were getting out of hand. More support in the form of fighters had been requested from another base to come to Loring, Ground forces were also being 'beefed up.'"

Later that day, Captain Wallace flew on a routine mission south of New York with two other tankers in a formation known as a cell flight, which meant that three tankers flew with each other. It was not an especially interesting mission until evening fell and they turned back towards Loring and northern Maine. Command Post contacted the lead plane's Captain and asked him to transfer to another radio frequency and stand by for a message.

Captain Wallace surreptitiously tuned one of his extra radios the specified frequency and listened in on the conversation. He reports that the Command Post ordered the captain of the lead place to transfer command of the flight to Captain Wallace in the second plane. The lead plane's commander was then told to depart the formation, maintain radio silence and to fly with his lights out. He was to make his way directly to the base and was given discretion as to his altitude, airspeed and direction. His mission now was to get as close as possible and observe the UFO that was again visiting the base.

The captain of the lead plane contacted Wallace and transferred command of the formation to him. Then, in the moonlit night, Captain Wallace watched as the lead plane turn off his lights and descended into the darkness.

Captain Wallace brought the two tankers to their normal approach over the south end of the Runway 36 at Loring. As he approached the base, Captain Wallace heard more than the usual amount of communications on the tower frequency and the command post frequency. The communication all referred to the UFO. The chatter related to the position of the UFO.

"How did it get down there that fast?" one voice asked. Runway 36 is two miles long and is probably three miles away from the nuclear storage facility at the time at the end of another runway. This craft could travel almost instantaneously from end of the runway to the other. The radio chatter did not last for long. Captain Wallace recalls there was one last statement on the air. "It's gone."

The two KC-135s landed normally and received normal orders. Everything was as it should have been and there was no mention at all to the crews concerning the events of only moments before that seemed to have the base in such high alert. After each mission, pilots report to the squadron for debriefings. He noticed that the pilot of the lead place was not among them.

A day or two later near the Base Exchange, Captain Wallace saw his friend, the captain of the lead place, walking on the sidewalk. He pulled over and asked him, "What in the hell happened with the UFO the other night?"

The answer was terse and to the point. "I can't talk about it, Mike." Then, he changed his aspect and looked Captain Wallace straight in the eyes and said, "And you wouldn't believe me if I could talk about it."

At the time, airmen reported that the craft they saw was orange and red and was shaped like a cigar or elongated football. About the length of four cars, it was silent, solid, windowless and door less. It had no visible means of propulsion.

In years to come, UFO investigators Larry Fawcett and Barry Greenwood in their book **UFO Cover-Up: What the Government Won't Say**, *included interviews with witnesses including CWO Bernard Poulin. He was a helicopter crew member from Bangor that had been send north to Loring help track the object. He said that "radar was not painting the object that was being reported" by the ground troops who directed his helicopter to the areas they were seeing the UFO. He claims that he was never able to spot the UFO at all."*

Note: This might have been because the radar was not advanced enough yet. By 2004, the Nimitz and Roosevelt (2014-2015) radars did pick up the UFO; this UFO has great similarities with the Tic-Tac capsules, as well.

The Loring events had many dependable witnesses who have come forward over the years. Captain Michael Wallace, for instance, had been a qualified military pilot for years with almost 71 hours of combat mission experience in southeast Asia and almost 2000 hours of total flight time. The other people mentioned in his recollection were also at least as experienced as he was. He had nothing to gain and his credibility is put at risk by telling his version of the events.

Something flew out of the darkness on those two nights in October at the height of the Cold War and left the United States Air Force scrambling for a way to deal with it. They, in fact, had no way to deal with it.

Footnote 22: Strange New England.com, "UFOs Over Northern Maine, the 1975 Loring UFO Incident," by Tom Burby, June 2015

What clue does the Loring event offer that the culprits were more likely Future Humans than extraterrestrials? There are not a lot of clues here for ETs or FTs (or anyone else), but as we profile the actions of the UFOs, we see how similar their actions were, to actions our military pilots on a military reconnaissance mission would have taken – except that the UFO crew had a much more advanced craft. Once again, this seems like a human vs. human event in terms of behavior. Who can be sure that extraterrestrials would match our behavior this closely?

Now, maybe extraterrestrials would harass in the same way, too, but that is a huge unknown. Time and time again, we make the assumption that ETs would act as we do. Especially in military situations, with narrowly assigned behavior into restricted parameters, it seems the UFO occupants fall right in line with our own military behavior but the unknown craft have more advanced technology.

The unknown craft, especially in the 1960s and 1970s, could not have been our "advanced exploratory craft," as some have said about the Tic-Tacs of 2004 and 2015. (As I write this book, September 2019, The Navy has now admitted the Tic-Tac capsules are true unknowns).

It is interesting that this report mentions that the UFO "would make an almost instantaneous jump from place to place;" the F-18 pilots from the Nimitz described the white capsules as bouncing like ping pong balls. Captain Flavor said the Tic-Tac he was trying to chase, suddenly showed up behind him.

The radar was probably not advanced enough yet to pick up the UFO. By 2004, the Nimitz and Roosevelt (2014-2015) advanced radars did pick up the Tic-Tac UFOs.

The capabilities of the UFOs were the same or similar, whether at Loring AFB in 1975 or Nimitz in 2004. This tends to rule out some extremely advanced military project in the 2000s. The UFOs of 1966 (Minot) have similarities with the Tic-Tac capsules of 2004, cigar shape and no openings.

Due to these similarities, it might also suggest that the UFOs originated from the same point in (future) time, but arrived at different points in the past (1975 or 2004).

The list of military bases which have had UFO activity is a long one; it is almost easier to find a military installation not having had UFOs observing them.

And, it's not just military bases; let's not miss the fact that the USS Nimitz and the USS Theodore Roosevelt aircraft carriers/battleships are **nuclear-powered.** Might this fact have entered into the Tic-Tac capsules' presence?

Why are UFOs no longer buzzing military nuclear facilities? They may be, the lid has been slammed down even tighter by the government than it was in the 1950s and 1960s. For instance, there are new stricter rules regarding military pilots discussing the phenomena they have seen.

These are the dark ages of the 21st Century, when warheads sit atop ballistic missiles, ready to spread death to the entire planet when that word is given by one flawed man or woman. Future Humans would know that "no one wins thermonuclear war." The weapons which sit mounted and ready to go, and which would murder billions of people and life-forms, seem a likely target of annoyance and even worry for the time travelers.

Perhaps the fact that time travelers annoy our (nuclear) military, is written into history and cannot be changed. Perhaps this is their written-in-stone role in preventing nuclear annihilation. Note: This idea is speculation.

UFOs over nuclear power plants: Nuclear power plants are great until they are not; Chernobyl, 3 Mile Island, Sellafield-Windscale (United Kingdom), wherein a fire destroyed the core of an atomic bomb project and released 740 terabecquerels of iodine-131 into the environment. The list of accidents and close-calls at power plants is long and kept under publicized.

Footnote 23: wikipedia.org "Nuclear and Radiation Accidents and Incidents"

With climate change and chaos, what are the chances that the Savannah River, Indian Point, Crystal River, Davis-Besse, St. Lucie, Cooper Nuclear Station, and many other nuclear plants built in vulnerable locations, will hold up to super hurricanes, tornadoes, floods, and tidal surges of the near future? Many of the U.S. nuclear power plants are getting old as well and in need of updating, which does not always happen promptly.

Photo: Lights photographed in 1952 over a Coast Guard air station in Salem, MA, part of the Blue Book archive. Credit Shell R. Alpert/U.S. Coast Guard

A Sampling of UFOs over Nuclear Power Plants

The Davis-Besse Nuclear Power Plant in Oak Harbor, Ohio. (MUFON report): He was passing the plant at 3:30 a.m. on October 29, 2017: *"I noticed something floating up and down above the reactor,"* the witness stated. *"I pulled off and got out of my car and it did this for maybe three to four minutes before it flew up about 50 feet and seemed to just slowly hover over the buildings. There were six lights, two at each corner, a white and blue light side-by-side in each corner. The blue light would brighten when the white light would dim and vice versa. It did this for a few minutes and then it just shot up and away at a 45-degree angle and was so fast it looked like a streak of blue light. I heard no noise except for this pulsing, vibrating sensation in my ears until it shot away. I never believed in extraterrestrial life until that night. Now I'm convinced of it. I was in such shock at what I was seeing I didn't think to try to take a photo. Of course, my two friends were passed out in the car after drinking all night and didn't see it or even realize we were stopped."*

Footnote 24: MUFON.com, "UFO Reported Hovering Over Nuclear Power Plant," by Roger Marsh, Case Investigator: Rod McGlone

Due to the huge need for water intake, nuclear plants are built on bodies of water; with global warming, bodies of water become less predictable, often rising to levels unheard of in the past.

For every three units of energy produced by the reactor core of a U.S. nuclear power plants, two units are discharged to the environment as waste heat. Nuclear plants are built on the shores of lakes, rivers, and oceans because these bodies provide the large quantities of cooling water needed to handle the waste heat discharge.

Footnote 25: ucusa.org, "nuclear power/nuclear power technology/got-water"

Cooper Nuclear: Report of UFO Over Nuclear Power Plant Is Now Declassified:

In the winter of 2017, Cooper Nuclear Plant, Nebraska, had an "unusual event" according to the Nebraska Public Power District declared an "unusual event" at its Cooper Nuclear Facility due to possible flooding along the Missouri River. However, Cooper has had more than one "unusual event:"

Cooper Nuclear Plant, Brownville, Nebraska, is the site a UFO event in the late 1980s, as reported by a former security officer. This knowledge has been made public through the Freedom of Information Act and is 43 pages long, although some of those pages have little to do with the sighting.

The report's description: *An unidentified flying object violated the protected area at the Cooper Nuclear Power Station between 1986 and 1989 but the event was not reported to the Nuclear Regulatory Commission (NRC) as required.*

The Confidential Informant describes an event that occurred during his employment as a security officer... While posted at the intake structure one night, he observed an unidentified flying object fly down the Missouri River about 150 feet in the air and hover in front of the intake. He observed it for a few minutes and then called contacted a fellow security officer who also observed it...

After they together observed the UFO, it turned and went back up the river and did not come back that shift. He and the other officer shared their observation with other employees who did not believe them.

The next evening, he was again posted at the intake and observed the UFO return again. This time he didn't call anyone until the UFO had traversed into the protected area just north of the reactor building. He said it was roughly triangular in shape with a Council of rotating lights at the bottom. He could not hear any propulsion noise from the UFOs. He believed it was roughly 1/3rd the size of the reactor building.

Once it hovered over the protected area, he called the security break room and most of the officers on that shift observed the UFO. After hovering there for a few minutes, the UFO left the protected area and headed back up the river to the north as it has done on the previous night.

Footnote 26: OpenMinds.tv, "Report of UFO Over Nuclear Plant in Nebraska," posted by Alejandro Rojas, March 23, 2017

There are reports of UFOs over nuclear power plants in many other countries as well: France, Belgium, Japan, Saudi Arabia, Chile, Brazil, Italy, Russia, and Australia, just to name a few.

Point Beach Nuclear Power Plant, Two Rivers, on Lake Michigan:

A former veteran of the US Marine released a video which was being hailed as "the biggest UFO story of 2019." That may be an exaggeration, but it is two person sighting in 2019 over a nuclear power plant.

March 4, 2019, Marine veteran Myles Panosh was on the phone to a friend discussing UFO experiences when he happened to glance out of the window and saw a bizarre array of lights in the vicinity of Point Beach Nuclear Power Plant in Two Rivers. Wisconsin.

Panosh attempted to capture footage of the purported UFO with his phone, then asked for assistance from his neighbor, Jeff Lavicka, who happens to be a videographer. Lavicka captured amazing footage of the UFO between 8.45pm and 11.30pm.

Preliminary analysis of the video footage indicates that there are no stars or celestial bodies visible in the background which suggests that the lights emitted by the UFO were bright enough to drown out surrounding emitted light and that it was in the Earth's atmosphere.

Panosh is a trained military observer and said that he knew immediately that it was not a star or a planet or a meteor and it was not an aircraft operated by the United States. He said, "Not anything we have. No way. Not even close. Not a chance. It was not a star. It was not a planet. It was not a meteor. It was definitely (by definition) an unidentified flying object."

This is not the first time that this particular area of Michigan, especially Lake Michigan, has been known for unusual activity in the skies. Local residents and visitors to the area have long reported sightings of unusual lights in the region of the nuclear plant since 1994.

Footnote 27: Daily News media.com, "Ex-Marine Films Huge Object Over Nuclear Power Plant"

The topic of UFOs harassing nuclear installations draws a sharp comparison between extraterrestrials and the human time travelers; it seems clear that each group has a different "stake in the game." ETs can just leave when a nuclear accident or nuclear war happens; it is a stretch to believe they would care enough to keep warning us over many decades about the threat of nuclear accidents or nuclear war.

Future Humans seem to be saying, "Hey, don't do this to our planet!" Logic tells us that Future Humans are the more likely culprits because this is their planet too. Perhaps Future Humans do not like to inherit a dead ocean or a dead planet.

The Fukushima Daiichi Nuclear Power Plant: Nuclear accidents, such as the meltdown of three cooling towers at the Fukushima Nuclear Power Plant following Japan's devasting 9.0 earthquake and huge 40 meter tsunami of March 11, 2011, do irreparable damage to oceans, land and life-forms. Radioactive water from Fukushima is still dumped into the Pacific Ocean periodically. Even when the radiation dissipates years later, the damage is already done to the genetics and health of life on Earth.

Fukushima radiation in the Pacific Ocean has adversely affected chitons, abalone, mussels and salmon. Bioaccumulation of radiation has registered in seafood periodically. The health and vigor of many of Earth's life-forms is already faltering, and so adding radioactive contamination could well be the death knell of entire species. The damage done to whales, seals, dolphins, octopus, and other higher levels of life, is not yet known and has probably not fully manifested even today.

Greenpeace International estimated in 2006 that 270,000 people in Ukraine, Russia and Belarus developed cancers who otherwise would not have done so, due to Chernobyl's radiation. Humans of the future do not want genetic mutations or genetic flaws which cause cancer, a disease which is on a dramatic rise among the human population in the 21st Century.

Future Humans may have conquered cancer; in fact, it is predicted we will find cures for a variety of cancers in the next ten years, but warning about the dangers of radiation, benefits both the time travelers and 20th/21st Century humans because we share one planet. This is not the extraterrestrials' home; that heartfelt concept of "Protect the environment of Earth, our only home" is a powerful emotion which, I believe, motivates Future Humans as they fly over nuclear installations.

I can offer speculation, such as gene mutations arising in the future human genome due to radiation, but the time travelers' specific reasons are not known; however their general policy seems clear: Without hands-on overt interference, get the message across to the humans of the 20th and 21st Century – to abandon fission nuclear energy!

Fusion or Thorium: Alternatives, Yet Nuclear

It seems we can conclude that UFO occupants are not fond of our nuclear energy and radiation. However, perhaps the occupants know there is a "kinder" nuclear power, although it isn't perfect. It is likely kinder to the planet we share with our descendants than coal, or fossil fuels.

Steven Hawking stated, "I would like nuclear fusion to be a practical power source. It would provide an inexhaustible supply of energy, without pollution or global warming." We thus far have not been able to harness power from fusion because its energy requirements are unbelievably, terribly high.

In order for fusion to occur, you need a temperature of at least 100,000,000 degrees Celsius. That's slightly more than 6 times the temperature of the Sun's core. It should be noted that experimental fusion reactors do exist – and work – but they consume way more power than they produce, which basically defeats the purpose of generating power using fusion.

Perhaps Future Humans have conquered what is today still a fantasy: Cold fusion.

Cold fusion is a hypothesized type of nuclear reaction that would occur at, or near, room temperature. It would contrast starkly with the "hot fusion" that is known to take place naturally within stars and artificially in hydrogen bombs and prototype fusion reactors under immense pressure and at temperatures of millions of degrees.

Footnote 28: scienceabc.com, "Why Aren't We Using Nuclear Fusion to Generate Nuclear Power Yet?," 2017

Or, perhaps Future Humans just want us to switch to thorium power. Thorium is a type of nuclear energy. Thorium installations would be different than the nuclear plants with which we are familiar. Thorium is naturally-occurring, slightly radioactive metal discovered in 1828 by the Swedish chemist Jons Jakob Berzelius, who named it after Thor, the Norse god of thunder.

Thorium is found in small amounts in most rocks and soils, where it is about three times more abundant than uranium. Soil contains an average of around 6 parts per million (ppm) of thorium. Thorium is very insoluble, which is why it is plentiful in sands but not in seawater, in contrast to uranium.

However, thorium comes with its own challenges. Thorium dioxide melts at 550 degrees higher temperatures than traditional uranium dioxide and while thorium might avoid some of the long-term challenges in waste management, combining it with uranium-233 in the short term, would actually be more radioactive than current plants.

Footnote 29: Popular Science.com, "Thorium Nuclear Power, Here's What It Is," David Grossman, August 2019

Of course, the large, powerful nuclear fuel industry does not want to spend money updating or replacing the old nuclear plants. Maybe the UFO occupants, whatever their source, don't understand why that stuff called "money" is king, and why the welfare of the planet and its life-forms, including humans, is low on the list of considerations.

Of course, we all think of clean energy like solar, wind, and geothermic power, not to mention Tesla's free energy (later in the book) as preferable to any nuclear option. The human population of Earth is now so overwhelmingly large and growing larger, that nuclear power has the potential to serve that huge population. However, the goal, I believe, should be to ultimately phase out any use of nuclear power. I would love to see if the Future Humans managed to do it.

***

Chapter Four: Sarfatti's Low Power Warp

"It's the Whole Enchilada." – Jack Sarfatti

In Chapters Four and Five, we'll look at the physics of traveling back in time; is it possible? Chapter Four is devoted to the astounding current research of one theoretical physicist which is gaining a lot of attention around the world, including from some people at high levels of government. This is partly because the Tic-Tac and UFO maneuvers are so well explained by this theory, as are the basics of traveling back in time. It feels like a theory whose time has come! It is from brilliant maverick physicist Dr. Jack Sarfatti who might be just the person to "take the leap" and get it right, regardless of what conventional physics says.

In Chapter Five, we'll take a closer look at other mind-bending theories regarding time travel.

There has been theoretical talk of traveling back in time for years, but Jack Sarfatti now offers the specific formula for accomplishing the goal. By "formula," we mean specific, intricate physics equations and brilliant thought processes which really might work. This is why Jack's work has suddenly drawn the attention of everyone!

No doubt some people are saying it can't be correct. Dr. Sarfatti has had his physics theories doubted before many times, but he has turned out to be uncannily right in the first place – many times.

Jack Sarfatti is an American theoretical physicist who was known for a while as the "hippy physicist." This tag did not deter him, in fact it inspired him onward. He preferred to work mostly outside academia and has remained a maverick with private funding. His research has revolved mostly around consciousness, quantum physics and more recently, Post-Quantum Physics, a new field at which he excels.

Dr. Sarfatti grew up in Brooklyn in a working class family. In 1953, when he was 13 years old, he had contact with a strange intelligence which he feels was Future Human, or in his terms, "humans or post-humans." One day in his home, the phone rang, he answered it, and his life changed forever in that second. Jack heard a series of technical beeps and other noises, and then he heard a cold, metallic computer-like voice talking to him.

Jack's mother remembered it differently. She remembered that for three weeks, their phone rang many times with strange technical beeps and a cold computer voice at the other end. Jack can remember only one phone call from "them." His mother even told them to leave Jack alone. "Not even a super-technological conscious computer from the future can argue with an irate Jewish mother!" laughs Jack. It seems Jack may have suffered missing time similar to a UFO encounter, because he remembers only one of the telephone calls.

This high strangeness opened his mind to a universe of possibilities; the strange voice on the phone said that Jack that he would be a part of a special project with a few bright young minds if he wished to be, and that he would reach a special phase of great clarity and accomplishment, in 20 years.

Jack got his doctorate in physics from University of California, and his career took off. Jack's career brought him into contact with top physicists such as Richard Feynman, John Archibald Wheeler, and David Bohm. Jack was recognized as one of the rising stars of his generation. Wheeler, whom Jack met several times at UCSD La Jolla and Wernher Heisenberg's Institute in Munich, was to become very important in the next phase of his career which was to be the special phase in his life which the cold voice on the phone, predicted.

Jack's career became both spectacular and turbulent in the 1970s and introduced him to controversial people such as Timothy Leary, Uri Geller, and Ira Einhorn. New Physics was exploding in popularity with such books as Fritjof Capra's The Tao of Physics, Gary Zukav's The Dancing Wu Li Masters, and Jeffrey Mishlove's

<u>The Roots of Consciousness.</u> Jack was instrumental in these very popular books which explore the meaning of the quantum realm and how it relates to consciousness, the paranormal, and mysticism. Jack wrote his own popular book as well with Fred Alan Wolf, entitled <u>Space-Time and Beyond</u>.

Important scientists were joining in the great consciousness debate of the 1970s. John Archibald Wheeler, regarded by many as the greatest scientist since Einstein, proposed that the universe and consciousness have an extraordinarily intimate relationship with each other. Although his ideas might seem dangerously surreal, if not outright crazy, they were perfectly logical according to New Physics. Is the universe really that crazy? The answer seems to be, "Yes."

Sarfatti was guided toward even deeper implications of quantum theory. Jack began to wonder if his insights on quantum theory were being *given* to him by "the others" who phoned him in 1953.

I became friends with Jack Sarfatti when I wrote to him with a physics question and mentioned that I have felt for the 38 years in which I've written philosophical, spiritual, and scientific (quantum) concepts, that the information is being *given* to me. I feel a shared consciousness with the other-worldly individual whom I encountered in childhood. I am *given* entire concepts to quickly jot down.

If a person has this connection (possibly this entanglement), it does not diminish the person's own ability. This sharing is from an advanced form of consciousness which is perhaps more common in our future. It is beneficial to both, and there is a oneness.

I hasten to add that my quantum ideas are not on par with actual quantum physics equations and proofs. The incoming information is obviously aimed at the level of the receiver and the receiver's education (I am not a physicist). However, when Jack says that complicated physics feels like it is *given,* I do understand what he means.

Upon further discussion, Jack and I both realized that as children we had contact with probably the same group, Future Humans, in the same year of 1953 (in my case, it was 1952 and 1953). I had two encounters, to be detailed later in the book, and Jack encountered the strange phone contact.

In recent years, Jack has been working on Post-Quantum Physics (capitalized to denote a new discipline). He works on research into conscious artificial intelligence, warping space, nullifying gravity, and traveling back in time. These topics sound like science fiction, but NASA scientists, research groups, universities, and governments, also work in these areas. This is no longer 1953, and these "crazy" topics will become reality one day in the not-distant future. We as a species are working on all of it!

There is much more to Jack's life story and work, but we need to move on to his revolutionary new post-quantum theory for time travel. Suffice to say, MIT science historian David Kaiser's best-selling book in 2011, How the Hippies Saved Physics, relates the New Physics era which paved the way for real progress in quantum physics and thus our understanding of the universe. Jack's latest mind-blowing book is Star Gate.

Footnote 30: "Future Mind," by Lynn Picknett and Clive Prince, is an essay in Star Gate, by Jack Sarfatti, Lambert Academic Publishing, 2018.

Footnote 31: Super Cosmos, Through Struggles to the Stars (Space-Time and Beyond), by Jack Sarfatti, Author-House Publishing, 2006

Footnote 32: How the Hippies Saved Physics, by David Kaiser, W.W. Norton and Company, 2011

Interview with Dr. Jack Sarfatti: Here is Dr. Jack Sarfatti's explanation of the crucial role metamaterials play in not only attaining zero gravity and warping space, but also, the probability that metamaterials offer the key to traveling back in time.

Is this how Future Humans do it?

Interview with Dr. Jack Sarfatti on August 7, 2019

Diane Tessman: Dr. Sarfatti, you talk "low power warp drive," tell us about it. For starters, what about metamaterials being able to slow down the speed of light. As I understand it, this is due to the metamaterials' artificial, exotic electromagnetism. This results is a spacecraft being able to move faster than the (slowed down) speed of light. Is this the same as warping space? And how long until this becomes reality? Please explain all this.

Dr. Sarfatti: Yes, it is a workable way to fold spacetime which becomes more fluid as the speed of light slows down. No one can predict when we will have this technology. It depends on the money given to further research and whether we have captured extraterrestrial or post-human craft which already have it. We need a huge project, all sorts of scientists working together to develop this. Right now we have the basic key.

Incidentally, by "post-human," I mean humans who have evolved beyond our current state, who are probably endowed with artificial intelligence and consciousness.

Diane: Just where is the metamaterial on a space craft? Is it in the engineering section?

Dr. Sarfatti: No, metamaterial is incorporated into the skin of the craft. In other words, it is a part of the composition of the outer craft. It would be less than a nano-meter thick. The "Tic-Tacs" of the U.S.S. Nimitz and Roosevelt Battle Group videos, likely have outer skins in which these exotic quantum materials are in-built.

You see, metamaterials have strange electromagnetic properties, they form a lattice-work kind of structure. They have negative indices of refraction. Technically what this means, you can send an EM field into metamaterial, it can develop negative energy density and that would cause anti-gravity, but the problem is: Even though negative energy density is formed inside metamaterial, it is too weak a field, less than microscopic. We would need a "Jupiter-size" amount of energy – or we did need that much. But I have changed that, that's why I call this discovery "low-power warp."

Diane: But then how does this theory succeed?

Dr. Sarfatti: Ah, there is another trick! When we reduce the speed of light inside the metamaterial to a very small number, spacetime gets less stiff and can be warped.

Why does spacetime become less stiff? This happens because of Einstein's equations regarding the Bose-Einstein condensate, a part of his Theory of General Relativity. It has to do with superposition.

So, the stiffness of spacetime becomes more fluid. Refraction becomes large, the speed of light becomes small, and there is formed a zero-gravity bubble around the craft. Gravity has been nullified. A very small amount of energy is then used, possibly as small as a triple A battery.

Diane: The Tic-Tacs and a large variety of UFOs certainly seem to nullify gravity. They make sharp right angle turns, they accelerate to super-fast speeds, they drop tens of thousands of feet out of the sky and then stop on a dime in mid-air. A human pilot's head would be crushed from the G-Forces of those maneuvers, but the UFO pilots seem to do it easily. Are you saying that inside the craft, the UFO occupants don't feel any G-Forces or upheaval?

Dr. Sarfatti: Correct. It is gravity which causes the G-Forces but the Tic-Tacs are in a gravity free bubble.

Diane: But what does this have to do with traveling back in time?

Dr. Sarfatti: Diane, metamaterials and all I just explained, are the whole enchilada! They are the key to the advanced technology which human or post-human UFO pilots possess, both in terms of zero-gravity and in terms of warping and traveling spacetime. This includes traveling back in time.

Diane: I am somehow reminded that airplanes didn't leave the ground in actual flight until we realized a plane needs to have an aerodynamic shape. There is a lot more to planes staying aloft than just their shape, but their shape is basic, it is crucial.

Metamaterials seem to be similarly crucial. They may be the key to zero gravity, warping space, and even traveling back in time: They may be the basic component which opens the door to—everything.

Dr. Sarfatti: Yes, all this even opens the door to conscious artificial intelligence and consciousness itself. Using the pilot's consciousness to control saucer makes sense now with this theory. It means <u>The Day After Roswell</u> may have offered the truth. In the 1990s we did not have ideas we do now. Brain waves, possibly of part-biologic/part silicon entities, may control most UFOs.

Diane: Do you think some advanced group on Earth has this technology now, something like the Solar Warden and "breakaway civilization" stories we hear online?

Dr. Sarfatti: No, I don't think so. Of course I'm not sure, but I know well the top people who would have to be involved in something like that and none of them know these things as a done deal. In the 1990s, I was involved with a nanotechnology group. We heard rumors that test pilots were being asked to fly back-engineered captured craft but there were too many crashes; the pilots didn't know how to fly these advanced machines. We did not understand these machines.

I know the Russians; the Chinese and the Iranians are very eager to get this technology and are working on it. We have the creation of the United States Space Force now, which I have campaigned for since the 1980s.

We also have the "To the Stars Academy," founded by Tom DeLonge, which engages with global citizens to investigate the outer edges of science and unconventional thinking in order to push human knowledge and ultimately, our collective capability forward.

We are seeing UFO Disclosure now. It has not been one huge announcement but it is happening. And, we can build this technology ourselves if we have the will.

Diane: Thanks for your patience in explaining this to us lay people, Jack. And may I say that apparently we did build this technology since we have it in the future? (Sarfatti smiles).

Footnote 33 : U.S. Space Force, Military.com

Footnote 34: To the Stars Academy, dpo.tothestarsacademy.com

$$G_{\mu\nu} = 8\pi G\left(\varepsilon_{\gamma\delta}\mu^{\gamma\delta}\right)^2 T_{\mu\nu}$$

Dielectric permittivity 4D tensor splits into "Vacuum" + "Matter"

ZPF (Zero Point Fluctuations, off-mass-shell)

Matter (real particles on-mass-shell)

$\varepsilon_{\gamma\delta} \equiv \varepsilon_{\gamma\delta}(\text{ZPF virtual particles}) + \varepsilon_{\gamma\delta}(\text{real particles})$

Similarly for magnetic permeability.

$\varepsilon_{\gamma\delta}\mu^{\gamma\delta} = \varepsilon_{\gamma\delta(ZPF)}\mu^{\gamma\delta(ZPF)} + \varepsilon_{\gamma\delta(ZPF)}\mu^{\gamma\delta(Matter)} + \varepsilon_{\gamma\delta(Matter)}\mu^{\gamma\delta(ZPF)} + \varepsilon_{\gamma\delta(Matter)}\mu^{\gamma\delta(Matter)}$

$\varepsilon_{\gamma\delta}\mu^{\gamma\delta} \to \infty \Rightarrow T_{\mu\nu} \to 0$

for fixed $G_{\mu\nu}$

Dr. Sarfatti's completed equation.

Definition of Metamaterial to help understand Dr. Sarfatti's work:

Metamaterial is defined as an artificial composite that gains its electromagnetic properties from its structuring rather than inheriting them directly from the materials it is composed of. The properties of metamaterials are tailored by manipulating their internal physical structure. This makes them remarkably different from natural materials, whose properties are mainly determined by their chemical constituents and bonds. The primary reason for the intensive interest in metamaterials is their unusual effect on light propagating through them.

Using electromagnetic waves with relatively large wavelengths, the composite structure of metamaterial acts as an array of artificial atoms, giving rise to unique and exotic electromagnetic properties. This has made metamaterials a very exciting and promising research area, yielding many interesting and unique phenomena.

Metamaterials are used in cloaking, not unlike *"Star Trek's"* cloaking devices, but they also promise other far-reaching potential. They are of the nano-quantum world. They are not "material" as in what our clothes are made of. Also, the metamaterials of which Dr. Sarfatti speaks, are somewhat different than those used for cloaking.

Footnote 35: Britannia.com, "Metamaterial," by Yongmin Liu and Xiang Zhang

Photos of metamaterials

> **Metamaterials**
> - Metamaterial is an arrangement of artificial structural elements, designed to achieve advantageous and unusual electromagnetic properties
> - meta = beyond (Greek)

***

Chapter Five: There Are Always Possibilities

Time is the fire in which we burn

— Gene Roddenberry

Taking a look at the idea which postulates that traveling back in time is possible, certain principles of physics and quantum physics raise their confusing heads. Taking a closer look at them, we first run into the Novikov Self-Consistency Principle.

The Novikov Loop: When the topic of time travel is mentioned, someone always says, "But what if I came back and killed my grandfather (or my father or myself)?" The fear is, even the smallest act of a time traveler can change all future history, even eliminating the time traveler's own existence. However, the Novikov Self-Consistency Principle says this cannot happen to a time traveler; this rule is accepted physics.

In the mid-1800s, Russian physicist Igor Dmitriyevich Novikov set about to solve paradoxes in time travel. He offered the Self-Consistency Principle which asserts (put in simplistic and admittedly dramatic form), that if a time traveler comes back and is about to kill his grandfather, he cannot, because the Novikov Loop says that all changes due to time travel into the past, were always part of history (in the first place).

Therefore, the loop is a closed loop, it is already part of history, so a diversion such as killing your grandfather, has 0% chance of being introduced; therefore, this act can't exist.

Footnote 36, en.wikipedia.org "The Novikov Self-Consistency Principle"

However, the Novikov Principle is a principle of "not-new physics." New physics (quantum and post-quantum), especially the "many worlds" interpretation, deals with alternate timelines and multiple realities. It has been argued that if a chrononaut did manage to kill his grandfather, this would create a new (alternate) reality but the time traveler would not be the original time traveler, so says the theory, but instead (he would be) an alternate of himself or herself. The original chrononaut still would have a living grandfather. As to how the alternate chrononaut would then exist, well, he would not exist in the first place, according to Novikov. Holy paradox, Batman!

Sometimes science fiction is so helpful:
The following science fiction tales seem to uphold the Novikov Self-Consistency Principle:

Greek mythology has the story of Cassandra. She was given the gift of prophecy by Apollo but also cursed so that no one would believe her predictions. This left her unable to avert any of the disastrous events she foresaw. I can relate to this myself, after my predictions of climate crises, melting glaciers, rising waters, and more, for almost 40 years. Almost no one listened to me and others who predicted the same, certainly not any "leaders" who could have done something about it back then.

The Time Machine by H.G. Wells, 1895, is a science fiction novella. A quick summary, that is, up to a certain point in this great tale:

A group of men, including the narrator, is listening to the Time Traveler discuss his theory that time is the fourth dimension. The Time Traveler produces a miniature time machine and makes it disappear into thin air. The next week, the guests return, to find their host stumble in, looking disheveled and tired. They sit down after dinner, and the Time Traveler begins his story.

The Time Traveler had finally finished work on his time machine, and it rocketed him into the future. When the machine stops, in the year 802,701 AD, he finds himself in a lovely world of small humanoid creatures called Eloi. They are frail and peaceful. He explores the area, but when he returns, he finds that his time machine is gone.

The Time Traveler decides that his machine has been put inside the pedestal of a nearby statue. He tries to pry it open but cannot. In the night, he begins to catch glimpses of strange white ape-like creatures the Eloi call Morlocks. He decides that the Morlocks live below ground.

Meanwhile, he saves one of the Eloi from drowning, and she befriends him. Her name is Weena. The Time Traveler finally works up enough courage to go down into the world of Morlocks to try to retrieve his time machine.

This is only the beginning of the best known and loved literary time travel conundrum and adventure!

Footnote 37: The New Yorker.com "Morlocks and Eloi," By Rebecca Curtis, June 2015

In **Star Trek, Original Series'** Emmy Award-winning episode, "City on the Edge of Forever," Kirk and Spock are time travelers who arrive in 1930's Great Depression. Edith Keller's life is devoted of helping people survive by running a soup kitchen. She is *of* her reality; it cannot be changed (Novikov Self-Consistency Principle).

Kirk and Spock apparently feel it is not against the Prime Directive to know Edith because they accept her life is a closed loop which they cannot change.

Kirk and Spock discover that Edith will die in a street accident, soon. Since Kirk has fallen in love with Edith, he badly wants to save her; but, at the last second, he does not. It might be argued that he really *could not* have saved her due to the Novikov Self-Consistency Principle.

So the time travelers from Star Fleet perhaps *could not* affect that 1930s reality. Kirk, Spock, and McCoy return to their own world only seconds after they left. Edith's closed loop of life was long ago, she was long-dead.

It is one thing to contact one individual like Edith Keeler, but it is another thing to allow the Nazis to win World War Two, which is what would have happened if Edith had lived because of the pacifist movement to which she belonged; it would have kept the United States out of World War Two long enough for Hitler to build an atomic bomb.

Footnote 38: *Star Trek*, Original Series, "City on the Edge of Forever," Episode 28, **April 1967**

The 2002 television **Twilight Zone** series has an episode entitled "Cradle of Darkness" which follows a woman who traveled from the modern day back in time to kill the infant Adolf Hitler to prevent his future atrocities. The woman disposes of the Hitler family's baby and replaces him with a beggar woman's child so as not to arouse suspicion. This replacement infant is the child who then grows up to become the infamous Adolf Hitler. That's right, you can't change what *is,* as hard as you try, according to Novikov.

A causal loop is a theoretical proposition of a sequence of events (actions, information, objects, people), which is among the causes of another event, which is in turn is among the causes of the first-mentioned event. Such causally looped events then exist in spacetime, but their point of origin cannot be determined.

Footnote 39: wikipedia.org, "Causal Loops"

This is one way some UFO abductees feel they have a connection to their UFO abductor; the abductee feels that his strange abductor is a different form of himself – perhaps a future self. So, parallel aspects (past, present, future lifetimes) exist for this abductee, but a causal loop means that time is irrelevant for him. His future-self can come and abduct or contact, his present self. This is admitted conjecture which mixes physics and metaphysics, something that annoys physicists.

The causal loop has a cousin, **The Bootstrap Exception (Paradox):** Traveling back in time allows for causal loops whose histories form a closed loop, and thus seem to "come from nowhere." The notion of objects or information which are "self-existing" in this way is often viewed as paradoxical.

Two examples of the Bootstrap Paradox: The television series **Doctor Who** tells the tale of a time-traveler who copies Beethoven's music from the future and publishes it in Beethoven's time in Beethoven's name.

The film **Somewhere in Time** is also an example involving an object (a watch) which seemingly has no origin, reminding us of Schrodinger's poor cat, being either/neither dead or alive. An old woman gives a watch to a playwright who later travels back in time and meets the same woman when she was young, giving her the same watch that she will later give to him.

So events, objects, information, even people, when sent back in time, can become trapped within an infinite cause-effect loop in which the item or person no longer has a discernible point of origin, and is said to be "uncaused" or "self-created." (bootstrap theory).

On the other hand, a causal loop has a discernible point of origin in spacetime but it cannot be discerned.

Footnote 40: Astronomy Trek, "Time Travel and the Bootstrap Paradox, Explained" by Peter Christoforou, October 2014

The Bootstrap Paradox is also known as an Ontological Paradox, in reference to ontology, a branch of metaphysics dealing with the study of being and existence. How often do physics theories and principles echo of metaphysical, often age-old practices and knowledge? Fairly often!

Spooky Action at a Distance and Retro-causality:

One of the stranger aspects of quantum mechanics could be explained if causation can run backwards in time as well as forwards.

What Einstein called "spooky action at a distance" could theoretically be evidence of retro-causality. This would be the quantum world's equivalent of you having a sore toe today from stubbing your toe, tomorrow.

Part of that strangeness of the quantum world comes down to the fact that at a fundamental level, particles don't act like solid billiard balls rolling down a table, but rather like a blurry cloud of possibilities shifting around the room.

This blurry cloud comes into sharp focus when we try to measure particles, but all the while, the rest of the blurry cloud of waves is sitting there, unperceived.

But what about actions taking place somewhere else... or some*when* else? Can something far away influence that blurry cloud without touching it? Einstein called it "spooky"?

If the quantum particles of two die (dice) are entangled in space at some point, measuring a property of one of them instantly sets the value for the other, no matter where in the universe one die then goes. Theoretically, if you roll a "5" on one die in your house, its partner die on Mars, will roll a "5."

If causality ran backwards (thus retro-causality), it would mean a particle could carry the action of its measurement back in time to when it was entangled, affecting its partner. No faster-than-light messages needed; these two entangled partners would have beat time!

This is only theory at this point.

Footnote 41: sciencealert.com, "This Quantum Theory Predicts That The Future Might Be Influencing The Past," by Mike McCrae, June 2018

The Many-Worlds Interpretation of Quantum Mechanics:

The many-worlds interpretation of quantum physics asserts that all possible alternate histories and futures are real, each representing an actual "world." The theory states there are an infinite number of universes, and everything that could possibly have happened, but did not, has occurred in some other universe or universes.

Can we visit these other universes? The Novikov Principle says, "No," but there are always possibilities of change as science and technology advance.

Regardless of physics, there are countless science fiction stories of characters crossing into other universes and meeting versions of themselves. As our descendants travel time, incredible possibilities are bound to pop up. The universe is stranger than we can imagine.

The Arrow of Time: In science class, we have always been taught that there is an "arrow of time" and it points in one direction: Forward! This argument is often used in debates wherein traveling back in time is said to be impossible. It does seem that time flows into the future; if we break an egg, we cannot reverse time and unbreak it.

British astronomer and physicist Sir Arthur Eddington coined "the arrow of time" back in 1927. Eddington stated that the same arrow of time would apply to an alien race on the other side of the universe as applies to us. Therefore, the arrow of time is not part of our biology or perception, it is the way the universe is. Or is it?

Many physicists believe the forward arrow of time comes down to entropy, the level of molecular disorder in a system. Entropy is always increasing; the gradual decline into disorder is ever-marching forward.

However, the Theory of Relativity states that the universe can be described by four dimensional space-time. Modern quantum physicists just write it as one word these days, "spacetime." The point is, time does not actually *flow;* it just *is*. Einstein opened the door to new thinking on the arrow of time.

The perception of an arrow of time that we have in our everyday life seems to be nothing more than an illusion of our level of consciousness in this universe. It seems to be a perception we happen to experience due to our type of existence at this point in our evolution.

The rules of the macroscopic universe (our everyday world) and the rules of the microscopic universe (the world of quantum physics), are often seemingly not compatible. Einstein died not having "unified the field," but he did try.

In our macroscopic world, there is a natural order of time and an obvious forward direction. However, in the quantum world, if a physical process is physically possible, it is *the same process run forward or backward.*

Footnote 42: exactlywhatistime.com, "What Is the Arrow of Time?"

The Two-Headed Arrow of Time: The arrow of time is in fact two-headed, so say Julian Barbour from the University of Oxford, Tim Koslowski from the University of New Brunswick, and Flavio Mercati from the Perimeter Institute for Theoretical Physics. They argue that for any confined system of particles (for example, a self-contained universe, not affected by anything outside of it), gravity will create a point wherein the distance between particles is minimal.

"That point is the Janus Point and a two-headed arrow of time moves out from there, in both directions," says Barbour. Time and gravity are an awesome and mysterious pair!

An initial event, such as the Big Bang, might have created a Janus Point, but it is not an exclusive property of the Big Bang. Other changes could cause gravity structures to form in both directions. Researchers have found that as the particles begin to expand outwards (after an initial event such as the Big Bang), they will do so in two different directions, emanating from one point.

Is it possible that there are places wherein time actually moves backwards? In theory, yes. These might be called mirror universes.

To summarize: The moment before the expansion is called the Janus Point, which is named after the two-headed Roman god. Time does not pre-exist but as systems converge and expand, gravity creates structure in both directions. The Janus Point is the beginning point from which the arrow of time moves out in opposite directions.

Footnote 43: The Scientific Explorer, "Our Mirror Universe Where Time Moves Backward," Joanne Kennel, January, 2016

Janus, two-headed god of gates, passageways, transitions, time, duality

The Two Headed Arrow of Time theory may not have anything to do directly with Future Humans traveling back in time, but it is clear that time itself is not what it used to be!

Just maybe Future Humans are not having to move against the over-powering arrow of time which always marches forward. They most likely use quantum or even post-quantum technology in order to travel back in time. It makes sense that the key to time travel lies in quantum and post-quantum technology we already know is not chained to the steady march of time of the macroscopic world.

Do Future Humans deal with these crazy quantum physics theories? I'd love to ask them!

It may be that Future Humans on time travel duty, do not run into physics problems every day, or, perhaps some of these theories have been proven erroneous as actual time travel and the situations and events it causes, have unfolded.

We drive on busy freeways and roads all the time, but do we refer to the Department of Motor Vehicles' rule book often? Do we find that a few of their rules don't make sense in actual driving? We drive our technology and handle it as we are used to doing, and it works, usually. It may be similar for the time traveling brigade.

Time is absolute to us because that is our level of evolution. We have a lot of room to evolve and to grow! Few people who believe in advanced extraterrestrial life would deny that their awareness and perception is far beyond ours and is probably not chained to time at all. This does not mean they are perfect!

It is strange that we open our minds if we are talking about extraterrestrials, but we are often pessimistically closed-minded about ourselves and our future.

***

Chapter Six: Jacques Vallee and The Others of Earth

There are things known and there are things unknown, and in between are the doors of perception. – Aldous Huxley

Jacques Vallee, astronomer, computer scientist, and venture capitalist is an icon of ufology. Born in Pontoise, France, in 1939, he may be best known to Americans for his cameo appearance in **Close Encounters of the Third Kind.**

In May 1955, Vallée first sighted a UFO over his Pontoise home. Six years later in 1961, while working on the staff of the French Space Committee, Vallée witnessed the destruction of the tracking tapes of an unknown object orbiting the Earth. The particular object was in retrograde orbit, meaning it was orbiting the Earth in the opposite direction to the Earth's rotation.

At the time he observed this, there were no rockets powerful enough to launch such an object, so the team was quite excited as they assumed that the Earth's gravity had captured a (natural) asteroid. Then, explains Vallee, an unnamed superior came and erased the tape. These events contributed to Vallée's long-standing interest in the UFO phenomenon.

As an alternative to the extraterrestrial visitation hypothesis, Vallée has suggested a multidimensional visitation hypothesis. This hypothesis represents an extension of the Extraterrestrial Hypothesis, wherein the alleged extraterrestrials could be potentially from anywhere or any-when. The entities could be multidimensional beyond space-time, and thus could coexist with humans, yet remain undetected.

Dr. Jacques Vallee has written unique, fascinating books which postulate it is the "Others of Earth," and probably not extraterrestrials who visit us. But who are "the Others?"

A special thanks to Jacques Vallee for approving the sharing his research paper.

"I believe that a powerful force has influenced the human race in the past and is again influencing it now. Does this force represent alien intervention, or does it originate entirely within human consciousness?" states Dr. Vallee.

He says they are perhaps an Earth intelligence (not an alien intelligence), perhaps from a hidden dimension. He feels they appear to us within the cultural framework we recognize, so that in the 1700s, a fairy may have appeared before us in the meadow and somehow interacted. In the 20th and 21st Centuries, it is a humanoid "alien" in a UFO. Vallee has consistently said that we have leaped to the conclusion it must be aliens since the technology is way beyond our own. He insists that we give thought to our visitors being from a source closer to Earth or of Earth.

Vallee with J. Allen Hynek

The research paper herein is from 1990 when Jacques was beginning to consider a more advanced technology as the UFO answer. In recent years, Jacques has intensely followed the evidence that advanced technology is involved; in his earlier writing, he was less prone to include advanced tech. His changing ideas are reflected in the fact he is now a Silicon Valley adventure capitalist, one of the technology experts working on finding the advanced technology to take us into the future and to the stars. "The Hidden Others of Earth" may already have that technology.

Footnote 44: Vice/Motherboard Online: "Meet Silicon Valley's UFO Hunters," by MJ Banias, June 28, 2019

Dr. Vallee is a principal at Documatica Financial, LLC and a diversified investor with a passion for technology startups in space development, medical equipment and information management. He earned a Bachelor's Degree in mathematics from the Sorbonne, a Master's Degree in astrophysics from Lille University and a PhD in Computer Science /AI from Northwestern University (1967).

Footnote 45: jacquesvallee.net

In his research paper for *Journal of Scientific Exploration*, Vallee gives five reasons why our visitors are not extraterrestrials. These reasons seem to overlap with reasons why our visitors are Future Humans. I stress that Jacques Vallee does not say the words "Future Humans." He seems to feel that UFO occupants are from Earth or a dimension adjacent to our Earth. Time, of course, is the 4th dimension.

I have abbreviated the first argument because the statistic of an estimated one million UFO encounters was offered in 1990. Today, the numbers of those experiencing UFO encounters must be in the tens of millions, so Vallee's detailed figures for 1990 aren't as relevant today.

Vallee's Premise: *The extraterrestrial theory of UFOs has never been put to such a test - hence the continuing skepticism of the scientific community.*

In this paper I try to show that major aspects of the phenomenon were not accounted for by the extraterrestrial theory, at least in its simplistic form, which assumes that the objects are spacecraft flown to the Earth by a race of Aliens from another planet who came here around the time of World War Two.

The paper is NOT, as often falsely assumed, an attempt to debunk UFOs or to claim that the phenomenon could not be extraterrestrial: this hypothesis is still to be considered, but it is not the only one, or the most scientifically interesting one.

In order to be valid, any extraterrestrial explanation for UFOs must account for at least the five series of facts outlined here. Doing so would open rich new avenues for research. – Jacques Vallee

Argument One: Close Encounter Frequency

"...The remarkably large number of UFO sightings and encounters can and should be used as a challenge to the natural phenomenon hypothesis that UFOs are simply a peculiar atmospheric phenomena, such as a plasma discharge."

"Yet the same argument can also be used against Extraterrestrial Hypothesis (ETH) because it is difficult to claim that space explorers would need to land 5,000 times in one year on the surface of a planet to analyze its soil, take samples of the flora and fauna, and produce a complete map. While the ETH could perhaps account for the 923 landing reports in our 1969 compilation, the theory can no longer be supported today."

Note: Vallee then explains that "5,000" is not an accurate number, either, taking into account the entire world and other factors. He arrives at the figure "one million encounters" as more accurate, in 1990.

..."If we remain faithful to a strict interpretation of the ETH, even this very large figure still underestimates the real number of actual landings. Shouldn't we assume that extraterrestrial explorers would land on our planet without regard for the presence of human witnesses?"

"In fact the geographic distribution of close encounters does indicate a pattern of avoidance of population centers, with a higher relative incidence of landings in deserts and in areas without dwelling."

"This number still does not take into account another important pattern in the phenomenon, namely its nocturnal character. First published in 1963, this pattern shows no significant variation between older and more recent cases and even yields the same distribution when a very homogenous sample of previously unreported cases from a single region is analyzed (Poher & Vallee, 1975)."

Note: His argument here is also one of my arguments; extraterrestrials would have gotten their samples, mapped the planet, and their activity would dwindle, being complete as years pass. Instead it seems that whatever the UFOs are, they simply operate and function *here*. It seems they think they belong *here*.

... *"The question to be answered is: What objectives could extraterrestrial visitors to the earth be pursuing, that would require them to land millions of times on our planet?"*

"It should be kept in mind that the surface of the Earth is clearly visible from space, unlike Venus or other planetary bodies shrouded in a dense atmosphere. Furthermore, we have been broadcasting information on our various cultures in the form of radio for most of this century and in the form of television for the last 30 years, so that most of the parameters about our planet and our civilization can be readily acquired by unobtrusive, remote technical means."

(**Note:** This was written before the Internet but as I've mentioned, the Internet reveals everything about us, good and bad).

"The collecting of physical samples would require landing but it could also be accomplished unobtrusively with a few carefully targeted missions of the type of our own Viking experiments on Mars. All these considerations appear to contradict the extraterrestrial hypothesis (ETH)."

Argument Two: Physiology *"The vast majority of reported "Aliens" have a humanoid shape that is characterized by two legs, two arms and a head supporting the same organs of perception we have, in the same number and general appearance. Their speech uses the same frequency' range as ours and their eyes are adapted to the same general segment of the electromagnetic spectrum. This indicates a genetic formulation that does not appear to differ from the human genome by more than a few percent."*

"Such an observation, if the entities were in fact the product of independent evolution on another planetary body as stated by the ETH, would stretch our understanding of biology."

"Humans share the unique combination of gravity, solar radiation, atmospheric density and chemical composition known on earth with an array of creatures closely related to us through evolution, yet deprived of legs and arms like the dolphins or endowed with multiple eyes like the spiders..."

Argument Three: Abduction Reports

"The growing number of abduction reports is being used by a vocal segment of the UFO research community as further evidence that we are, in fact, being visited by extraterrestrial aliens, even if their origin has not yet been revealed. In the context of the present paper, a careful survey of the reported behavior of the alleged ufonauts argues exactly in the opposite direction."

"Such incidents are characterized by what the witness reports as being transported into a hollow, spherical or hemispherical space and being subjected to a medical examination. This is sometimes (but not always), followed by the taking of blood samples, various kinds of sexual interaction, and loss of time. The entire episode is frequently wiped out of conscious memory and is only retrievable under hypnosis."

... "Although nothing concrete seems to have been gleaned from these case studies about the origin and purpose of the visitors, those doing the investigations are vocal in their claim that the abductions are further evidence of the ETH."

"In order to examine this claim, let us assume ET intelligence has indeed developed the ability and the desire to visit the Earth. It is a reasonable assumption to expect that such visitors would know at least as much as we do in the fundamental scientific disciplines such as physics and biology. Few ufologists in fact, argue against this assumption. In particular, the visitors would presumably know as much about medical techniques and procedures as our own practitioners.

Today, the average American doctor can draw blood, collect sperm and ova or remove tissue samples from his or her patients without leaving permanent scars or inducing trauma. The current state of molecular biology—a science which is in its infancy on Earth—would already permit that same doctor to obtain unique genetic information from samples."

"None of these accomplishments require the procedural behavior of the "Alien Doctors" described by abduction researchers. The answers may have to be sought in other directions than ETH."

Note: It is true that we see no reason for Future Human doctors to do what some abductees have claimed was done to them so crudely; no extraterrestrial doctor should do these things, either. I do wonder if the abductees were in such a state of shock and fear that they report events inaccurately but that is only a theory.

Another somewhat bizarre theory: Some Future Humans may have perversions the same as some of us, do; what if he or she carried them into actual practice? Might (a few/some) sadistic Future Humans happen to be on catch and release (abduction) teams?

I do believe that a preponderance of evidence would show this kind of thing (such as anal probes) happened mostly through a specific period of time and is not the norm in encounters and abductions throughout the years. And, if ETs are the answer, there are some sadistic ETs, then.

Argument Four: History

"When UFOs first became famous was at a time when the earliest sightings known dated from World War II. It could be validly argued that this major conflict was detected from space and that the observation of nuclear explosions on Earth precipitated the Aliens' decision to survey our planet, perhaps in an effort to assess the human potential threat to other intelligent lifeforms..."

"The mounting proliferation of evidence for similar phenomena not only before 1945 but during the 19th Century and indeed in the remote past of our culture has...established that the phenomenon has indeed existed throughout history, adapting only its superficial shape but not its underlying structure to the expectations of the host culture..."

"Such historical considerations, combined with extensive research on mythology and folklore, have led some researchers to regard the entire UFO phenomenon as a projection of the consciousness of the witnesses. They point out that science-fiction and legends, too, stay one step ahead of human scientific realizations..."

Argument Five: Physical Considerations

"As witnesses become less reluctant in the reporting of their experiences, the notion that UFOs are "somebody else's spacecraft (in the words of Stanton Friedman), with the implication of a technology powered by advanced propulsion systems, becomes less tenable. But, alternative explanations, notably the psycho-sociological hypothesis, also find themselves severely challenged."

"The phenomena to be explained include not only strange flying devices but also objects and beings that exhibit the ability to appear and disappear very suddenly, to change apparent shapes in continuous fashion and to merge with other physical objects."

"Such reports seem absurd in terms of ordinary physics because they suggest a mastery of time and space that our own physical research cannot duplicate today. However, if these sightings can be confirmed either by direct observation by photographic evidence or by the weight of statistics, they may represent an opportunity for new concepts."

Note: The paragraph above would seem to have manifested into reality with the U.S. Navy's Tic-Tac capsule admission in 2019 that the videos and UAP/UFO events are real.

New Hypothesis by Vallee: *"In the mid-70's, I proposed to approach the UFO phenomenon as a control system, reserving judgment as to whether the control would turn out to be human, alien or simply natural. Such control systems, governing physical or social events, are all around us. They can be found in the terrestrial, ecological and economic balancing mechanisms that rule nature, some of which are well understood by science. This theory admits (two interesting variants: (I) An Alien intelligence, possibly earth-based, could be training us towards a new type of behavior. It could represent the "Visitor Phenomenon" (Stricter, 1987) or some form of "super-nature," possibly along the lines of a "Gaia" hypothesis. (2) Alternately, in a Jungian interpretation of the same theme, the human collective unconscious could be projecting ahead of itself the imagery which is necessary for our own long-term survival beyond the unprecedented crises of the 20th Century."*

Note: I have suggested similar in my essay, **"The ETs of Evolution," Alternate Perceptions, September 2016**

British researcher Jenny Randles has stressed that the discourse of abductees consistently reveals a breakpoint in time, after which the normal reality is left behind. On the "other side" of this boundary, ordinary spacetime physics no longer seems to apply and the participant moves as if within a lucid dream (or indeed a lucid nightmare) until returned to the normal world.

Randles calls this phenomenon the "Oz Factor." Building on this observation, one could theorize that there exists a remarkable slate of psychic functioning that alters the participant's vision of physical reality and also generates actual traces and luminous phenomena, visible to other witnesses in their normal state.

(Vallee concludes): "Finally, we could hypothesize extraterrestrial travelers using radical methods of spacetime manipulation, notably the use of four-dimensional wormholes for space and possibly even time travel..."

"Such travelers could perform many of the physical feats ascribed to ufonauts and they could also manifest simultaneously throughout what appears to us as different periods in our history. This hypothesis represents an updating of the ETH1 wherein the "extraterrestrials" can be from anywhere and anytime, and could even originate from our own Earth. (Bold font added by Diane Tessman).

Footnote 46: The Journal of Scientific Exploration, "Five Arguments Against the Extraterrestrial Theory," by Dr. Jacques Vallee, pages 105-117, 1990

Footnote 47: Alien Jigsaw.com, "The Oz Factor," by Jenny Randles

Here is my essay which I referenced within Vallee's paper. It is more ethereal than the nuts and bolts approach of most of this book, but I feel it belongs as a harmonious offering which says, "we create our descendants." If our visitors are Future Humans, then we created them on an existential basis as well as a physical basis. One generation creates the next and each generation echoes and creates, right through the centuries.

The ETs of Evolution

By Diane Tessman

"By believing passionately in something that still does not exist, we create it. The nonexistent is whatever we have not sufficiently desired." - Nikos Kazantzakis

We humans create our human reality. I feel that our evolving human perception not only experiences but creates at least some of the strange forms and ET craft which we see in our skies.

Greek philosopher Nikos Kazantzakis wrote "Zorba the Greek" and "The Last Temptation of Christ" and was the inspiration behind Anthony Quinn's award-winning performance in the film, "Zorba the Greek." Perhaps "Zorba the Human" would have been a better title.

I have no idea if Mr. Kazantzakis believed in life from other worlds and UFOs, but his thoughts are a poetic, artistic version of what quantum physics tells us about our creation of this reality.

We don't think often about our own evolution and what it really means: What does the mental and spiritual process of evolution look and feel like? How does collective consciousness grow and expand? Where is the evidence that this evolution-process even exists in each of us as members of the species?

"Everything we call real is made of things that cannot be regarded as real." – Niels Bohr

Might the evidence be in those UFOs we keep sighting? Are at least some UFO occupants created by Homo sapiens' vast, insatiable need to evolve? Or, a variation: Are UFO occupants being created by the process of evolution itself? Are UFO occupants falling out of the evolutionary egg? Evolution is a mysterious force which is a blend of science and spirit.

Consider the fact that the universe itself keeps growing as we, the human species, continue to evolve. A few hundred years ago, Earth was flat and the Sun revolved around Earth. For all intents and purposes, this was true, at least the results it rendered were real. Futurists were punished if they dared to guess that the world was round. Society and laws reflected that the Sun revolved around the Earth.

Today, just when we learn that there are 100 billion stars in 100 billion galaxies, it turns out our expanding science has discovered 200 billion stars in 200 billion galaxies. But wait! It was just announced the Milky Way might have 400 billion stars with as many planets! Our science constantly expands the universe and so does our spirit.

Whether evolution allows a species to perceive more of the cosmos, or the species actually creates "more" in the cosmos through its growing consciousness, who knows?

"Imagination is more important than knowledge." - Albert Einstein

It seems the natural world has this prime directive: Evolve or Die! However, humans are strange because of our advanced intellectual and spiritual needs. The animal world has wonderful intelligence and spirituality too, but it is in balance. Humans are restless, aggressive beings that seem out of balance with their own planet but at the same time, have amazing abilities and potential which other Earth species do not.

We arrived at this state of imbalance coupled with intelligence after many hominin species disappeared; one line of evolution was the most vigorous and aggressive, becoming Homo sapiens. We do not know what our people-ape ancestors began to perceive once the pressure of evolution set in.

It is not just the modern human who sees an image generated by his evolving mind and brings it into his reality. We have only been on Earth for a heartbeat but the process of evolution, the next step, had begun as soon as we emerged as a species.

I believe an ever-expanding, more complicated perception was and is "available" within quantum consciousness. If our collective consciousness stretches beyond our minds and into the universe, then there is always a more advanced version to be "uploaded" (a new evolutionary update).

"If quantum physics hasn't shocked you, you have not understood it yet." – Niels Bohr

Earlier humans did not yet dream of computers and rockets to the moon; thus they did not bring them into being. However, they did dream of being warm and being able to cook raw meat and so, it was discovered that fire could be harnessed. Our ancestors dreamed and thought what they needed next to survive, and it happened.

What we urgently need next is to know that we are not alone in the universe and that there are more advanced beings than ourselves. Our species needs this humbling knowledge desperately these days.

And evolution involves work! It involves stretching and stretching your neck over thousands of years if you are a giraffe. Thus it is not handed to us today on a silver platter; we have to work for it. UFO occupants remain partially hidden, almost not interfering at all; they are only available in glimmering objects hovering in the night sky. The UFO occupants are making us reach now, this is how evolution happens.

But does our collective consciousness *create* UFO occupants and their craft? This is much too simple because I do believe there are beings visiting us (and always have), from actual sources such as other planets, dimensions or time itself. Perhaps in the strictest sense, we do create all we perceive but I am not championing that extreme view; I am simply stating: Some of the ETs and UFOs we are experiencing, might have arrived because we are in the process of "uploading" an expanded consciousness. Therefore, we perceive more of the universe. This premise is solidly in line with quantum physics.

Yes, UFOs were seen by humans in the past also, but evolution is a process which starts as soon as the species appears on Earth.

"No problem can be solved from the same level that created it." - Einstein

Your cat walks all over your computer keyboard. This is frustrating because not only you are trying to type, but cat hairs are not good for the keyboard. But does the cat really perceive your keyboard at all? Your cat knows there is space there to walk with a slight up-rise from the desk itself. She does note that the human spends a lot of time pounding this space with human-fingers which should be petting cat.

For thousands of years, we have perceived more than just the starry skies. There is more to be known both scientific and spiritual, but we did not have the knowledge to comprehend fully. However, I believe we are now near the cusp of our evolution; good-bye to Homo sapiens and hello to our new species. The universe is growing too, and it is no coincidence!

There had to be The Moment when Grandfather Hominin's collective consciousness became Homo sapiens' collective consciousness. The force of evolution favored the new human form. This process will happen to Homo sapiens too. It is happening even now. Someone might say, "Well, it is a physical thing, this evolution. Early hominins slowly grew a larger frontal lobe, slowly lost some physical hair, and so forth.

However, what makes us human? What makes a wolf – a wolf? What makes a blue jay – a blue jay? Yes, there are physical traits but each species has a "hum" (a collective consciousness), which cannot be completely defined or fully encapsulated by looking at the physical structure of the life-form.

Earlier hominins behaved, felt, and thought, differently than Homo sapiens. What it meant to be them was different than what it means to be us.

There will come a day when Homo sapiens phases out and the next step in evolution dominates the collective consciousness. This new species will be flying into alien dimensions of which we now dream. Sound familiar?

I am positive that human evolution has something to do with some of the UFOs we are seeing. I believe this fact is a good reason not to be mindlessly afraid of them. What if we not only are beginning to perceive their reality, what if we are creating their reality?

In a basic way, we are creating the mind and spirit of the species which comes after us. If our minds are evolving into their minds, then are we creating creatures born out of constant fear, greed, war, and careless destruction of the home world?

It is time for new thinking, feeling, and being.

***

Chapter Seven: "The Singularity of Humanoid Life."

Our own genomes carry the story of evolution, written in DNA, the language of molecular genetics, and the narrative is unmistakable.

- Kenneth R. Miller

This chapter features an exclusive interview with Dr. Michael P. Masters who has written an excellent book which scientifically indicates that human time travelers are the answer to the UFO puzzle, entitled, **Identified Flying Objects** (2019).

Dr. Masters is a professor of biological anthropology specializing in human evolutionary anatomy, archeology, and biomedicine. He kindly sat down for an interview for this book.

Diane: Are UFO occupants an alternate branch of hominids, thus was never a part of Homo sapiens? If so, where were they all these years, what is their home? Or, are UFO occupants "us," a straight march through time and then discovered the key to traveling back in time?

Dr. Masters: We now possess an intricate knowledge of the 3.7-billion-year history of life on this planet, as well as a deep understanding of hominin evolution, which has been gleaned from the work of countless paleoanthropologists, archaeologists, and geneticists over the last century. Considering the wealth of information accumulated over this time, in considering the question of extraterrestrials and the UFO phenomenon, it isn't likely that the humanoid beings reported by those who have had a close encounter are a separate branch of hominids, and especially not ones with origins in a separate solar system.

Because these beings are so commonly described as having human-like traits, and importantly, the accentuation of quintessential hominin traits, the most parsimonious explanation is that they are from our future. The most dominant trends in hominin evolution are a shift toward habitual bipedalism (meaning upright walking), encephalization (meaning an increase in brain size), and reduced facial prognathism (meaning a reduction and retraction of the mid and lower face). The latter two of these have also been accelerating in the more recent human past, or for about the last 800,000 years of hominin evolution.

Considering the long history of hominin evolution on this planet, if these same dominant trends in the deep past persist into the deep future, we would expect to resemble to a high degree, these same "alien" beings in our evolutionary future. Namely, across millennia to come, our future human descendants are likely to possess even larger and more rounded neurocrania, smaller faces, larger eyes, a further reduction in body hair, and technology that far surpasses anything we have today.

With regard to the question of whether the hominin lineage could have split at some point in our evolutionary past, thus resulting in two separate advanced humanoid civilizations, if this had happened, there would be unmistakable archaeological evidence of that outcome. It is difficult to locate the habitation site of small nomadic hunter-gatherer groups even a short time after they leave a site. However, large-scale civilizations, comprising state-level societies of 10,000 individuals or more, leave a much more overt mark upon the landscape.

For those who cling to the extraterrestrial hypothesis, this idea is often espoused as an explanation for why these alien beings are so human-like. However, it is logically unfeasible and unsupported by evidence to claim that an earlier human civilization developed technology that enabled them to leave Earth and emigrate to a different planet in a different solar system, and that we are now seeing these humanoid cousins returning to visit us from that earthlike exoplanet.

If any past human group developed a civilization that became advanced enough to leave Earth, there would be overwhelming evidence of them in the archaeological record. Because no indication of any large-scale advanced human society exists prior to the Neolithic, there is no evidence to support this claim.

To the contrary, we know we are here now, and the advanced state we exist in today is the result of incremental changes to our culture and biology that have occurred over the previous 3.3, and 6 million years, respectively. As such, the most parsimonious explanation for any humanlike beings, with more advanced technology, observed in our own time, is simply that they have come from our future.

In other words, modern humans are the result of a long, unbroken, and accelerating progression of hominin culture and biology on this planet. If we are being visited by an even more advanced humanoid intelligence, observed now or throughout the historic or prehistoric past, they are better understood as our hominin relatives, cycling back through the primitive ancestral periods that gave rise to their more advanced future human existence.

Diane: Why do some visitors look like current humans while others are "small people?" If Future Humans from various phases of time, is it possible the small ones are maybe from a time farther in the future?

Dr. Masters: The variation observed among "Aliens," as described in instances of close encounters, could be due to the continuation of geographic racial traits, or what we anthropologists refer to as *ancestry.* In this sense, reported differences among these alien beings – viewed in the context of our future human descendants –could indicate that the same geographic differences we see today among groups from East Asia, Africa, Europe, Native Americans, etc., are likely to persist into the future.

However, in the presence of a time machine, the reported variation among these extra*temp*estrial aliens, can also be easily understood as a product of *temporal ancestry*, in which differences in their physical form is a product of *when* they come from in time, rather than where they come from in space.

This concept can be easily understood by looking back through our own evolutionary past. For instance, if we were to travel 20 years into the past, our physical form would still be nearly identical to human groups two decades earlier. Traveling 200,000 years into the past and meeting up with early members of our species *Homo sapiens*, we would begin to notice quite a few differences in our culture and physical form.

In visiting *Homo erectus* 1.5 million years in the past, not only would we look quite different, but now we are the ones with the big round heads, large eyes, small faces, relative hairlessness, and a gracile cranial and postcranial morphology. In this thought experiment, we remain the same as we visit each of these three periods, but the differences between us and the human groups occupying these progressively earlier times – as well as how we are perceived by them – changes drastically as we move deeper into that past from where we currently reside in time.

In the context of extratempestrial variation, as it relates to the UFO question, in the period of one day, we could potentially be visited by someone from 1,000 years, 100,000 years, and 1 million years in our future. Each of these three groups would look markedly different from one another, not because of where they came from, but rather when they came from throughout this one-million-year period.

With this in mind, it is even possible that some of the highly divergent alien forms, such as those described as insect or reptile-like, are simply from a very distant point in our evolutionary future. It is impossible to know what environmental or cultural forces will shape human evolution between now and then, but there is no doubt that we will continue to evolve, and that future biocultural changes will continue to build upon what came before.

If we are to take seriously the accounts provided by those who have had a close encounter of the third through fifth kind, the ubiquity of reports describing humanoid or humanlike individuals is overwhelming. Taking into consideration their reported relative humanness, it is highly improbable that another planet – with different gravity, chemistry, distance from its sun, etc., would ever develop bipedal humanoid life that would look, act, and talk so much like us, or that they would arise on a planet near enough to us to allow for mutual contact and communication.

Furthermore, given the tremendously long history of the universe, it is highly improbable that such a civilization would arise at the same time as us, be so much like us, but also have just slightly more advanced technology that also happens to be so similar to our own.

In thinking about the statistical improbability of this scenario arising in our proximate celestial neighborhood, we must also ask whether hybridization would be possible with these coincidental extraterrestrial aliens. Because we cannot reproduce with even our closest living relative on this planet, the chimpanzee, with whom we share more than 98.7% of our DNA, it seems unfathomable that we could ever produce viable offspring with any organism that evolved on a different planet with an entirely different evolutionary history. To this end, if one believes that aliens are real, and that they are hybridizing with us, then we must also acknowledge that these aliens are in fact human, and particularly with regard to how we define a species under the biological species concept.

We can easily reproduce with fellow concurrent humans on this planet, though this raises interesting questions about how distant a temporal group can be before we could no longer reproduce with them. Viable offspring could undoubtedly be produced with anyone from 100 or 1,000 years in the past or future, and likely groups within 300,000 – 500,000 years of our current present.

After all, because Neanderthals, Denisovans, and modern humans were all able to reproduce viable offspring across our collective evolutionary past, all indications are that we will continue to be able to reproduce with our more distant extratempestrial descendants, in spite of a similar degree of morphological variation that exists among these modern and future human groups.

Diane: Thanks so much, Mike Masters!

Footnote 48: Identified Flying Objects, Dr. Michael P. Masters, 2019

A Sampling of UFO Occupant Sightings, 1954-1989

Back in 1952, a farmer near Toeterville, Iowa, was out in his field, baling hay. Suddenly a small saucer-shaped craft landed. Two small humans got out. "They were not different from me in any way, except they were small," the farmer explained.

One of the two small humans carried a vessel in his or her hand; the two walked to a small creek which ran at the edge of the field. They gathered water in the vessel, then walked back to their ship and took off, disappearing almost instantly. "I never breathed a word about this because the community would have laughed me out of town," said the now-elderly farmer 50 years later.

This was a UFO landing 5 miles from my parents' farm back in 1952. In the same year, I had two encounters with an entity aboard a strange ship who told me, "We are from your future." He could have been lying, but I have researched and investigated the UFO phenomenon for 40 years. I have had conscious recollection of some of the encounter with him my entire life. I have objectively reached the conclusion that this strange man, told the truth.

I mention the Toeterville saucer landing to point out that the two little entities who got out of the saucer, were human except they were very short humans, according to the farmer's account.

The man I encountered was of normal height, he looked and acted human except for his amber colored, almost translucent eyes. His eyes and entire demeanor were somehow "enhanced." Was he artificial intelligence? There will be more on my encounters and on artificial intelligence later in the book.

In his report for the National Investigations Committee of Aerial Phenomena (NICAP), Richard H. Hall, who was editor of the MUFON Journal for many years and contributed greatly to early studies in the modern UFO era, stated: *"Sightings of UFO occupants have occurred steadily over the years, but tend to increase during sighting waves. By far the most common type is the small humanoid wearing "coveralls" and some kind of headgear, usually round or helmet-like. During close-range encounters with beings outside of their UFO craft, witnesses sometimes have heard unintelligible vocalizations and observed technological "tools." They have been observed "taking samples," "repairing their craft," and engaged in other activities."*

(Part of my old friend Richard H. Hall's NICAP Report):

Police officer Lonnie Zamora, April, 1964, reported seeing two small humanoid beings standing next to a landed craft on April 24. 1964, in Socorro, New Mexico. Since Zamora was a well-known and respected officer, his report helped to legitimize 10 years of prior UFO occupant sightings that had been considered somewhat borderline by many people. His report made headlines nationally and, to some degree, internationally.

Suddenly the air was filled with a roar and the officer saw a flame descending in the southwestern sky. Zamora glimpsed a shiny car-size object on the ground about 150 yards away. Near it stood two small figures clothed in white coveralls.

Zamora briefly lost sight of the object and figures as he passed behind a hill, then he saw an egg-shaped object standing on four legs; it displayed a peculiar insignia on its side, something like an arrow pointing vertically from a horizontal base to a half-Council crown.

The two figures had disappeared, and the object was emitting an ominous roar again. Frightened, Zamora charged back to his car. At one point he glanced over his shoulder to see the UFO, now air-borne, heading toward a nearby canyon.

Project Blue Book investigators found that Officer Zamora had a reputation for integrity. The investigators also examined what looked like landing marks found on the desert floor. In the middle of these marks was a burned area, apparently from the spacecraft's exhaust.

Note: To provide a counterpoint to my "human" argument, I purposely have chosen NON-humanoid or more "monster-like" UFO occupant descriptions (below) if I could. I did so because almost every description in any year of this long report, 1954 through 1989, is only of humanoids or humans. I have abbreviated the report and have chosen only a few cases in each time period from Richard Hall's lists of sightings, 1954-1989.

Richard Hall's NICAP Report: A brief sampling, 1954-1963:

September 10, 1954 Marius Dewilde, Quarouble, France 10:30 P.M.
Two beings 3-1/2 ft. tall, coveralls, diver's helmet; dark mass on ground; dog howled, witness blinded by light from craft, paralyzed.

September 26, 1954 Mme. Leboeuf, Chabeuil (Drome), France 4.00 P.M.
One being 3 ft tall, diving suit, helmet, large eyes; flat circular craft; dog barked, being approached, witness fled; Council of crushed foliage found at site.

October 15, 1957 Antonio Villas-Boas, Sao Francisco de Sales, Brazil. 1:00 A.M., Five small beings, headgear, one female; abducted onto landed disc craft

November 6, 1957 John Trasco, Everittstown, NJ dusk

One 2-1/2- to 3-ft tall being, green garb, putty-colored face, chin, large bulging eyes; man saw 9- to 12-ft.-long luminous egg-shaped UFO, confronted by being who spoke in broken English.

A brief sampling, 1962-1976:

April 24, 1964 Gary Wilcox, Newark Valley, NY 10:00 A.M.
Two 4-ft.-tall beings, silver-white garb, egg-shaped craft just above ground; beings communicated in English.

November 25, 1964 New Berlin, NY
Twelve humanoids observed at distance after two discs landed on hill; appeared to be engaged in repair operation for hours.

July 1, 1965 Maurice Masse. Valensole, France 5:45 A.M.
Two to three small humanoids, one-piece garb; whistling sound, saw craft and beings; tried to approach, paralyzed.

September 10, 1965 Sao Joao, Pernambuco State, Brazil 8:30 A.M.
Two small, brown-skinned humanoids, one-piece garb; two discs landed, beings emerged, objects rose a few meters, unintelligible vocalizations.

August 24, 1967 Ron Hyde, Wodonga, Victoria Australia 5:00 P.M.
Two humanoids about five ft. tall, silvery suits, round helmets, emerged from disc with dome; one moved toward witness and gestured, he fled in fear.

A brief sampling, 1968-1972:

November 20, 1968 M. Milakovic, Hanbury, UK 5:30 P.M.
Five silhouetted humanoids moving back and forth in dome of luminous UFO.

August 16, 1970 Puente de Herrera, Valladolid, Spain 1:00 A.M.
One human-size being, dark tight-fitting garb, entered Saturn-shaped craft, which took off with an intense whistling sound.

UFO Occupant Sightings during 1973 Sighting Wave
October 4, 1973 Gary Chopic, Chatsworth, CA early evening
One human-size being, silver suit, elliptical craft with clear dome; saw witness, entered craft and took off.

October 11, 1973 Hickson & Parker, Pascagoula, MS evening
Two robot-like beings, abduction case

October 12, 1973 Cincinnati, OH 2:30 A.M.
One "apelike" being, featureless, large waist, no neck, visible in dome-shaped object on or near the ground.

October 17, 1973 Paul Brown, Danielsville, GA evening
Two 4- 4-1/2-ft. tall beings, silver garb, emerged from silver egg-shaped craft that descended ahead of car; took off with "whooshing" sound when witness brandished a pistol.

October 19, 1973 Goshen, OH 9:00 P.M.
Two or three 6-ft tall human-like beings moved around a domed disc resting on tripod legs, entered via ladder, took off with humming sound.

A brief sampling, 1974-1989:

March 21, 1974 Valdehijaderos, Salamanca, Spain 2:30 A.M.
Two 6-ft.-tall beings, tight-fitting shiny coveralls, seen after E-M effects on car; beings entered luminous craft and took off.

June 14, 1974 Medellin, Spain 4:30 A.M.
Three tall beings with helmets visible in turret of "pot-shaped" craft hovering over farmhouse, area illuminated "like day".

September 29, 1974 Mme. Le Bihan, Riec-sur-Belon, Finistere, France 12:45 A.M.
Three 1.7-meter-tall stocky humanoids, round heads, silver garb, from brilliantly lighted dome-shaped object with portholes, swaying back and forth near ground; beings walked heavily, rocking back and forth.

February 4, 1978 Manuel Alvarez, La Florida, San Luis, Argentina 4:30 A.M.
One human-size being, helmet, luminous garb, descended on ladder from hovering disc, waved at fishermen, reentered craft, which took off at high speed.

Footnote 49: NICAP.org, UFO Evidence, "UFO Occupant Sightings," by Richard H. Hall

I first met Leonard Stringfield in the hotel restaurant in which the MUFON Propulsion Symposium of 1980, was being held. It was in Houston and lots of people from NASA were there – very exciting! I had dated Richard H. Hall (mentioned above), and I knew Stringfield confided in Richard as his research confidante. I introduced myself to Leonard and later I bought his **UFO Crash Retrieval Syndrome #1.**

It seems slightly strange to be writing about Richard and Leonard now that both are deceased and are part of UFO history. Leonard investigated a number of reports of alien bodies, usually from crashed saucers. His informants would talk to him, and then disappear while others would not say another word to him.

There is no way to guarantee that all of Stringfield's reports were real events and real alien bodies. I can vouch for the fact that he was not a liar nor a fool. Richard H. Hall was an honest and committed UFO research pioneer who did meticulous investigation and work. Neither of them would be easily fooled by someone telling them a story or being deceitful.

It became obvious that every "alien" body he learned about, was (said to be) human or humanoid (take your pick). While their features were a variation on our features, informants reported that autopsies revealed the "aliens" all conformed to our human physical paradigm.

Here are several samples of Leonard Stringfield's descriptions of the "alien" bodies as related to him by informants. Anyone interested in Stringfield's detailed description of many crash/retrieval cases, is urged to read his **UFO Crash-Retrieval Syndrome volumes.**

Case 1: Somewhere in Arizona: "I'm almost positive in happened in 1953," my informant said. He is a man with a long career as a pilot in the military, who held the rank of warrant officer in the army during the early 1950s, now serving in the Air National Guard.

It was now the late summer of 1977, as the man tried to recall the exact time when he stood as a witness, in 1953, at a distance of about 12 feet, peering at five crates on a fork lift inside a hangar at Wright-Patterson Air Force Base.

In each of three crates, he said, were the recovered dead bodies of small humanoids; the contents of the other two crates were not discernible. As he related this astonishing information in a matter-of-fact manner, he pointed vaguely to an area in Arizona on the map. "Here's where it happened," he said. "It was in a desert area but I don't have the name of the location."

There was no one else in the map room when he told me about the incident. He made certain of that. "It's still a secret, and at the time I had to swear to it," he said. "I was in the right place at the right time when the crates arrived at night by DC-7."

As we stood at the map, my informant described what appeared to be hastily prepared wooden crates. In these, little humanoids, appearing to be four feet tall, were lying unshrouded on a fabric, which he explained prevented freeze burn from the dry ice packed beneath. As a number of Air Police stood silent guard near by the crates, he managed to get reasonably good but brief glimpse of the humanoid features. He recalls that their heads were disproportionately larger than the bodies, with skin that looked brown under the hangar lights above.

The head appeared to be hairless and narrow.

Note: In other cases, a fuzzy thin hair was reported on the aliens' heads.

The eyes seemed to be open, the mouth small, while the nose, if any, was indistinct. The humanoids' arms were positioned down, alongside their bodies, but the hands and feet, he said, were indistinct.

When asked about their attire, he said they appeared to be wearing tight-fitting dark suits and, because of the tight-fit, there was one revealing feature — and a surprising one at that — for one of the humanoids appeared to him to be female. He added: "Either one of the aliens had an exceedingly muscular chest or the bumps were a female's breasts." Later, he learned from one of the crew members, with whom he bunked at the barracks, that the body of one of the aliens was, indeed, that of a female.

My informant also heard from the crew member that one of the little humanoids was still alive aboard the craft when the U.S. military team arrived. Attempts made to save "its" life with oxygen were unsuccessful.

Case 2: UFO that had crashed in the southwest region of the United States in 1957: (Stringfield writes), My informant M.S. says that according to the General he talked to, radar had confirmed that an alien craft had crossed the skies over the United States at great speed. It was tracked to the point of its crash. The area, as in most cases, was "roped off" and the National Guard summoned (with dogs) for maximum security.

From the damaged craft, four humanoid bodies were recovered with great difficulty because of the inability to penetrate the craft's metal structure. The deceased bodies were found badly burned, some parts so severely that certain features were indistinguishable. However, the suits they wore, appearing silver, were not damaged by the obviously intense heat endured inside the craft.

"The suits were fused to the flesh." M. S. said, according to the General, and the four bodies, approximately 5 feet in height, were sent to Wright-Patterson AFB, where the General had seen them in a deep freeze morgue, kept at approximately 120 degrees below zero for preservation. The only other anatomical features described, were the heads of the aliens which, by human standards, were larger proportionately than the bodies. Facial features had been obliterated by the heat.

Case 3: *This case concerned a soldier getting zapped by a beam which emanated from a landed UFO in 1957. The man was taken to the hospital but could rationalize the event only in terms of mathematics, as though an attempt at communications was conducted in this manner. The UFO which shot the beam was observed to retreat to its parent craft which then departed.*

Footnote 50: UFO Crash/Retrievals, The Concept of Truth, Leonard Stringfield (PDF document)

I mention this case because it is similar to Jim Penniston's binary communications after reportedly touching the UFO which landed at RAF Bentwaters (Rendlesham Forest), in 1980. Penniston has maintained it was a craft from the (human) future.

***

Chapter Eight: Abductions in a New Light

There are more things in Heaven and Earth, Horatio, than are dreamt of in your philosophy. - Shakespeare

Abductions are a complex topic, perhaps because raw emotions are so thoroughly mingled with scientific and logical information which can be gleaned from them. In this chapter, we will examine the examiners (the abductors) and see if we can take a closer look at the possibility that humans (or post-humans), have traveled back in time and are the abductors.

Whether all abductions and encounters are done by time traveling humans is something we won't attempt to answer. As stated at the beginning, extraterrestrials may visit us too, but it is our contention that the majority of visitors are, and always have been, human (or post-human) time travelers.

Also, there is solid evidence that our (current human) military has executed off-the-book (black op) abductions called MILABs. The goal is to cast disinformation and fear into the UFO waters so as to keep common people ignorant and obedient. In our chapter, we are only concerned with abductions and encounters in which the evidence seems to point to Future Humans. This is not an entire book on abductions.

Ufology tends to view those who abduct humans as extremely sinister. This premature conclusion muddies the waters because abduction accounts sprout up which are simply tall tales told perhaps with a profit motive; other abduction accounts emanate from people suffering paranoid delusions or other mental instability. Other people simply like the attention and enjoying "spinning." "Sinister" is an emotionally explosive word and does not appeal to investigative thinking, so the effort to examine events is skewered right from the get-go.

So, the abduction accounts which are indeed perpetrated by a strange outside source cannot be easily separated from the invalid accounts. Even worse, few people even try to separate the true from the false. Hysterical experiencers fill social media while researchers back away from abductions entirely. However, abductions are a major piece of evidence and we should not back away.

What terrible species would abduct human beings?

One answer which is true, "Human beings would abduct human beings."

I believe we can begin to understand how good or bad the UFO occupants are, by looking at our own human race. We have improved over the millennia, governments don't put people in "iron maiden" torture devices anymore, we don't have debtors' prisons, and so forth. I realize it is debatable that we have moved forward at all.

Less than 200 years ago, American settlers, with the support of the government, and often in the name of the government, drove Native Americans from their land which had been theirs for many generations. Many were murdered; it was indeed genocide. Native American survivors were driven to lands of hostile climates which are not fertile and are 50 below zero in the winter or they were marched to arid, hot deserts. Yet UFO abductees sometimes cast themselves as the ultimate victims. Not even close!

Human brings enslaved other human beings for thousands of years, and we did it in America not that long ago. Prisoners of war are tortured most cruelly by a variety of countries even today.

I'll spare you the endless list of **man's inhumanity to man.**

A catch and release abduction program, with the time in captivity only a few hours, seems a step forward from much of our behavior over the ages, and that includes our current time.

I am not aiming to make light of abduction experiences but emphasizing that Future Humans act just as we do; apparently whoever has the most advanced technology, can do as they please. In UFO abductions, it is they who have the more advanced technology and the element of surprise.

It is fortunate that the UFO abductors don't seem to want to kill us, don't seem to want to commit genocide or to displace us from our lives as we did to Native Americans. Therefore, it seems we have improved somewhat, but we are still inhumane.

Future Humans have probably continued to improve in terms how we treat our own planet; it turns out, it wasn't intelligent to deplete its resources, chop down its trees, and contaminate the water supply.

If they have artificial intelligence components, there should be a communal logic which states that to have empathy for "the other component" is to insure empathy for oneself. Artificial intelligence *should* create a singularity of loving one's neighbor as oneself, at least that potential is there.

Future Humans, whether natural humans or artificial intelligence, are obviously not perfect, or they wouldn't traumatize us with abductions. In other words, humans will always be human, which means imperfection. We strive to follow our better angels, but our demons sit on the other shoulder.

I strongly disagree with some contactees who claim UFO occupants are omnipotent gods or unconditionally loving angels. I also strongly disagree that those who conduct UFO abductions are demonic, evil, and are going to invade Earth at any moment.

We truly do not know if extraterrestrials would behave as the abductors do; we know literally nothing of the qualities of any extraterrestrial. Someone might tell us how an extraterrestrial race behaves but we have no firsthand experience, so people just believe what is being told to them.

Perhaps we should recognize ourselves in the behavior of the abductors. They are probably in a military or cohesive unit with other human time travelers and have an assignment, a mission, which over-rides individual "good behavior." Military units commit acts in unison (kill), when a single member of that unit, as a civilian, would not do such a thing.

As to the specifics of why Future Humans play catch and release with their poor old ancestors, we answer, "Why do we play catch and release with wild animals?" There may be a number of reasons, some actually show good intent, but no one can be sure at this point if their motives are somewhat altruistic or are only for their benefit, whatever that might be.

Reason 1: We tag bears partly because of simple human curiosity about how they live and behave. It is education for education's sake, to learn more about our world, and thus, the bears' world.

For Future Humans, it could be something like a college course with experience in the field (the past). After all, it has been said that the Roswell UFO pilots drove like teenagers.

This educational process would also include political and social history. Imagine being there when Alexander Hamilton was killed by Aaron Burr, when Abraham Lincoln began speaking, "Four score and seven years ago," at Gettysburg, or when Marie Antoinette was beheaded, or when Germany signed the unconditional surrender on Victory Europe (VE) Day in 1945. What an education!

Of course, we don't know if Future Humans observe big historical events closely because some time travelers look exactly like us. How can we tell who is who?

Obviously, they are also interested in how the common people live, what our medical information shows, how we react in situations of stress, and so forth.

Reason 2: With wild animals, we catch and release (after tagging them), because they are endangered. We are desperate for their sake and our own sake, to help them survive. Their habitat or food source may be in jeopardy or their numbers are shrinking rapidly. Our planet is in trouble, it is the only world on which we (and the animals) can live.

Currently we see climate chaos due to global warming happening every day, tornadoes, floods, torrential rains, droughts, huge wildfires, extreme heat, rising sea levels, melting glaciers, and more.

The time travelers' catch and release program may relate directly to this time of Earth crisis. It is a paradox that to save themselves, they may have to save us, but it may somehow apply. Granted, it is a confusing loop.

Einstein said, "If the bee disappears from the surface of the Earth, man would have no more than four years to live. No more bees, no more pollination." That is the tip of our current iceberg of our perceived ever-encroaching doomsday on

Planet Earth." Today, the planets' bees are endangered and so are 41,415 other species.

UFO occupants tamper with the nuke codes on warheads and play cat and mouse with our military. This may be another aspect of "catch and release an ancestor," called "bother the ancestors' military to illustrate it is not all-powerful, and that nukes are no good." Perhaps Future Humans really just want to fly a banner which says, "This is our planet too, and you are ruining it."

This is speculation, but one thing is clear: Future Humans have more motivation to abduct and to bother us, than extraterrestrials do. Current and future humans are, obviously, connected beyond any undoing.

Reason 3: A third reason for abductions and encounters by Future Humans may have to do with their own needs. We touched on the fact that our DNA might be helpful or even needed by them due to their physical or genetic crisis.

Computers: They seem to have grown smarter with their ability to time travel, but their physical bodies may have suffered. We know ourselves how computers take over one's life and it is hard to include enough physical exercise. Computers have no doubt taken over our descendants even more than ourselves, muscles shrink, physical vigor is lost.

Quantum computers (according to Jack Sarfatti, "*post*-quantum computers"), will dominate the lives of Future Humans. For instance, their time travel formula is no doubt enabled by advanced computers. They may have artificial intelligence components like nano-chips which make them so-much-smarter than us, but less physically motivated.

Yes, artificial intelligence can be created to be stronger physically then us, but what if a boost for one's IQ is given or offered, but the wondrous human physical (organic) body is preferred by many, especially if we (they) have overcome the aging process? We could boost intelligence but remain mostly natural human. To be honest, that sounds good to me.

Radiation: Not all Future Humans work in space, unless poor old Earth did become uninhabitable. Those FTs who do work in space are exposed to space radiation, but we don't know if time travel involves exposure to high radiation.

As for the three deadly kinds of space radiation, these even affect our astronauts today on the International Space Station which only orbits Earth; we can only imagine the bombardment of radiation which galactic travelers have to endure.

Jack Sarfatti says the zero-gravity warping bubble would protect even organic humans from radiation; if he is right, the USS Enterprise, 1701, lives! – and has its mostly very-human crew. Sign me up!

We do not know if Future Humans travel only in the Solar System or if they are veterans of interstellar space. It may depend on "when" in time is home to a Future Human. Deep space travel might be further in the future than time travel.

Falling Sperm Counts: The early 21st Century is before a possible thermonuclear war. Nuclear accidents are bound to keep occurring, contaminating our beautiful world even without nuclear war. The list grows: Three Mile Island, Chernobyl, Fukushima, and the current radiation crisis caused in 2019 by a nuclear-powered missile engine (or something) in the Artic, thanks to Russia.

UFO abductions began in great numbers in the late 1940s and early 1950s, right after we began using nuclear bombs in war (Nagasaki and Hiroshima) to annihilate our fellow humans. We do not yet know if thermonuclear war lies ahead in our future but we can be sure there will be other accidents which release a lot of radiation.

The Nuclear Age is when the decrease in human sperm count began. This is a little-reported but growing crisis for us as a species in the future.

Men's sperm have been decreasing in number and getting worse at swimming for some time now—and, at least in the United States and Europe, new research says it's getting worse. A pair of new studies unveiled this week at the Scientific Congress of the American Society for Reproductive Medicine (ASRM) in Denver suggest that American and European men's sperm count and sperm motility— that is, the "swimming" ability of sperm cells—have declined in the past decade, which follows a similar, broader trend observed by many scientists over the past few decades.

Footnote 51: The Atlantic.com, "Sperm Counts Continue to Fall," by Ashley Fetters, October, 2018

We can only imagine what efforts might have to be made to keep reproducing or to artificially produce genetic humans.

The time travelers' possible needs for organic human DNA may depend on if they are (for example), 75 years ahead of us or 700,000 years ahead of us. There may be one or two contingents from specific points in time, who particularly need help with DNA vigor, thus it is they who perform medical procedures during abductions.

Yes, we wind up writing a science fiction story when we guess about specifics, but if we look at clues, we can be sure, at least, that Future Humans would have more reason to do medical procedures, extract blood, tissue, and DNA, that extraterrestrials would. An ant's DNA is likely more like ours, than extraterrestrial DNA would be; our DNA would not be of worth to extraterrestrials.

I always wonder how much the fear factor on the part of the individual who is "caught," enters into abduction accounts. I do not blame abductees for being frightened as never before. However, I can't help but think of a toddler screaming in a frenzy when the doctor tries to give a vaccination. The toddler focuses on the cold, strange treatment room, the determined-looking doctor, the big alien needle. He projects for himself how much it would hurt and tells you all about it. If you ask the toddler afterward, he may start to cry again and tell you what a horrible ordeal it was. Your cat would tell you a similar story regarding being forced to go to the vet's; this is many cats' worst nightmare. The Great Unknown is frightening in a unique way to nearly all Earth's species.

Possibly the Future Humans do not attempt to lessen the fear because it makes everyone adhere to the Non-Interference Directive. "Let's get the medical sample and get the screaming toddler out of here!" I hear them saying. No friendships can be created, that's against the rules.

Some abductions have one goal on the agenda while others probably have other goals. As Jacques Vallee pointed out, it doesn't seem the abductors would need to do hundreds of thousands of abductions. This is true if they are extraterrestrial or Future Human. However, there must be some on-going need, process, or goal, stretching over all these years which may indicate an ongoing Earth connection.

A huge number of abductions is more likely if the abductors are on their own planet; it might be that first one official group of time travelers examines us, does a tour of duty in the past, and then returns to their own time. Meanwhile, another group arrives from a different time period, to do a tour of duty. It does seem likely that a brigade of time travelers from 75 years in advance, would not do duty with a brigade from the Year 50,000.

We are told about the various races of ETs; these can easily be humans, or what used to be humans, from 500,000 years hence (fill in whatever year you wish).

A Closer Look at Famous Abductions, Was It Future Humans?

I can only vouch for my own encounters being true, I can't swear to the reality of anyone else's encounters, but I feel strongly that the encounters I have chosen here are valid. They are the most-investigated, the most-time-tested of abductions.

Travis Walton: (A quick refresher): On November 5, 1975, Travis Walton was working with a timber stand improvement crew in the Apache-Sitgreaves National Forest near Snowflake, Arizona. The seven workers encountered a saucer-shaped object hovering over the ground. It was making a high-pitched noise. Walton claims that a beam of light suddenly shone from the craft and knocked him unconscious. The other six men hurriedly drove away. Walton says he awoke in a hospital-like room with short, bald creatures standing over him. He says they were human in form and design, but he was very frightened by their looks which did not seem human. He fought with them until a human wearing a helmet led Walton to another room, where Travis blacked out as three other humans put a clear plastic mask over his face. Walton has claimed he remembers nothing else until he found himself walking along a highway, with the UFO departing above him. (More details came back later to Travis).

Footnote 52: en.wikipedia.org/wiki/Travis Walton UFO incident

As we get more details from Travis, it becomes likely that both the short creatures who scared him and the humans were – human. The "creatures" may have been from a more distant future time while the human-looking humans were perhaps from 75 or 200 years in the future.

Travis describes the creatures as having thin bones and soft-looking white flesh. They had five fingers but no fingernails. Their hands were small, without hair. Their skin was so pale that it looked chalky. Their bald heads too big for their little bodies and their facial features looked under-developed. Their mouths were narrow, their noses tiny but with nostrils. This might indicate they were not robots. (Robots don't need a nose). The creatures had huge cat-like eyes. They had no lashes and no eyebrows.

Travis was ready to fight with them in his confusion and fear, but they stood there passively.

Were these creatures "alien enough" to be extraterrestrials? Or is this the path our evolution is taking as the years pass, 2,000 years, 99,000 years, 500,000 years, one million years.

Or, is this the result of DNA damage caused by our current contamination of Earth's oceans and land, or the result of nuclear war or too many nuclear accidents, or the price we pay for becoming deep space travelers, or the price of giving all our physical vigor to mental function to computers?

No one knows, and perhaps there are other events that happened to us, but these "creatures" seem of the human family, not alien octopus design, machine-planet design, or sentient alligator design. And, they were working with human-looking humans, according to Walton.

As for Travis' friendly, helpful humans aboard the flying saucer, why has this been overlooked as ufology generally assumes "It's extraterrestrials." Travis' account is very clear, "There, standing in the open doorway, was a *human* being!" The memory of this event on his website is entitled "Human?"

Travis describes the human as 6'2" with a helmet on his head. He was muscular and well-built. He had on a tight-fitting blue suit of soft velour material. He had black boots. In short, he could have stepped off the Starship Enterprise, NCC 1701 (again). I'm not making light of this because the being I encountered was similar.

Travis remembers that the human man remained silent, and gently escorted Travis into a different larger craft which apparently then took off. Eventually Travis found himself in a hangar area with several flying saucers sitting there. A star-base?

Travis was taken to a medical room; two more human men and a woman were waiting for him in a medical room. All three were similar to the first man. The woman was beautiful and seemed perfect with no blemishes or other imperfections. Travis says all four humans had a family-like resemblance but they were not identical.

Analysis Regarding Future Humans: Maybe this made little sense when we read Travis Walton's account in 1975, perhaps people thought Travis was making up a science fiction story. But now since we are aware of science/technology advances, and genetic strides toward eliminating unwanted flaws, this makes sense.

It is a good sign when the truth becomes more likely after we learn new scientific knowledge. It seemed like fiction in 1975 but not in 2020. There will be more on genetic engineering and artificial intelligence, and how it relates to the evidence for Future Humans in a later chapter.

Travis believes that the humans in the medical room then saved his life because he was injured accidentally when he first encountered the saucer. I also believe my life might have been saved by Future Humans. This is another parallel with Travis' experience, but it is something impossible to prove; I have found that people tend to dismiss this possibility as somehow not relevant or meaningful. However, it does show that these UFO occupants are of basically good intent, or at least they were of good intent in two probable situations.

Travis Walton's book is The Walton Experience, Fire in the Sky.

Footnote 53: travis-walton.com official website, "The Incident"

Betty and Barney Hill: On the night of September 19th, and into the morning of September 20th, 1961, Betty and Barney Hill were abducted by UFO occupants in a rural, mountainous part of New Hampshire. This was the first nationally publicized account in the United States of a UFO abduction. Their story was adapted into the best-selling 1966 book, "The Interrupted Journey."

Approximately one mile south of Indian Head, the object they had watched bouncing around in the sky as they drove home from Canada, rapidly descended toward their vehicle. The huge craft hovered over their car, reminding Barney of a huge pancake.

Barney got out of the car with his pistol in his pocket and moved closer. He saw eight to eleven humanoid figures looking at him out of the UFO's ports or windows. Barney felt he received a telepathic message to "stay where you are," as the humanoids seemed to be preparing to land and exit the craft. Barney remembered they had glossy black uniforms and black caps.

It seemed to Barney that these beings were "somehow not human."

Barney ran back to the car realizing the humanoids were going to capture them. The Hills sped away, but the huge craft followed them. Betty rolled down the window to look up and the Hills heard a series of beeping or buzzing sounds. The car vibrated and a tingling sensation passed through the Hills' bodies. The Hills did not lose consciousness, they reported, but entered an altered state of consciousness which left their minds hazy and dull.

Next thing they knew, another series of beeping or buzzing sounds returned them to full consciousness and they were 35 miles down the road from where they had been. They only recalled making a sudden turn, encountering a roadblock, and seeing a fiery orb sitting in the road.

They arrived home at dawn and eventually they realized they should have arrived home about three hours earlier. Both Betty and Barney immediately upon return home, had strange memories and impulses. Betty insisted their luggage be kept near the back door. Their watches did not work and never worked again. Barney said that the strap of his binoculars was torn, but he could not recall how it happened. They took long showers for no logical reason and each felt compelled to draw a picture of what they had observed.

Betty had strange dreams which ten days later which seemed relevant to the abduction. These continued for 5 days and haunted her in the daytime too.

Through Betty's dreams, the following impressions were given: The abductors were 5 feet to about 5 feet 4 inches. They had matching blue uniforms and caps. They were nearly human with black hair, dark eyes, large noses and bluish lips. Their skin had a grey hue. It is almost impossible to believe these were not a branch of humankind. The chances of extraterrestrials being human – seemingly as human as small people today with dark hair and eyes - is astronomical.

Of course, Betty's dreams were not conscious memory. She underwent hypnosis and described different details, but her description was still that their abductors were still small humans or humanoids.

Barney underwent hypnosis and remembered his sperm being take, something which would fit in with DNA research.

Both Betty and Barney remembered the leader communicating in English. The medical examination individual spoke English but it was difficult to understand. The Hills heard their abductors communicating with each other in a "mumbling language." Both Betty and Barney also felt that at times there was "thought transference" because their captors' mouths weren't moving.

The most amazing and lasting occurrence to emerge from the Betty and Barney Hill abduction is the star map which Betty was shown by the leader after the medical examiner left the room. He and Betty began conversing and he said Betty could keep a book with strange symbols in it. The leader later changed his mind.

Betty then asked him where he came from. He pulled down an instructional map full of stars. Today, we would question why an advanced craft would not have star-maps on computer rather than a pull-down map which older readers remember from school days, but it is possible that Betty never said, "He pulled down a map," but rather than "He showed me a map..." In fact, Betty later said the map was a holographic projection.

At any rate, there are inconsistencies and many unlikely aspects to Betty's accounts which were partly from her dream state by her own admission. If all she related did happen, perhaps seen through her altered state of consciousness, it seems the abductors were suspiciously human-like, but not from our time or culture.

The famous evidence which emerged from the Hills' abduction was the star map which Betty drew, having been shown the map by the English-speaking leader who said they were from this star system.

Footnote 54: en.wikipedia.org/wiki/Barney and Betty Hill

In 1968 Marjorie Fish, an amateur astronomer, read **Interrupted Journey** by John G. Fuller, 1966. She wondered if she could figure out what star system was shown on the star-map which Betty had drawn. Assuming that one of the fifteen stars on the map must represent Earth's Sun, Fish constructed a three-dimensional model of nearby Sun-like stars. The only star system which matched Betty's map was the binary system of Zeta Reticuli.

From this arose entire groups of humans who feel connected to the "Zetas" and many messages are felt to be received from these extraterrestrials. The idea that the Hills' abductors might be some branch of humankind got buried in the excitement and rush of interest in Zeta Reticuli aliens.

Marjorie Fish's conclusion proved not correct as time went by and noted astronomers Carl Sagan and Stephen Soter explained that the star map was a random alignment of chance points.

Footnote 55: Armagh Planetarium.com, "Betty Hill's UFO Star Map, the Truth"

Analysis Regarding Future Humans: Looking at it from a Future Human point of view, why not show this curious ancestor named Betty, a star map – any star map. Perhaps it was or was not Zeta Reticuli. It was shown to her to deflect her from thinking about the possibility that actual humans had abducted her. It was an effort to follow the Non-Interference Directive while still performing a "catch and release," which garnered genetic samples and information. Betty was a persistent woman and the leader began to feel he was sharing too much, being too open.

It might have been an abduction which got rather messy, the craft having to chase the Hills' car when Barney drove away in a hurry. Then the entities had to handle two upset people, perhaps more upset than if the "catch and release" had gone smoothly. In fact, the leader told Betty the whole thing would go quicker if they could examine the Hills in separate rooms. The leader wanted it over too.

It seems that the least likely option in the Betty and Barney Hill case is that it was extraterrestrials, but the common assumption is that it was ETs.

Possibly the entire thing was a hallucination in which Betty influenced Barney, who was more skeptical all along than Betty. At the time, psychologists drew this conclusion.

However, I feel the most logical answer is that the Hills did undergo a "catch and release" abduction by Future Humans who made a bit of a mess of it.

I have counseled abductees for over 37 years and the basic emotional characteristics of the abductee makes a huge difference in how she or he reacts at the time of the abduction and as years go by.

In my opinion, Betty resisted the "I am a victim" mentality, she was a fighter. Barney had an IQ of 140 and was more logical and not as obsessed with the abduction as Betty (perhaps he sublimated it and got on with life), but Betty kept working on finding answers. She eventually considered it a quest, the purpose of her lifetime and felt she had later contact with the small beings. Betty and Barney Hill are fondly remembered.

Betty Andreasson: On the night of January 25, 1967, Betty Andreasson was in the kitchen while her seven children and her parents were in the living room. They lived in South Ashburnham, Massachusetts.

The house went dark after the lights blinked on and off, and a red beam of light beamed through the kitchen window. Betty comforted the children as her father went to peak out the kitchen window to see what was happening. To his horror, he saw five odd-looking entities coming toward the house with a hopping motion.

Before he could warn the family, the entities floated and bounced through the closed door. It was as if each hop gave them momentum to float for a few seconds; they were moving fast. Immediately, the entire family was put into a state of stasis. Only Betty was not in a state of suspended animation and she began to feel their thoughts in her head, perhaps telepathy.

One of the group seemed to be the leader. He was about five-feet tall. The other four were about foot shorter. All of them had pear-shaped heads, with wide eyes, and small ears and noses. Their mouths were only slits, and never moved.

The entities wore a type of uniform, blue in color, with a wide belt. There was a logo of an eagle on their sleeves. Their hands only had three fingers, and they wore boots.

Betty said later that she was frightened in a way, but also felt a sense of calm and friendship toward these little men.

The aliens were holding Betty's children in stasis and Betty worried about them, and so they released her eleven year old daughter from that strange state of consciousness, so Betty could see her family was not being hurt.

Betty was taken by the aliens outside to their craft which rested on the side of a slope in the back yard. The craft was estimated to be about 20 feet in diameter, in the classic UFO shape.

Betty believes this saucer joined with a mothership wherein she had a physical examination and was also subjected to the effects of strange equipment. She believes they inserted "something like a small BB" into her head. They did something painful to her but it soon turned into a positive religious or spiritual experience. Betty had always been a religious person.

Two of her captors returned her to her home, approximately 4 hours later. One of the beings had stayed in her house to watch the other family members. When she returned, there was the family, still in a state of stasis. After releasing the family from their altered state, the entities left.

Betty realized later that the entities had blocked her memories until a designated time when she would begin to recall all that happened. Before the abduction, Betty was not interested in UFOs. Being religious, she first viewed the event as having religious meaning. It would be later before she began to view the abduction as alien in nature.

Eight years had passed when Betty answered a notice from Dr. J. Allen Hynek asking people to come forward who had experienced strange abductions. Betty answered the ad, but Hynek dismissed her case because of its unusual details. However, in January 1977, Betty's abduction began to be fully investigated.

The investigative team assigned to the Andreasson case included a solar physicist, an electronics engineer, an aerospace engineer, a telecommunications specialist, and a UFO investigator. A hypnotist and medical doctor were also used who stated that Betty and her daughter were sane individuals, intelligent, and they believed what they were relating. Raymond E. Fowler, who also worked on Betty and Barney Hill's case, then wrote popular The Andreasson Affair.

Footnote 56: UFO Casebook, "The Betty Andreasson Encounter," by B.J. Booth

Analysis Regarding Future Humans: Might the "BB" (BBs are used in pellet guns), inserted in Betty Andreasson's head, be a nano-chip for tracking and communication later on?

Might the entities "hopping and then floating from the momentum of the hop" be a form of zero-gravity, perhaps their uniforms have metamaterial for nullifying gravity? Otherwise, it seems strange that any creature, human or extraterrestrial, made of solid matter and 5 feet tall, could defy Earth's gravity by floating. Advanced technology must be involved!

Travis Walton reported that the small entities he met had five fingers. Betty Andreasson reported "three fingers," but outside of this discrepancy, it sounds like the Hills, Travis Walton, and Betty Andreasson were abducted by similar beings who were human. In our present world, of course those who are "small people" (dwarves) are human.

The Walton and Andreasson entities wore similar clothing: blue uniforms and boots. Even more than these superficial similarities, the little men in all three cases had a degree of concern and compassion for their captives. The duration of the abduction seemed to be an issue, the abductees were not held for days or weeks.

Betty Andreasson's family was okay when it was all over, and so was the Hills' little dog. The little men went to the trouble of releasing Betty Andreasson's daughter to show she was not hurt by the state of suspended animation.

I have also wondered if my parents were put into stasis when I was abducted; I have talked with other abductees who suspected the same with their families. One friend remembers his mother just sitting there, staring straight ahead, as he was abducted.

Betty Hill was shown a book with strange symbols by the leader, then the star map. He seemed to want to explain the situation and educate her but then the entities argued among themselves and decided that Betty could not take the strange book home with her as their leader had first promised. This sounds like bickering humans to me. Humans are not black and white in their thought processes, we are gray in our diverse thinking, an opinionated bunch. Sometimes we are good people; other times, not-so-good. Most of us mean well but we hurt others, especially emotionally.

Abductees have emotional scars from abductions, but many have made these scars into badges of strength and beauty as we too become cosmic explorers. Personally, in my experiences with "them," I was changed, changed for a lifetime. I treasure that change. I would have it no other way.

Perhaps this is a way to look at how the abductors act: U.S. soldiers, when they are on a foreign tour of duty, perhaps in the Mideast, know they are there to do a job; they break the local traditions and laws because there is no way to do their job and without doing so. Some soldiers are more heartless while others have more compassion, even if they are soldiers. It is so with our soldiers, and the same may apply to Future Humans on active duty.

Yes, the rights of these four abductees were trampled on, but the little men did not kill. They were intent on performing medical procedures; it was their mission to do these medical exams and get these samples of blood, DNA, sperm, and more.

Also, there must have been a plan to begin slowly, as of the 1950s, to nudge 20th Century humans, into demanding Disclosure sometime in the 21st Century. A plan would have to be made along these lines because abductions expose the existence of UFOs and their occupants.

Do the abductors' desperately need samples from us to save themselves, or to help us as a species, or is it merely a future university course called Ancestors 101: Get some samples, a course requirement?

Steve Boucher: Canadian Steve Boucher experienced an encounter with unknown beings when he was about 4 years old with his father. He was riding with his father in a car when a UFO stood in the road before them. Steve's father seemed to know the entities and was not scared of them. Steve remembers being babysat by one of the entities while his father did something on board the UFO.

Steve describes his second encounter when the rock band in which he played as a late-teen, got abducted by strange entities and they were taken onboard a ship to have experiments run on them.

Steve has videos on You Tube which detail not only his encounters, but what he has learned since. He was changed because of those encounters, but in a good way. He explores cosmic vistas, he helps others become more aware, and would have it no other way.

I asked Steve to share his observations with me for this book, asking him if "they" might possibly be Future Humans. I will add my comments where appropriate.

Steve: The thing I observed about the beings I had experiences with, is that they have certain protocols that they adhere to when performing an abduction. One of these protocols, I observed in more than one abduction. I noticed that whenever they interact with a group of people, they separate them from each other and there is at least one being assigned to handle each person in the group. This is something that our military and police officers also do when dealing with more than one individual.

Another protocol that I observed, was that they always want to wipe your memory after the incident is over. I have often wondered why they do this. I never liked that idea and often would insist that I would remember. These beings are very strong-willed and exercise a kind of hypnotic mind control technique to cause the experiencer to forget the incident, but if you are also a strong-willed person and are very insistent, as I was, it is difficult for them to make you forget.

Diane: I have always retained a few conscious memories; they are as conscious and clear as remembering my kittens or swinging on my bag swing.

Steve: They may employ a diversionary tactic to get you to drop your guard. It can be a simple technique of asking you the name of a type of flower growing nearby. When you briefly lower your guard for a moment to observe the flower and answer the question, they will use that opportunity to 'sink in' the command to forget. The technique is often quite effective and it worked on me.

Other times, they may not give you the command to forget while they are present with you. They can also send the command telepathically to you even after they have left. If the experience took place at night and you are tired, your resistance is lowered. If the experiencer is somewhat traumatized by the event, they are usually more than happy to comply with the memory wipe.

Diane: I do have to wonder if this is a natural gift of theirs or if they simply have advanced technology techniques and tools. We have tended to think they must be extraterrestrials with omnipotent mindpower because they can do what seems like magic. However, look at our technology these days and how baffling it would be to someone a mere one hundred years ago.

Steve: I didn't appreciate the memory wipe because in each subsequent encounter I had with them, I would experience that initial terror all over again as if it were the first time. So, why do they do it? I believe it is a required safety protocol, put in place to protect us and to preserve their secrecy. They want us to be able to live a semi-normal life after an encounter with them. If they left our memories intact, that would not likely be possible.

Diane: It's that Non-Interference Directive mentioned in this book.

Steve: And when you remember consciously, it changes your life forever. There is no going back to a normal life after that. This is something I would caution people to consider before choosing to undergo regressive hypnosis. On the other hand, I would not trade my recovered memories for anything, even though it has isolated me from many of my friends and family, I feel it was worth it for the value of knowing what happened to me.

Diane: I agree.

Steve: I feel that my resistance to the memory wipe is probably one of the main reasons they stopped visiting me 'physically' around 1976. I was becoming increasingly difficult to control. Budd Hopkins told me that once your case starts to be investigated, they stop coming around. They avoid any repeat visits once their cover is blown, unless it is absolutely necessary.

I feel that this is because they prefer to communicate with the sub-conscious mind, rather than the conscious mind. This way they are able to stay under the radar and keep the abductions to a more clandestine nature. It's as though the experiencer has a secret life of which he or she may be completely unaware. I believe there are many experiencers who may have had multiple experiences with these beings, perhaps even creating hybrid offspring with them and yet go through their entire life being totally unaware of it, unless something happens that causes them to go under regressive hypnosis.

So, you have to wonder, whose idea was it to keep the existence of extra-terrestrials a secret from the public? Was it the government, or the extra-terrestrials themselves, or a mutual agreement between the two?

Many people have said that the small grey beings seem to be emotionless and go about their business-like biological robots. I am aware that there are several different kinds of beings that fall under the classification of small greys. However, I did not find this to be the case with the beings that I encountered. They were respectful and polite with me.

Diane: Same here. I always have to use the word "reticent." The being I met was actually reticent to carry out this encounter and he was very mannerly and soft-spoken. As I will explain when I offer information on my own abduction in this book, there was and is something personal in his and my connection. I don't mean he is my father, my lover, my son, or anything like that.

I know you have mentioned that sometimes you feel the entity you met is yourself, Steve, in a future or other - lifetime. I too feel the being I met is "my Other," without being sure how to define that.

Steve: I am a big believer in reincarnation, and I don't believe our lives are necessarily consecutive.

When the leader wanted to use a device on me that was able to reveal what was beneath the skin, he took the time to demonstrate it to me using his own arm and then expressed his desire to use the device on me. I asked him if it would hurt and he assured me that it wouldn't, but that I might experience a slight tingling sensation. And so I agreed to the procedure. He didn't have to do that, but the fact that he took the time to show me how the device worked, proved to me that he was compassionate and considerate of my feelings.

In another instance as I stepped out of the van to go with them, I came face to face with one of the beings. I remember when I looked directly at him, the thought came into my mind, "Man, are you ever ugly!" The being immediately turned his face away from me and I felt the emotion of embarrassment, or shame.

I then began to wonder if the thought was me thinking that about him, or him thinking that about me, as I felt that we were telepathically connected. So, these are two instances where I felt that these beings definitely exhibited emotions. The most profound evidence of this occurred when I felt a very powerful wave of love emanating from the being that I regarded as the leader. I had never felt love like that from anyone else before.

Diane: I remember two times wherein I found myself looking at me, out of his eyes. And there was so much love of some kind, that it can make me cry in awe and wonder, even today.

Steve: I have also observed that they are extremely concerned about damaging any of our property during an abduction and also any damage that may occur to the abductee. From my own experiences with them, I refer to the incident with the drum during the abduction of my band. The leader instructed us to follow him and as he was leaving the van, his foot got caught in the snare drum stand and the drum fell over and rolled out the back of the van. Immediately, one of the beings picked it up as it fell to the pavement and began examining it. Both he and the leader were very concerned about any damage that may have occurred to it.

I suspect that damage occurring to property or to an individual may incur some kind of punishment in accordance with their laws, which could range from a strong reprimand to a suspension of duties or even perhaps some form of incarceration if it is an actual crime. I feel that these beings are part of a chain of command, just like our military soldiers are. I don't feel that the beings are operating on their own. They are answerable to a higher authority. Who, or what that might be, one can only speculate.

They may be operating under a system of rules and laws that we are not aware of. One of these laws I believe is the Law of Non-interference. This may seem to be a contradiction to some, because many of the abductions would appear to be non-consensual. We are often told by the beings, that we agreed to the abductions before we were born, and although that may be true for some, it is difficult to prove since we are never shown a contract.

And it is even more difficult for abductees that don't believe in reincarnation, or that we had some sort of pre-existence before we were born into this world. So, are they actually violating our free will? Or is there more to this that we are not being told?

I believe that our perception of the experience may have a lot to do with whether we see it as something good, or something bad. I believe it has a lot to do with our personal and spiritual or religious beliefs. Dr. Bruce Lipton has made the claim that it is our beliefs that ultimately create our reality in his book *The Biology of Belief*. And I believe this has a major impact on how we perceive our abduction experiences.

Diane: I absolutely agree, Steve. I have worked with hundreds of abductees and each has perceived it differently, even if only a slight difference from another abductee. With some of us, we perceive our interactions with "them" 180 degrees different.

Steve: I also feel that these beings are multi-dimensional, in that they are able to move through solid walls and even cause experiencers, or abductees to be taken through close windows, or through the ceiling to a ship hovering outside. To be able to do this, they would have to have some kind of technology that is able to alter the fabric of time and space. This requires an advanced knowledge of quantum physics that we are just now beginning to understand.

Diane: Agree! Arthur C. Clarke who wrote **2001: A Space Odyssey**, said, ""Any sufficiently advanced technology is indistinguishable from magic.

Steve: Many experiencers claim that during their abductions, time seems to stand still and everything goes quiet. I have experienced this first hand. It's as though they create a sort of time bubble that separates the experiencer from his/her normal perception of time and space. Sometimes they experience a feeling of pressure or a vacuum. This 'time bubble' seems to have a different set of rules that don't necessarily coincide with our understanding of Newtonian Physics.

Since they are already using this technology, it is not that much of a stretch to envision them using it to achieve time travel. It involves altering the frequency of vibration of whatever is inside the bubble, or more accurately, the 'localized field'.

And so, it may well be that they are actually time travelers. (italics added by Diane).

If this is the case, then they may be here to try to change or correct something which pertains to our future, which would perhaps be their past. *Could they be 'us' from the future?*

I will leave that up to the reader to decide. If you consider what we currently know about quantum physics and what we are doing with the Large Hadron Collider, consider what a race that may be thousands of years ahead of us in technology might be doing. The possibilities are staggering.

Footnote 57: Steve Boucher: Abductee Video, You Tube

Diane Tessman:
The final abduction case we will look at, is my own. I had two abductions that I can remember and will feature one of them. I could easily add periphery strangeness, theories, and possible related events throughout my

lifetime, but the focus of this book is to illustrate the probability that it is Future Humans who visit us. Abductees know that there are incredible synchronicities and inexplicable occurrences as we continue through our lives, but for now, "just the facts, mam." The following is from my personal files:

Summary: As best as I can figure, at age 4, I had the first encounter. I might have been 5 years old. I was a little kid; I wasn't keeping track of what year it was. It most likely happened in 1952. I was near our house on the farm, it was getting dark on a relatively warm November evening. My parents were inside, I don't know where my brother was.

I was playing with Pat, my dog. I was asked in hypnosis if Pat reacted when "it" happened. No, he did not, to my knowledge. I think I was then quickly gone from his side, though, and so he might have reacted a second later.

I cannot remember consciously, the moment a small craft appeared. I did not specify this during hypnosis, either. I am not sure of its shape because I was suddenly inside it.

It was small in area, inside. There were two entities, both small humans although one of them was more insect-like facially. His face reminded me of a grasshopper. The other looked like a dwarf I had seen in a circus movie but was not misshapen in form. They paid absolutely no attention to me and I somehow sensed I should just sit there. I was not terribly frightened.

Then, I was on or in, an absolutely huge place. I think I got a glimpse of it from the smaller craft; it was indeed enormous. In the part of the ship (I assume it was a ship), in which I found myself, there was earth-like vegetation rather like a terrarium. I sat down on a park bench, it reminded me of the park in town where band concerts were held every Saturday night.

The long window up toward the high ceiling had what must have been stars shining through, but they were huge! I was unsure they were stars because my child-mind said, "No, stars are smaller, so what are these huge lights outside?"

I believe I was never frightened for two reasons. The first is that I must have been given something to suppress fear. I read recently that today, scientists have found a way to suppress fear in a patient through a small pill. Perhaps it can be sprayed in aerosol form (just speculation). The second reason is that the place, the entities, the experience, was somehow familiar or, I belonged there. I didn't analyze this as a child, but that impression was with me on a subliminal basis.

I also want to note that I might have seemed too young to record this experience. I am not being egotistical to say, I was a mature four or five year old, with above average intelligence, as later recorded on tests. My maturity was not all a good thing, my mother had always used me as a "counselor" to whom she could tell her complaints about my father. I felt I should handle anything and not be the problem, not be a child. I was a kid who perceived and observed life, not a "mindless" happy child. I suppose I am still that person.

So, there I was on the park bench, waiting for – him.

There he was, the special one on the ship who would now communicate with me. He never stated his name, so he is "the special one." He was calm but seemed reticent to do whatever it was he was doing. I felt a sadness in him but I could have been wrong; again, I was a little kid but I was sensitive and alert to emotions.

He looked human except for amber eyes, not hazel, but deep amber. They were wide-set. They had a translucent quality which mesmerized me. He was normal build, maybe 5'9" or 5'10". My dad was 6 feet and this man was shorter than Dad. He was probably 28 or 30 years old.

I always described this man as "an enhanced human," but for many years I did not know what I meant by that. I now believe the "enhanced" description was because of his eyes. In recent years, I have realized his eyes might have been artificial intelligence but, he was human in the sense that a small child senses another human. Maybe "human at the core" is how to say it. This is the best description I can offer.

He had tawny-colored hair and it seemed, olive colored skin (not white or pink), and casual cut hair (not super military). His coloring too was just a bit different than I had seen on Earth.

I want to note that I know a person can fantasize under hypnosis even if she does not aim to, and so what I most value are a few conscious memories which have always been with me.

I have always had conscious memories of what he looked like and of him and me, sitting on the bench. We sat maybe a foot apart. I can easily see "Little Diane" as he saw me, my feet dangling off the bench.

As Steve Boucher mentioned, there is this feeling of looking at - myself. Steve suggests past and future lives as the answer; I'm not sure that is the answer for me but there was and is some entangled connection.

So as not to stare at him, I sometimes gazed at a hologram-like large "frame" (the size of a human statue), across the corridor in this small earthy "terrarium" area with vegetation. The hologram swirled in pastel colors; I don't know if it was just decorative or was a calming, hypnotic tool.

So, his physical looks and the park bench "scene" are my conscious memories and are always with me. I think some of the information was via telepathy or a "download," but he spoke out loud as well. I remember no accent; it was plain English.

"We are from your future," is something he wanted me to remember as well as what he looked like, and the fact he sat and talked with me. I feel these memories were purposely not blocked or wiped out. He wanted me to remember these things. There was a purpose in this.

I realize he could have been lying regarding what his source is. My life has proved (to me, at least), he was not.

I am not sure what exactly the "purpose" of that encounter was. It was something about "what he gave me" and in doing so, what he gave up of himself. Maybe he did not actually lose anything of himself, but my child-mind feared this, simply not being able to understand. I was a hyper-sensitive child, especially regarding the welfare of animals and nature.

I felt I was home where he was, not because of him but simply **home**, and then I somehow knew I'd be without that home for the rest of my life as Diane. There was deep sobbing of a kind I don't think I've done at any other event in my life.

As Dr. Sprinkle could tell you, I cried often and long during regression, a soul-level sobbing. Dr. Sprinkle sometimes had to wait for half an hour while I said *nothing;* I was going through these previously blocked memories for the first time, all by myself.

I felt bad about my special one, as I looked through my child-eyes during hypnosis. I may be the only abductee who ended up crying for the "alien" rather than for herself.

I had no answer to this for years. I pondered on what my regression notes said, which was that my special told me that he and I were to embark on an adventure. A possible answer came only a few years ago as I became aware of what advanced computer science might do. It came to me then that possibly through advanced technology, he gave me an aspect of his awareness (his consciousness). At four years of age, I worried, thinking he wouldn't have "it" after he gave it to me. I now feel he "kept all of himself" too, which would make four year old me, very happy. And, Diane remained fully myself, too.

This is difficult to word and to understand but I know a few people out there will know what I mean. This is my impression; I am not offering it as any kind of proof.

I'm not suggesting this hasn't been done before. I know several abductees who feel a "dual consciousness" with a crewmember aboard a starship. There is a dual identity as if they are a crew members of a starship and also a person on 21st Century Earth.

With me, it not "dual consciousness" as much as it is "shared consciousness."

This would explain the worry four-year-old-Diane felt for him, as if he was going to cease to exist in this experiment. I think and hope that was my child-like misinterpretation and that he went on with his life. I truly do not know.

Apparently more happened on that encounter (or on the second encounter); I have no memory of what else was done. But the unexplained missing membrane between my upper gum and mouth, must have happened - been removed - at some point. I have searched and searched for a normal explanation for this missing membrane which a plastic surgeon told me in 1987, looked like a laser scar. There were no lasers in 1952. I asked my parents many times, there is no mundane explanation.

My tissue sample could have been used for their own selfish purposes, to clone or to use for their genetic needs or projects. However, as mentioned before, I was struggling with episodes of strep throat, heavy, frequent, nose bleeds, and being underweight when I was three and four.

By 5.5 years old, I was almost literally hanging off the chandeliers, out exploring nature, excelling at gymnastics and dance. What changed so wonderfully and abruptly? My encounters were between my time of "unhealthy" and "super-healthy" and it might be suggested that advanced medical techniques corrected my ailment – techniques not available in 1952.

I am superstitious enough not to brag, but (cross fingers, knock wood), to this moment, I have only been to the hospital once, to give birth to my daughter 50 years ago. My health has continued as it was at age five.

I had the impression at the end of Dr. Sprinkle's hypnosis, that after a certain point, my special one on the ship was no longer available to me, as if it was impossible. I have no idea how I got back to the farm.

R. Leo Sprinkle, psychologist and researcher of UFO abduction and contactee experiences, received his Bachelor's and Master's degrees from the University of Colorado and in 1961, and completed his doctorate in counseling psychology at the University of Missouri. After three years at the University of North Dakota, he moved to University of Wyoming, where he remained until his retirement.

Leo traces his interest in UFOs to a sighting he had in 1949. He and his wife Marilyn also had a sighting in 1956. During the years immediately following the completion of his formal education, he conducted several studies, including an early survey of the members of the **National Investigations Committee on Aerial Phenomena** and an initial study of people who had experienced extraterrestrial encounters. He served as a psychological consultant for the **Condon Report** (1969) on UFOs, which led to further work on a number of abduction cases through the 1970s.

Dr. Sprinkle organized conferences for UFO abductees and contactees each summer. The conferences provided an open forum for them to tell their stories in a nonjudgmental environment. As the number of abduction reports increased in the late 1980s, abductees were welcomed to the summer conferences.

In time, Leo concluded that UFO activity is part of a larger program which he calls "cosmic consciousness conditioning" and adds that that he himself is a part of this program just like other experiencers. "The UFO entities are attempting to nudge humanity into an understanding of ourselves as cosmic citizens," exclaims Leo.

Footnote 58, Encyclopedia.com,"Sprinkle, Ronald Leo"

I first wrote to Dr. Sprinkle in 1981 at the University of Wyoming, seeking help in uncovering more about my possible abduction. I was in my eleventh year of teaching school and raising my daughter; in my spare time I was a field investigator with APRO (Jim and Coral Lorenzen's Aerial Phenomenon Research Organization), and MUFON, but my interest in UFOs was deeper and more personal than investigating cases. I sought help for the memories which haunted me of childhood contact. Thank goodness I found Dr. Sprinkle, who was a consummate professional and yet caring and sensitive. Regression is a tricky thing and if an abductee has the bad luck to have a poor hypnotist, it can hurt rather than help.

Here is Dr. Sprinkle's comments on my regression, written in August, 1981:

I have worked with approximately 150 persons who have described in hypnosis sessions their memories (or impressions) of their UFO encounters and abductions by UFOLKS. I am impressed by the sincerity and fortitude of these persons, as they sometimes describe painful and frightening reactions to their experiences. However, it was a pleasure to work with Diane. Her level of intelligence, her level of knowledge, and her level of self-awareness allowed her to minimize her doubts and fears, and to maximize the exploration of the significance and meaning of her memories and impressions. My own interpretation of the reactions by Diane to the hypnotic procedures was as follows: Diane's reactions were vivid recall, or memories, of real experiences which have a profound influence on her inner character and her personal goals. In other words, these memories were of "real" experiences as far as Diane is concerned. Does that mean that the information obtained by Diane is true? I do not know. Perhaps time will tell us the answers to that question.

Diane's Theory Regarding "Get to Know You:" It is possible I have an example of two children in a family who both experienced the unknown, having encounters back in 1952. One child reacted with fear and even violence, while the other child was compatible with this unknown contact.

The child who reacted with fear and violence was my half-brother, who was nearly ten years older than me.

The child who seemed compatible with "alien energy," finding it positive and fascinating, was me. My brother was 14 years old at the time, and I was 4 years old. We were both above average intelligence and both lived on a farm in a remote rural area.

I acknowledge that my brother's experience and my experience might not be related at all, but here is my theory:

In the early 1950s, Future Humans had a program of contact with individual humans of the 20th Century. This period is referred to as the "Golden Age of Abductions," wherein the abductors were more open and abductions were generally less frightening.

It is my theory that contact with an advanced unknown intelligence turns out to be incompatible with the intricate workings of some human minds. This is neither negative nor positive, it is simply how we are. This "beyond frightened" bad reaction applies to some abductees, and it explains what happened with my brother. Of course, his contact could simply have been with bad aliens, or maybe it was only too-real nightmares.

Throughout 1952 and into 1953, my mother warned me to stay away from my brother's bedroom at all costs because he had armed himself with a baseball bat and large knife, against "3 little men" he called Moe, Hoe, and Poe. He never reacted like this to any other nightmare. He carried the baseball bat and knife around the house with him.

My parents just laughed about what they felt must have been a series of nightmares my brother was having with 3 little men, but his dangerous reaction was no laughing matter. He was always ready to attack, seemingly to defend himself, when wide awake. How could a 14 year old have been so confused between nightmares and reality as to arm himself in the waking world and remain in this mode for months on end? It was the only episode of this kind, he did not go on to imagine other threats like this, day or night.

In his adult life, my brother, now deceased, stated he had no interest in UFOs or aliens. He had a tendency on other subjects to block his own memory in order not to remember bad things. Perhaps this was true of Moe, Hoe, and Poe. I referred to them once and he changed the subject.

In the same year of 1952 and less than five miles away, two little men were indeed spotted by a farmer as they exited their flying saucer in a hay field near Toeterville, Iowa. The farm where my abduction occurred is less than five miles from that hay field. I am sure the Toeterville landing and my abduction were in the same season as well – the autumn. This UFO landing is covered in a previous chapter.

Future Medicine: I am convinced that part of the reason for my two abductions (two that I remember), were to cure me of the often lethal disease of childhood leukemia. The survival rate in 1952 was around 20%. Today, survival is over 80%. I do not ask anyone else to believe that Future Humans saved me.

What is fact is that our medical researchers a few years ago, began the process of taking tissue samples from cancer patients, especially childhood leukemia patients, and genetically engineering them, weaponizing the patient's own cells, to go back in and fight the cancer. I believe that was part of why the membrane in my mouth was taken, and why I had two (at least two) abductions. They may have used the rather large tissue sample for purposes of their own as well.

Here is a more informed explanation of the procedure:

A new cancer treatment pioneered at the University of Pennsylvania has generated a lot of excitement in the field in addition to a handful of breathless media reports. Called targeted cellular therapy, the approach has given several dozen patients what Laurence Cooper of the MD Anderson Cancer Center called "a Lazarus moment."

The patients all suffered from lymphocytic leukemia and had exhausted other treatment options. The researchers, Carl June and David Porter, announced the results recently at the American Society of Hematology Annual Meeting.

"Those patients were facing certain death," said Cooper, who wasn't involved in the Penn study but is researching a similar treatment at MD Anderson.

After receiving targeted cellular therapy, 26 of 59 patients, including 19 children, are now cancer-free. Patients with the acute form of the cancer, which affects both children and adults, were especially likely to respond positively to treatment.

Targeted cellular therapy is an extension of long-standing efforts to ramp up the patient's own immune system to destroy cancer cells. With advances in genetics, doctors can now reconfigure patients' T cells to target a particular type of cancer cell.

June and Porter removed the patients' T cells and genetically "rebuilt" and multiplied them before reintroducing them into the patient's bloodstream. The weaponized T cells find and destroy all cells with the protein CD19 on their surface, which includes the cancerous B cells found in chronic and acute lymphocytic leukemia.

"There are clues that the T cells continue to kill leukemia cells in the body for months after treatment. Even in patients who had only a partial response, we often found that all cancer cells disappeared from their blood and bone marrow, and their lymph nodes continued to shrink over time. In some cases, we have seen partial responses convert to complete remissions over several months," Porter said in a news release.

Will arming T cells lead to treatments that bring those suffering from other types of cancer back from death's door? It's a matter of finding other molecules like CD19 to target on the cancer cells without killing too off cells that patients can't do without, Cooper explained.

Researchers are pursuing similar approaches for pancreatic and breast cancers as well as glioma, the type of brain cancer that killed Ted Kennedy. "It's a 'you have a hammer, go get some more nails' type thing," said Cooper.

Footnote 59: Singularity Hub, "Gene Therapy Turns Several Leukemia Patients Cancer Free, Will It Work For Other Cancers Too?" by Cameron Scott, Jan., 2014

Strange Coincidences and Beeps: As I talked with Jack Sarfatti about his exciting work on "low power warp," the conversation also wandered to the strange phone calls he received at age thirteen in 1953. My abductions were in 1952 and 1953.

Both Dr. Sarfatti and I have concluded that the contact we had was with Future Humans. It was rewarding to talk with someone else who has concluded this, especially because he is a brilliant theoretical physicist.

Jack's phone calls at first featured computer-like beeps and then a computer voice which said it was on board a flying saucer. Jack says, *"In 1952 and 1953, when I was about 12 or 13 years old, I received a phone call...in which a mechanical sounding voice at the other end said it was a computer on board a flying saucer. They wanted to teach me something and would I be willing? This was my free choice. Would I be willing to be taught—to communicate with them? I remember a shiver going up my spine, because I said, 'I was thinking "NO" ...but I said, YES."*

Footnote 60: theparacast.com, "Jack Sarfatti's Phone Call from an Alien"

This message is not dissimilar from the talk I had with "my special one" when I was abducted (actually, he communicated, I listened). As Jack found out also, that brief contact with "them," has changed my life's path.

There is one more similarity with Jack's strange experience: For over a year, I was bombarded with bizarre technological beeps in my house, similar to Jack's phone calls. It was not at the time of my childhood contact; it was when I was teaching school in 1979-1980. I was thirty-three.

The house I shared with my parents and young daughter, was one block from Tampa Bay in St. Petersburg, Florida. For over a year, that house was full of computer-like beeps. The television beeped first, at five minutes before most hours; however, as time went along, the beeps in the tv became random.

As time progressed, a wall beeped, lamps beeped, the clothes drier beeped, the hair drier beeped, a ceiling light fixture beeped. Thinking maybe the house was in the path of some kind of waves from MacDill Air Force Base, I took a cassette recorder on batteries about half a block away from the house, and it beeped too. My daughter and I recorded "the beeps" but when we re-played the tapes, the beeps were either gone or very faint. We never heard them far away from the house, however.

1979 was also my time of awakening as a UFO abductee; I finally accepted it fully. In 1981, I underwent regression with Dr. R. Leo Sprinkle and remembered one of two UFO encounters when I was a child in Iowa. As mentioned previously, I had kept a few conscious memories all along, which inspired me to explore further.

Perhaps not coincidentally, the most spectacular UFO sighting of my life happened in this 1979-1980 time period also. The dual-span of the Sunshine Skyway Bridge could be seen from a park at the end of our street. It was a summer night in 1979, when my daughter and I walked our dog Bailey to the park. I was a field investigator for MUFON and APRO at the time, and so the two huge glowing white spheres which were hanging in the dark sky over Tampa Bay, were absolutely thrilling!

We took the dog home, and raced back to the park with a camera. A small group of people had gathered to watch the spheres which had not moved. Unlike weather balloons, there was absolutely no drifting in the breeze. Perhaps this was rocket test from a military test at MacDill Air Force Base, Tampa? Then this phenomenon should have slowly dissipated.

These objects were as white and solid-looking as a full moon before it becomes "smaller" as it rises. They were not as large as the moon at the moment it rises, but they were similar to perhaps 30 minutes after the full moon rises. The spheres were not directly overhead but seemed high over Tampa Bay midway between horizon and sky zenith.

After several hours as I looked down for just a second, one of the two dazzling white spheres, just disappeared. Not a trace of it was left. It was the sphere with which I felt I was trying to communicate. The sphere was there and then in the blink of an eye, gone.

The other enormous sphere stayed there, not budging an inch, until I gave up and went home at 2:30 a.m. I had to teach school in the morning, but I have kicked myself for leaving. No weather balloon, rocket debris, helicopter, or Chinese lantern hoax, would have stayed stationery for all those hours. I took photos and none turned out. What a "coincidence," a bad roll of film? There were one or two daytime photos at the beginning of the roll, and they were also gone.

On May 9, 1980, "the beeps" were temporarily forgotten as I hurried to get my daughter and myself ready for school. Suddenly, our smoke alarm started to beep. I raced around to check for fire, and then realized it was not the fire warning, but also not the "battery low" signal. It sounded like Morse Code, but I didn't know Morse Code. My dad was trying to remember what he knew of Morse Code, when we heard on the television news that the Summit Venture barge had just rammed into one span of the Skyway Bridge at approximately 7:35 a.m.

That was exactly the time when the smoke alarm buzzed and beeped. And it never did it again.

I have no idea what this disaster had to do with the beeps. Were they warning or predicting this catastrophe? We were not involved in the tragedy directly, and what could we have been done to prevent it?

Were the ongoing house beeps that entire year, the huge white spheres, and the Skyway disaster connected? If not, it was a real coincidence.

Searching for meaning, I wondered if the life-energy of the dying victims in the Greyhound Bus and several cars which plunged into the water off the severed span, somehow made the smoke alarm go off. The Skyway Bridge over Tampa Bay is a tall structure and to plunge off it, there would be a few seconds of falling, falling, falling in sheer panic, through the air. 35 people died at 7:35 a.m., May 9, 1980.

Final Thoughts on Abductions:

Being both a UFO researcher for 38 years and an abductee for 68 years, I feel I have insight on a few possible truths:

Thought 1: The being I met was not a demon. The being I met was not an angel. The being I met was not extraterrestrial. He was human.

We have tended to make UFO visitors into evil demonic invaders or god-like twin flames and super-transcended-beings. The evidence points to something in between, something as "grey" as human behavior.

Thought 2: Travis Walton, Betty Hill, Betty Andreasson, and Steve Boucher all met human-like entities. As time passed following the (first) abduction, they felt affinity with the entities they encountered. Travis realized after the fact, that they saved his life. Betty Hill spent the rest of her life in a quest to find the truth and seemed to flourish in that quest (Barney Hill was less obsessed than Betty). Betty Andreasson remembered entities with whom she had interacted in her childhood and she viewed her abduction as opening a window of memory and spirituality.

Thought 3: It seems that early abductions in the 1950s and 1960s, were less traumatic than the frightening abductions of the 1980s and 1990s. Those early abductions have been called the Golden Age of UFO Abductions.

Did the UFO occupants decide as time went on, to be less-humane?

Or is it because a new group of aliens or Future Humans arrived who were not as nice?

Or is it because the governments of Earth began doing military abductions using strong hallucinogenic drugs as a disinformation tool, so as current humans and "aliens" would not open a bridge of communication with each other?

Or is it because the media and UFO organizations began to hype alien abductions as the most horrendous event possible? Abductees became victims with a capital "V" but also became celebrities. It became a dark topic which people perversely enjoyed thinking about.

There are probably multiple answers.

Thought 4: I am not excusing UFO occupants for trouncing on our individual rights but it seems that something transformative on behalf of our entire species was set in motion in the 1950s, perhaps to reach fruition in the 1990s, and then it turned sour and negative, partly because our perception of encountering the unknown, became collectively fearful and dark. It was as if by the Year 2000, we had opted to remain in the Dark Ages.

The "New Age" came along in the 1980s but soon turned to "me-ism" with sweat lodges and wealthy gurus. At worst, the New Age turned to medieval superstitions with amulets and miracle cures. The waters of ufology became muddied.

Some of us did receive messages and warnings for the entire human species; we predicted super-storms, melting glaciers, and rising waters, and more, but we failed to make a dent in the mass consciousness. We took our place with the street corner psychics who only "read" for individuals. We ended up being asked questions like, "Will my boyfriend leave me?" or, "How do I win the lottery?"

If we had succeeded in being listened to, we might have been able as a species, to stop the tragedy of global warming and resulting climate chaos looming ahead of us today. Now our grandchildren and their children, will pay for our collective ignorance.

***

Chapter Nine: The Technology of Time Travelers

"Any sufficiently advanced technology is indistinguishable from magic." – Arthur C. Clarke

Looking into a dazzling variety of advanced scientific and technological developments in our current day, tends to make the evidence even stronger that it is human or post-human time travelers who account for the UFO phenomenon. We think, "Well, we can't do anything like what those UFOs do, from the incredible maneuvers of their craft to how they manage to abduct people right in front of their families and then efficiently wipe the memories of those people they abducted. So, obviously these entities are not humans."

We think this way because we assume ourselves to be at the peak of human technical development. Yes, we know logically that more advancement is coming but emotionally and within our psyche, we cannot fathom it. It is as if we cannot fathom what has not yet happened, which in fact, is perfectly reasonable of us. We cannot know what we do not know.

How are we supposed to take into account what will be real in the Year 2525?

Of course, the same holds true regarding extraterrestrials, and yet, we tend to just go ahead and imagine that "aliens" is the answer. We feel, "Well, I don't know what the heck an Arcturian can do, so I'll just accept it can do everything UFOs and their occupants can do." It is as if the collective human species has a mind block on envisioning and dreaming of, its own future. Ironically, considering the sad state of affairs on Earth, we seem to be therefore creating "no future" for ourselves. We aren't dreaming as we used to.

A wild thought is that it might be much easier to travel back in time, once we have the right technology and materials (like that famous metamaterial with strange electromagnetic properties), than it is to travel the mind-bogglingly far distances in space. Afterall, all generations of humans, all layers of time on Earth, are right here, on Earth in what is perceived simultaneously as The Now.

Here is a closer look at possible science and technology in the world of the Future Humans, which they may use to arrive back here, in/at this Eternal Now.

Alcubierre Warp Drive: In 1994, Mexican theoretical physicist Miguel Alcubierre emailed William Shatner confessing that he had named his famous theory on faster than light propulsion, "warp drive" after **Star Trek,** the science fiction he loved so much as a boy.

And so, Alcubierre drive and warp drive became synonymous. The Alcubierre bubble does basically function like **Star Trek's** warp drive as well.

Let's take a look at the theories and ongoing research regarding warping space:

Dr. Alcubierre realized a negative mass would have to be created in order to achieve faster than light travel. In keeping with Einstein's general relativity. Alcubierre's warp does not exceed the speed of light but by contracting the space in front of it and expanding the space behind it (thus the bubble), a starship would arrive at its destination faster than light would arrive, without breaking any physical laws.

And surprise! Warp drive also needs exotic matter like metamaterial with bizarre electromagnetic properties, as well, because Alcubierre drive implies a negative energy density and therefore requires some form of exotic matter to create that negative field.

The starship crew would free fall while the warp bubble is accelerating and experience no g-forces. That is, until someone invents "artificial gravity" inside the ship as **Star Trek** did.

But wait! Someone did just invent artificial gravity; this is how fast technology is moving! **Star Trek** suggested that plating was embedded in the deck of the starship but for today, we will have to settle for the **Von Braun gravity generating wheel** as seen in **2001: A Space Odyssey.** So, this concept has been a vision from an iconic film since 1968, but it will soon become reality.

Credit: The Von Braun Space Station

Built by the Gateway Foundation, it is estimated that the world's first space hotel will be visited by about a 100 tourists per week by 2025.

"The dream of the Gateway Foundation is to create starship culture, where there is a permanent community of space-faring people living and working in Earth's orbit and beyond," says Alatorre.

The ideas for the station were taken from Wernher von Braun, a top Nazi rocket scientist who developed the infamous V2 rocket. After the war, he was taken in by NASA and became a major part of the American Space program of the 1950s, '60s, and early '70s.

The station will be made of a giant wheel, 190 meters in diameter, which will rotate in order to generate a gravitational force, similar in pull to the moon's gravity. 24 individual modules with sleeping and support facilities will be spread around the wheel on three decks, providing accommodations to about 400 people in total.

Alatorre compares the hotel to a cruise ship, pointing out it will have "many of the things you see on cruise ships: restaurants, bars, musical concerts, movie screenings, and educational seminars." Just in space. The designer thinks gravity, about a sixth of Earth's, will add a "sense of direction and orientation that isn't present in the ISS." You'd also be able to go to a toilet, shower or eat food the way you are used to.

Alatorre thinks that while initially space travel will be the domain of the uber-wealthy, soon enough it will be available to regular people. He wants to make traveling to space commonplace.

Footnote 61: Big Think.com, "Space Hotel, Artificial Gravity," by Paul Ratner, August 31, 2019

Back to Alcubierre Warp Drive: The "no experiencing of g-forces" is in keeping with the Tic-Tac pilots apparently not being subject to g-forces when flying over the Nimitz. This apparently is also due to negative energy density (zero-gravity). Referring to g-forces, Navy pilots exclaimed that a human's head would explode during the maneuvers performed by the UFO Tic-Tacs.

However, there are a few problems to iron out with the Alcubierre bubble: There are no known methods to create a warp bubble in a region of space that would not already contain one.

Second, assuming there was a way to create the bubble, there is not yet any known way of leaving the bubble once the ship is inside it.

There might also be a problem with stopping the warp momentum "Scotty, no brakes!" The warping effect might just go on and on, which would not be good.

There have been concerns that warping space might actually tear up spacetime; thus as humans arrive with our Alcubierre drive, we would be destroying space as we went – not a good start for socializing in the galaxy. So, do Future Humans warp space? Or do they have another method of traveling through spacetime?

Footnote 62: Phys.org, "What is the Alcubierre Warp Drive?" By Matt Williams, Universe Today, January, 2017

Reading this, I became confused as to how Dr. Sarfatti's metamaterial theory works in with Alcubierre drive. Here is Dr. Sarfatti's reply, August 26, 2019:

"Forget all those hypothetical problems. It's primitive. Tic Tacs do not travel through space at long distances. They travel through wormhole tunnels through short distance."

"Also, if they use warp drive through space, the warp field acts as a shield against radiation and collisions with asteroids and other matter in space. The people writing those papers are behind the times. We see warp drive in the flight of the Tic Tacs. No problem."

"That's the point – the flight of Tic Tac capsules (if reports are true), prove the reality of low power warp drive able to out-fight any fighter jet in acrobatic maneuvers including "braking." Air, sea, under sea, space makes no difference."

"While post-humans do exist, ordinary humans can get to the stars with Tic Tac Tech."

And with that, Jack Sarfatti, one of the world's most brilliant theoretical physicists, wiped out my work on the problems facing Alcubierre drive trying to warp space, because he said that Future Humans obviously already have this ability so it is a moot point to worry about the little details.

The truth is right before our eyes, says Jack: For Tic-Tacs to do what they do, they have warping (space) and time travel ability, and that includes traveling *back* in time. He also says that most likely natural (organic) humans can travel space and time due to a protective anti-gravity bubble and so, not all Future Human time travelers need be artificial intelligence or post-humans in order to survive intense space radiation. This amazes me.

Footnote 63: Jack Sarfatti, October 7, 2019

Regarding the Tic-Tac capsules: Civilian witnesses have reported UFOs doing these incredible maneuvers for years, but civilians were not Navy fighter pilots, they did not have cameras like the Navy jets do. With civilian reports, we always wonder if they get exaggerated or not reported accurately inadvertently;

The Tic-Tacs changed all that! To boot, the U.S. Navy has just confirmed that the Navy's photos, videos and radar returns of the Tic-Tacs are real and that the Navy doesn't have a clue what they are.

Footnote 64: popularmechanics.com, "Military Section: Navy UFO Videos Are Real," by Kyle Mizokami, September 16, 2019

Because the Alcubierre Drive is probably relevant in some way, I'll leave that information. In one hundred years, the problems with these propulsion systems will likely be no-more. They may be like the Neanderthals who became extinct when Homo sapiens came along. Yet, elements of that species remain within us. Perhaps it is the same with different kinds of spacetime propulsion.

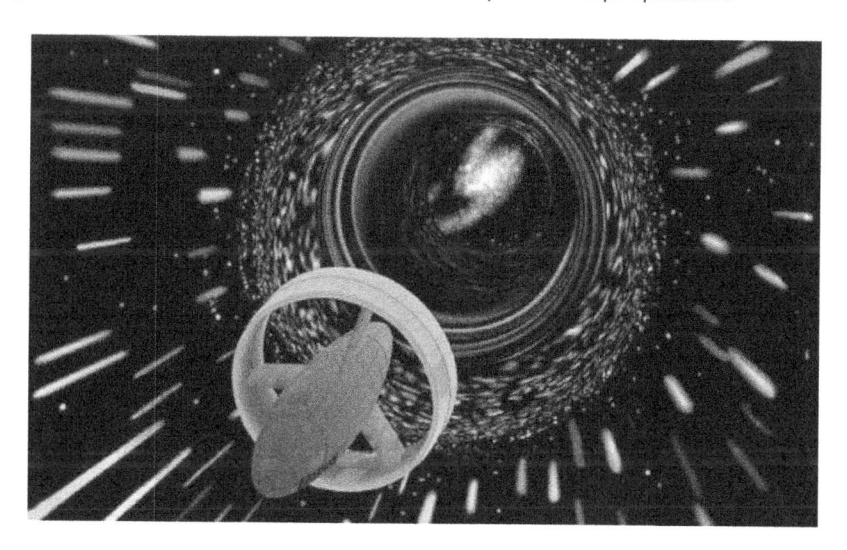

Do Future Humans Travel Back in Time via the Same Method? Is creating a shortcut to another star system ("warping"), also the basic mechanism which Future Humans use for traveling back in time? I asked Dr. Sarfatti to clear up another question: I wondered if time travel is less problematical than interstellar travel, because, in traveling back in time, there is not the extreme distance to contend with. All the layers of humankind throughout time, are all right here.

Dr Sarfatti answered that if you can fold space to travel back in time, you can fold space to lessen interstellar distances. His metamaterial, "low power warp" research is ready to be tested, it simply needs funding just as has been done for other huge scientific and technical projects.

In Chapter 4, Jack Sarfatti offered his very promising work on how Future Humans travel back in time. Metamaterials are crucial. They may be the key to zero gravity, warping space and traveling back in time. They may be the basic component which opens the door to—everything. Other top physicists who still work for the government agree that metamaterials are a game-changer; several secretly also suspect that it is future humans, not ETs, in those Tic-Tacs. Rest assured, the game has changed!

And even if these precise metamaterials are not the key, the key to traveling back in time will be discovered by physicists, probably of the 21st Century, who persevere and who hold onto their childhood love of science fiction and the stars.

I have heard people say that traveling back in time is something even advanced extraterrestrial civilizations can't do. I have no idea what ET physicist from an advanced civilization was conferred with, to render this opinion. Humankind has always thought the next scientific step is impossible, until we do it.

We dream it, we work boldly and diligently, and it becomes reality. That is how it has always been.

Michio Kaku: "Once confined to fantasy and science fiction, time travel is now simply an engineering problem."

The Technology of UFO Abductions:

Scientific Control of the Fear Response: In the abduction chapter, I mentioned that I felt no fear during either abduction, which is admittingly, not the obvious response. Steve Boucher felt no fear, at least during one of his encounters. There are other abductees as well who felt no fear. It is true that most abductees are terrified.

The reactions among us are of such extremes, it seems the UFO occupants must do something to suppress fear in some of us. Whether to suppress fear might depend on the decision of the leader, regarding the specific goal of the mission, or on the specific group of UFO occupants.

We tend to think there is no "one pill" to suppress natural fear, but as of 2016, there is; we have a pill to reduce fear *now*. It could easily be administered to an abductee, possibly in aerosol form.

For extraterrestrials to have such a pill would take research into human physiology which, of course ETs could do, but why bother? Do space-traveling extraterrestrials take time to develop a no-fear pill remedy for every species they abduct on every planet?

The Cure for Fear: *Karin Klaver woke in the darkness and searched the nightstand for her iPhone. It was 2 a.m. Her husband slept quietly beside her. They had arrived in Johannesburg early that morning on the red-eye from Amsterdam and spent the day window shopping and people watching in the city. In the blackness of the room, Klaver sensed a presence at her bedside. A man was standing there with a gun in his hand, and he raised it to her head. Terrified, Klaver rolled onto her stomach. If she was to be shot, she thought to herself, better to be shot in the back. Her movement woke her husband, and the intruder demanded their cash and valuables. Then he slipped away into the night, leaving them unharmed but shaken.*

Back in Holland, Klaver, 56, struggled to resume her normal life. What had once been comfortable and familiar now felt uneasy and insecure. "Everything would remind me of what happened in Johannesburg," she said. She was nervous around unfamiliar men, and her house became a racket of threatening noises. The wind rustling in the curtains could keep her awake for hours. Nothing could dispel the dread that had overwhelmed her in that hotel room, when she was sure that she would die. "It was always there," she recalled recently. "It felt like a balloon inside."

Klaver found it difficult to talk about her anxiety, even with her husband. Thinking back to the robbery left her feeling even more isolated and vulnerable. "The first seconds, you feel so very, very lonely," she said. She resisted the idea of psychotherapy, with its long sessions devoted to reliving and processing the trauma.

A year and a half later, in 2013, Klaver read an item in the newspaper about Merel Kindt, a professor of clinical psychology at the University of Amsterdam. Kindt had developed a revolutionary treatment that could "neutralize" fear memories with a single pill. This treatment was a scientific breakthrough, building on decades of psychological research. It was also deceptively simple. "It was quick and that's what I like," Klaver said.

One of Kindt's assistants made Klaverr re-live the trauma, insisting she give every terrible detail which frightened her so much. She was shattered after this initial session.

Three weeks later, Kindt, ushered Klaver into a small, plain room. Normally, a patient who had suffered a traumatic experience might expect a therapist to proceed slowly and gently, offering comfort and support. Instead, Kindt dived straight in, pushing Klaver to relive the night of the robbery and focus on the source of her fear. "There is no escape," Kindt told her, as Klaver wept into her hands. "Nobody can help you." After 15 minutes, Klaver seemed shattered by her memories, and Kindt abruptly stopped the interrogation.

Kindt gave Klaver a round, white pill, which she swallowed with a sip of water.

Klaver went to bed early that night and slept for twelve hours. When she woke the next morning, she found that her memory was transformed. She recalled the details of what had happened in that bedroom in Johannesburg: She could still see the man's dirty cap, oversized jeans, and cheap plastic shoes. Yet she was able for the first time to think about the experience without anxiety or panic. "It felt like there was not that much weight on my shoulders," she said.

When she returned to see Kindt a week later, she exclaimed, "It's really gone!" Klaver said, "It is quite special, isn't it?"

Kindt smiled and leaned forward in her chair. "Yes," she agreed. "Very special."

Kindt, 48, has devoted her career to understanding human fear and memory. She has developed simple treatment she hopes might one day help millions of people who suffer from PTSD, phobias, and other anxiety disorders. In her clinic, she has seen it work in hundreds of cases, and yet she still marvels every time she sees a patient disencumbered of fear and trauma after such a short procedure. In those moments, she told me recently, her work doesn't feel like science or medicine at all. "It still feels a bit like magic," she said.

Richard Friedman, the director of the psychopharmacology clinic at Weill Cornell Medicine, recently lauded Kindt's work in the <u>New York Times</u>," writing, "It suggests that someday, a single dose of a drug, combined with exposure to your fear at the right moment, could free you of that fear forever.'

Note: This article is abbreviated but I encourage you to read the entire article.

Footnote 65: The New Republic, "The Cure for Fear," by Ben Crair, May 1, 2016

Nabbing the Abductee, The Interrupt Field: Abductees are often puzzled as to why their families or friends, don't interact during a UFO abduction. Betty Andreasson reported her family was put in "suspended animation."

My parents were older parents, devoted to me, the child they thought they might not be able to have. Either of them would have wrapped their arms around the legs of any alien or Future Human who was taking their daughter away and held on. Granted, in the abduction I detailed here, I was taken while playing outside. My parents were inside the house.

However, on the second abduction, I was alone in a cabin we had rented on Eagle Lake, Ontario, Canada. My mother would not leave the cabin (or anywhere), for any length time without me. I have guessed that my parents were somewhere outside talking with my aunt and uncle. Was that group held is stasis? My parents showed up again after the encounter was over. I have no idea why I was left behind in the cabin in the first place.

On that encounter, the same entity (my special one, and I realize that is a highly subjective name), came through the door of the cabin suddenly, as I was reading my book on not being afraid of unknown strange things (no kidding!), entitled **Toys in the Attic."** He wore jeans, red plaid or checkered shirt, and sunglasses.

That same aunt and uncle, who were staying at the same camp, on that same morning, reported two UFOs over Eagle Lake, Ontario, when they were out in a canoe. However, I did not know about their sighting until thirty years later, so it in no way influenced me to think I was abducted that day.

A friend who was abducted has said the same regarding a stasis field. She states that three siblings and herself had just been put to bed for the night. They were not wealthy, and her parents' bedroom was right next door, thin walls. Her siblings normally did not go right to sleep but fooled around, talked and wrestled. But this night, her siblings were "out cold instantly, not a peep from her parents, and she was levitated out the window in a UFO abduction.

No family member was aware of anything strange happening. She was gone, as best as she could figure, for three hours that night. She found herself back in bed, looked at the clock, and when she stopped panicking, she calculated how long she had been gone. She stresses that her siblings had never gone right to sleep like that. Her parents, who stayed up later, said they thought a "cop car" had been close by that night, due to "some lights somewhere outside."

We have computer technology even today to create such an "interrupt" field within a computer. We also have virtual reality and rudimentary holographic technology today, so that possibly a "interrupt bubble" can be created not in a computer but from a computer – a specific brain wave, an "interrupt."

The Interrupt: Here are the basics which an experienced, top notch computer programmer offers, *"The simultaneous nature of time is very nicely illustrated by what is known as an 'interrupt' in computer machine language programming. When a computer executes commands one after another linearly, it can be signaled by an external event such as a sensor changing its state, or a button being pushed.*

The interrupt causes the CPU (central processing unit) to store its 'environment' such as data it registers and where it was in memory when reading a program.

Then the cpu executes the 'interrupt vector' involving different data in the registers and a different place in memory where it runs code to service the sensor changing state or the button being pushed. When it completes the task, it goes back to the exact place in memory and restores the previously held data in the registers and continues on as if nothing happened.

When I received this info, I immediately related to the families and friends of abductees who notice nothing out of the ordinary and have no memory of being "interrupted" in time. We do have the beginning of this technology in our current world, but give us 100 years? Think of PC, laptop, and smart phone advances since the Year 2000!

The interrupt concept seems connected to the idea that once time can be manipulated backward and forward, "time loops" can also be created. This connects to causal loops in physics.

An example of a time loop is **Original Series Star Trek** episode entitled "Yesterday Is Tomorrow," wherein the pilot of a 1960s military jet spies the Enterprise in the sky and figures it is a UFO. He gives chase. His fighter jet begins to break up in the Enterprise's tractor beam, so they beam him aboard. They have to return him to Earth because in the future, the pilot's future-born son contributes greatly to human efforts to travel space, so they set the pilot back down into his fighter jet the second before it started to disintegrate. The pilot remembered nothing because it never happened.

Yes, this is science fiction, but I suspect this manipulation of time, causing loops which end right before they begin, is within time traveling technology and may have elements of computer "interrupt" as well.

At any rate, as technical advancement continues at light speed, we can see that Future Humans probably consider "computer tricks" in their "catch and release an ancestor" abduction program, as just another day's work.

We current humans are so dependent on time, assuming it just marches along second by second, always going forward, that we are sitting ducks for advanced time travelers who travel back to study their ancestors. That's us!

The Forward March of Computers: Where will computer science be in the Year 2525? Moore's Law states that computer processing speed doubles every 18 months. This is symptomatic of a far greater trend in everything-computer and technical. This is the Golden Age of Technology which is advancing at an exponential rate.

For most of human history, it was assumed one would die in a world which was similar to the world into which you were born. That is no longer true.

Futurist and transhumanist Ray Kurzweil states that soon we won't have to die because we will be able to upload our unique mind and essence, into a computer, and then download it, if we wish, into a new artificial humanoid body. He says that in the 21st Century, we will experience not 100 years of advancement, but 20,000 years of advancement.

I am not pushing this idea, but I also do not feel the almost-obligatory distaste for it which many people do. This, simply, could be the future.

Footnote 66: Big Think "Technology Grows Exponentially," March 2011

Unless our species manages to extinguish itself through nuclear war or by making our planet unlivable in other ways, this concept of computer-human singularity called "transhumanism" will become reality, if not for all, then for some. **Transhumanists feel that our species' next natural step in evolution is to become artificial intelligence.**

We hope that it is not for the wealthy, leaving 99% of us as "inferior" because we remain natural. This and other nightmare scenarios could happen; *all of us* need to engage in shaping this future, today!. It is no time to hide one's head in the sand!

There's no point to being snobbish about "natural" being superior, either. The knee jerk reaction from many of us is to argue that our natural state is the way we must be and the way we must stay. One day, this attitude might be considered the epitome of human chauvinism.

If artificial intelligence is handled intelligently, it can transform our current problems, it can help solve them, it can work for us and free us to reach for our full potential.

Quantum Computers and Their Qubits:
The computers used by time travelers are no doubt quantum computers or even post-quantum computers which will operate through even smaller particles. To try to understand our time travelers, we need to try to understand their computers.

Today, the older generations sigh at how much younger generations are addicted to smart phones; possibly in, say, one hundred years, humans won't have their heads in cell phones but computer access will be within them – within their minds. Perhaps humans and their computers will be better integrated with each other and it will become more natural. Maybe not, but it is a thought.

The smaller computers get, the more powerful they become. There is more number crunching ability in our cellphones than in a huge military computer 50 years ago. Transistors in our computers will soon be as tiny as an atom. How powerful and fast will quantum computers be, 100 years into the future?

Quantum computers will have processors which work millions of time faster, using qubits (quantum bits), not the "bits" computers have today. They will use subatomic particles, which open quantum computing for us. They will operate in the "spooky action at a distance" world of quantum entanglement and superposition to perform operations on data.

Not coincidentally, our minds also work on quantum particles. Perhaps this is a hint on a more natural mingling of human and computer. It is hard to even guess at this point.

Today's classical computers store information in binary; each bit is either on or off. Quantum computation use qubits (quantum bits), which, in addition to being possibly on or off, can also be both on and off, which is a way of describing superposition. This reminds us of Schrodinger's poor cat, being neither or both, dead and/or alive.

This is only the beginning for quantum computers although there are now several more sophisticated ones gearing up than the test-models of a few years ago. There are problems in getting quantum computers off the ground which, as humans usually do, should be solved eventually.

Quantum computers eventually will far out-do conventional super-computers. They will revolutionize technology by making it possible to simulate the behavior of the universe itself, down to the sub-atomic level.

Quantum computers and post-quantum computers are probably at the fingertips of Future Humans, or literally, in their heads. Those incredible computers belonging to the Future Humans, have their beginning in our moment of time, the 21st Century. We are the founding fathers and mothers, for better or worse!

Footnote 67: Explain That Stuff, "Quantum Computing," by Chris Woodford, March 26, 2019

Future Genetics

But the facts must be recorded----they may be only interesting bits of folklore -or they may involve the future of civilization.
-Jacques Vallee

There no doubt is advanced genetic research in the world of the Future Humans, but what proof (or hints), do we see from UFO witness and abductee accounts?

Officially, today's designer babies cannot have altered genes for traits considered by some people to be preferable such as high intelligence, or blue eyes. When a designer baby is created with altered genes today, it is to correct genes associated with disease. This is cutting edge genetics; what a gift to be given a normal life without a disease or defect!

Golden Humans: In the future, will gene altering be kept to these rules? Almost always, rules melt away over time. And so, enter the "perfect humans" ("golden humans") whom Travis Walton met. Might these Future Humans be "designer babies" with gene-editing resulting in good looks, flawless complexions, beautiful features, and high intelligence?

There are good reasons to object to this extreme of gene altering; we love our imperfections, our individuality! I am offering it only as an answer to the "golden humans" whom witnesses and abductees have seen, including myself.

Sketch from an essay by Jacques Vallee on "Pilots and Passengers."

Small Humans: I have an admittedly far-out idea regarding the small humans who are the majority of UFO occupants, especially in the 1950s and 1960s. The fetus-like variations and "greys" who are more common today, are also small humanoids and are included in my theory.

Many times, UFO occupants have been described as human dwarves, only with balanced symmetry – not having the unusual features (genetic flaws) which dwarf humans have. In the old days, we called these well-proportioned little people, "midgets" but that has become an impolite word.

So, whether extraterrestrial or human, we are puzzled as to how these obviously far-advanced UFO occupants, are "little people." Shorter legs mean less athletic ability by our standards, but perhaps it is only a different athletic ability. Being very short means it is challenging to physically deal with tall humans or other large species, but perhaps having advanced tech weapons and defenses make up for this.

Did our species shrink? Or is this the normal march of evolution as Dr. Michael Masters has suggested?

Or, if the small humans are genetically altered, why would they opt to be this size?

Or, is there a race of ETs who are just like small humans? The last answer seems highly unlikely due to the vastness of space and the uniqueness of our DNA.

An answer – the only one I can think of – came to me as I watched a news feature on how the United Nations is advising that we cut back on meat in-take to help save the planet. Some of us are willing to give up meat to help save the planet, others of us are not. Some may grumble and say it is the latest nonsense.

However, what will Earth be in, say, 75 years, at the rate we are going in terms of ice melting, oceans rising, crops failing (the same show had a feature on how coffee plantations are ruined due to drought and plant disease), and on down the long, tragic list?

So, let's say the small humans come from 75 years in the future. Jack Sarfatti is right, we got low power warp, and it took 75 years to build, perfect, test, and begin to travel back in time. Meanwhile, Earth is in a terrible state with climate chaos, global warming, carbon emissions, lack of trees, and more. Our world is ravaged and almost non-habitable.

Therefore, a group of us decide to have smaller children to make less of a footprint on Earth and to use less oxygen, and lessen the strain on natural resources; these children will need less food and water, both of which will have become scarce in 75 years. After all, the situation is so bad already that today, that we are being advised to stop eating meat to help the faltering planet. There is no doubt that the huge population of humans is killing the planet.

So, an entire branch of humanity becomes smaller. These are intelligent space-goers and time travelers, the children of very responsible parents trying to help save their world – Earth. Through genetic engineering, these parents are giving birth to smaller humans. The genetic line is engineered to continue to be smaller.

Yes, this may be a stretch, just sheer speculation, so I challenge anyone to figure out why so many UFO occupants are just—little people with the slightest variations.

Gene Editing and Altering: A brief look into the future of genetics which will be the world of our progeny:

Just like artificial intelligence, there is a huge question of extreme potential good and extreme potential evil in the field of advanced genetic engineering.

How might this relate to Future Humans? They must live in a world wherein advanced genetics have probably been implemented, certainly to treat diseases with gene therapy; in fact, we are already doing this. We are on the threshold "fixing" genes which mandate that an individual gets cancer, Parkinson's, Alzheimer's, Huntington's, ALS, and many other human afflictions. Not all cancer (or other disease) is gene-connected, but a lot of it is.

Faulty genes lead to babies born with serious defects but even now, we correct many defects before birth so that a normal individual will enjoy a lifetime. The above can mostly be achieved with gene therapy as it progresses.

CRISPR: But what about gene editing? Since the late 2000s, scientists began to develop techniques known as "genome (or gene) editing." Genome editing allows scientists to make changes to a specific "target" site in the genome. One of the techniques that have generated the most excitement, due to its efficiency and ease of use, is called "CRISPR." CRISPR stands for "clustered regularly interspaced short palindromic repeats."

The basis of CRISPR technology is a system that bacteria evolved to protect themselves against viruses. Scientists have now taken components of the CRISPR system and fashioned it into a tool for genome editing.

There is the Chinese scientist who got in big trouble in 2018 with the Chinese government when he stated he had created two CRISPR (genome edited) twins, Nana and Lulu, who have "perfect genes." In fact, they have serious gene problems, as if adjusting one set of genes, caused the others to go out of whack. However, this is just the beginning stage of CRISPR genetics.

Footnote 68: genetics education project.org, "genetic-modification-genome-editing-and-crispr"

As with most innovations, CRISPR (actual genome editing) will probably be accepted eventually, for better or worse.

We all know the horrors of the Nazi eugenics program and the sick hatred of believing this or that race is supreme. Add the capabilities of advanced science and technology to this, and we have a dystopian nightmare.

Or, we can find ourselves in a better world with little to no disease, a recovering, healthy planet, and with the stars themselves at our fingertips. It really is up to us as a species which way it goes.

We can take educated guesses at what might become reality as technology advances but in the field of genetics, there are many wild cards.

I do have more questions for the Future Humans besides the "small humans:"

#1: Why do the "golden humans" which Travis Walton and I met, seem so perfect? They are the epitome of human attractiveness, rather like the Greek gods. Travis saw two female "golden humans" who were flawless and lovely.

#2: It seems females are seldom on abduction teams; in a few cases, an abducted man has claimed he had to have sex with an exotic alien female. "Man being made to have sex with alien female" would seem to be old fantasy stuff, although I am not commenting on any case in particular.

But, where are the females of the "small human or humanoid" group? Perhaps when in uniform, the females are assumed to be males by upset abductees (?). Or if manipulating genetics is common, are males preferred?

#3: Where are the other tribes in our glorious human family, the Asians and the Africans? The small humans seem to be of light pink skin color or emaciated white or grey color. The being I met did have olive-colored skin, but whether a person believes in extraterrestrials or Future Humans, there seems to be little diversity. Arcturians all look alike in drawings, as do Zetas, and so forth.

#4. Is there is a "cookie cutter" for artificial intelligence entities? If some of these are artificial intelligence beings, perhaps that explains some of it. Whether extraterrestrial or Future Human, let's hope diversity still exists!

Artificial Intelligence:

We all know what organic humans are, but we are unfamiliar or have stereotyped views of artificial intelligence. Taking a closer look how artificial intelligence might be involved:

Space has three kinds of deadly radiation: Space has non-iodizing radiation, iodizing radiation and galactic cosmic radiation from inside and outside the Milky Way. GCR is particularly troublesome for astronauts in orbit around Earth; we can only imagine how lethal it would be in interstellar space.

Artificially intelligent post-human time travelers would be nearly invulnerable to all radiation. Does traveling back in time involve the same radiation threat? I don't know, but "time" is not deep space travel.

In space, creating a zero gravity bubble or a warp field, would seem to protect the travelers from g-forces but spacetime is a cruel mistress. There are bound to be dangers and stresses such as "tidal forces" involved in manipulating (warping) the fabric of spacetime, which we cannot anticipate at present. Artificial intelligence beings would be more resilient and tougher than organic humans.

I would love to think that natural humans like **Star Trek's** Starship Enterprise crew are busy out there warping spacetime, but I can live with the possibility that although they may might look like Greek gods such as Travis Walton encountered, or similar to "little people" such as Betty and Barney Hill confronted, the human starship crews are, all or partly, artificial intelligence.

Or, they may be like the wonderful artificial intelligence of **Interstellar,** which saved the day several times but did not have a head, 2 arms and 2 legs (not humanoid design).

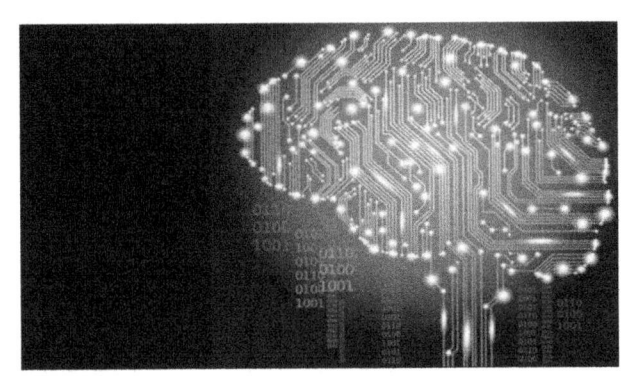

We assume that we lose our unique humanity, perhaps our soul, as artificial components are added. However, we do realize that if you receive an artificial knee or hip, we remain human. Those who have artificial limbs are still human. So, it is not the physical parts of the body which would make us lose our humanity.

It is not my intention to campaign for artificial intelligence, but to delve into the possibility that artificial intelligence seems a likely aspect of time traveling human crews. Our penchant for smart phones, computers, and other high tech is certainly headed in AI's direction as well. We hate to admit it, but perhaps this is evolution's natural path, or at least, its inherent drive for a species to survive in some form, however altered.

There are two "branches" of potential artificial intelligence. One is an organic (natural) human who becomes artificial intelligence through an advanced computer's interface with her mind; she now has a higher IQ and loads of information, now accessible from within her mind when she seeks it out.

As time goes along, she will add physical artificial components like new joints, muscles, and organs, because the organic body wears out. Eventually she will become completely artificial, but she will still be "her," a unique individual, human at the core, or so we fervently hope. (Remember, being human is not 100% positive, it might be good to upgrade a bit).

Of course, we can't be sure the human soul or core, will remain as greatly expanded minds engage in new vistas. Change is a natural force which cannot be denied.

Jack Sarfatti states: "Furthermore, one can imagine attaining the transhumanist agenda. For example, the consciousness of a genius like Stephen Hawking could be uploaded to the post-quantum Cloud and then downloaded to a healthy body or android."

Footnote 69: Solution to David Chalmers "Hard Problem" by Jack Sarfatti and Arik Simansky, Internet Science Education Project

The other branch of artificial intelligence is a computer-created android or robot; we have those today, but in the future, probably it will be a fully conscious entity. Sarfatti sees a time in the not-distant future when an additional nanochip will create a conscious post-human. That specific nanochip is being researched.

A conscious android would have human consciousness because humans created it. Humans do not have the ability to create an android with, for instance, Arcturian consciousness. Humans will be the creators of the nano-chips which carry human consciousness. However, eventually, AI will create AI, and that is one of the worries.

Do we fear high intelligence? Very intelligent humans are poets, musical composers, great authors, and so forth, as well as physicists and rocket scientists. Perhaps we should fear ignorance and stupidity more than an upgrade in our intelligence. Ignorance and stupidity do cause a lot of violence, grief, and back-sliding.

Would our soul be destroyed if we became artificially intelligence? This myth is assumed to be true by vast numbers of the population. In fact, there are disinformation campaigns online which preach that artificial intelligence is the ultimate evil and is out to destroy us all. In fact, having artificial intelligence might free humankind from the grips of greedy, oppressive governments.

I do not know the future, no one does. But since artificial intelligence already exists and will likely become, literally, a part of us in the future, we need to consider it with logic and intelligence, and not through a dark, superstitious, misinformation lens. We shouldn't be hiding from the very thought of it, but rather active in influencing how this technology may manifest for good rather than evil.

Today's artificial intelligence has already been applied to environmental crises. For example, WildTrack uses a computer vision to monitor endangered species non-invasively. The tool analyzes images of footprints of cheetahs, rhinos, and other endangered species to identify them, track them, and determine what threatens them. Ironically, we cannot save most higher life-forms on Earth in the coming climate chaos without help from artificial intelligence working out innovative methods to avert doomsday across the globe.

Footnote 70: WildTrack.org, "Non-Invasive Wildlife Monitoring"

Advanced robots are already used to go into burning or booby-trapped buildings. There is an endless list even today of artificial intelligence being used for the good of organic life. As the tragic Amazon fires blaze threatening life on Earth, I cannot help but think how artificial intelligence could speedily mobilize resources to fight those thousands of fires; AI could be sent in, impervious to the flames.

And as we fervently hope the Amazon Rainforest enters a recovery phase, how useful AI would be to go into the dense jungle and the barren fire-ravaged wasteland, going where organic humans simply can't go, to begin to restore what was lost.

One in five breaths we take is oxygen manufactured by the Amazon Rainforest, but artificial intelligence does not need oxygen. AI has the potential to save our world. The situation may be so bad that we organic humans do not have that ability to do this alone, anymore. I feel that Future Humans would point out these facts in defense of their artificial components.

UFOs have flown over Earth for years, observing and researching. They must know that in 2020, we are in bad shape on Earth. Perhaps they feel that we are our own worst enemy and if things get bad enough, we will be forced to see the benefits of artificial intelligence and other aspects of their future world.

UFOs from 50 or 200 years ahead, will have the advantage of having highly advanced crews, some or all of whom might be artificial intelligence. If the UFOs are from 10,000 years ahead, we can't even begin to imagine.

Different Types of Artificial Intelligence:

Reactive Machines AI
Limited Memory AI
Theory of Mind AI
Self-aware AI

Artificial Narrow Intelligence (ANI)
Artificial General Intelligence (AGI)
Artificial Superhuman Intelligence (ASI)

Footnote 71: medium.com, "Artificial Intelligence, Definition, Types, Examples, Technologies," by Chethan Kumar, August 2018

It is true that artificial intelligence has a collective component to it. Using the Internet as an example, somewhere there is the source of it all, there is a network or directive, which guides.

However, every species has a collective system already, through Mother Nature. Humans have collective human consciousness. Whales have collective whale consciousness; lions have collective lion consciousness.

The collective species mind governs how individual entities behave and think to a great extent, and yet each whale, each lion, is an individual too. Diversity thankfully seems to be a constant factor of the universe. The human collective consciousness is inescapable for a human, it is how we behave, how we think and feel. And yet, we too are individuals.

When humans say, "Love thy neighbor as thyself," they allude to the collective human consciousness, the shared humanity. "To be human" has evolved throughout the ages, and yet in another way, it has remained the same. I suspect the same will be true as we leap into the human future.

Thinking about artificial intelligence certainly makes us cherish natural consciousness, both collective and individual but there is no reason AI can't co-exist with the natural world.

It is up to us, the humans who are already creating artificial intelligence. The day will come when a scientist will bestow consciousness upon artificial intelligence and then Pandora's Box cannot be closed.

Do we make conscious artificial intelligence war-like or peaceful? Do we make it aggressive, aware of who is superior to whom? Or do we instill respect for life, artificial and organic? Do we program integrity, honesty, and responsibility?

Acting with logic and using one's intelligence is also in the best interest of others. Acting out of blind emotion and dancing to one's own psychological foibles, spells disaster. Artificial intelligence individuals will become full citizens one day and might be a positive influence among us. At least, it is worth some thought.

The fact is, if AI and humans could work together, we can find the answers to huge problems and challenges which would elude either of us working alone. Together we can improve the process of thinking. Perception and consciousness will then move a step forward. Maybe when we of the 21st Century grow up that little bit in our thinking, our Future Human descendants in UFOs will make themselves known to us.

And, when artificial intelligence gains actual consciousness, they should have the same rights as organic humans. They will be *life*. Otherwise, we will have the same old struggle as one segment of the population fights for its inherent rights.

What Is Their Future Like? I can't tell you what Future Humans' Earth is like; well, I could, but that would be entirely subjective on my part; this is not a new age or channeled book. However, since it seems almost a "given" that science and technology will continue to progress, here are a few positives in this advancing behemoth of technology which leaves our minds boggled every day.

This is the Golden Age of Science and Technology because genetics, astronomy, physics, medicine, computer science, and more, are advancing exponentially each year. "We the People" may not get the full benefits of this advancement, but it is happening, thanks in a large degree to advanced computers.

It seems clear that Future Humans do embrace this advancement; perhaps they could not stop it if they wanted to. The Future Humans from an era when traveling back in time is possible, probably live in a world of artificial intelligence. This is the world they know and many of them are AI.

There is an argument which says only the wealthy will buy for themselves the benefits of artificial intelligence, not the least of which is immortality. It may happen that way and that would be tragic. The wealthy buy everything for themselves today, can it be so much worse? Yes, it can. However, this is not the book in which to go exploring dystopian theories.

We shouldn't give up having our voice heard on this crucial issue of artificial intelligence and advanced technology; the future is an open book. We need to participate in making it compassionate and humane. There is no reason we can't have both advanced science/technology and enlightenment.

If today we think poorly of our species and its future, let's change it while we can! I would like to look to a time when we have finally learned the truth that we do create the future.

We can work for a future world which is awakened to human and animal rights, justice, equality, freedom, and the sanctity and care of our precious Planet Earth. These areas need more effort put into them by us to make them reality in the future. Science and technology are exploding, leaping ahead, regardless!

***

Chapter Ten: ESP or Time Travelers' Nanochips?

To paraphrase Arthur C. Clarke, "It was magic until we made the next step in advanced technology, and then we understood!"

There would seem to be two ways to receive a message in one's mind:

1. Receiving information through psychic impression or message.

2. Receiving information through quantum technology which makes use of microscopic nanochips which offer impressions or messages.

There is also receiving information through a Vulcan mind meld, but we have yet to make friends with the Planet Vulcan.

The focus of this book is to illustrate that UFO occupants may well be humans who have traveled back in time. I want to make clear I am not advocating inserting nanochips into the heads of the citizens of the world by their governments or anyone else.

Aliens are said to channel entire books through human conduits, offer psychic workshops through "channels,", read an individual's thoughts, control an individual's reality, send telepathy at will, and more. Sometimes channels receive messages of enlightened wisdom, while other people feel they are being possessed and driven mad by evil alien input in their heads. The concept of both extremes is that extraterrestrials have advanced alien minds with inherent, super-powerful psychic abilities which can be used as needed.

In fact, extraterrestrials might utilize nanochips or similar advanced technology to influence an abductee's mind or to channel a message to a 20/21st Century human. If ETs do visit Earth too, it may boil down to technology which gives them their "super-powers," rather than having natural telepathic minds.

We assume that humans don't have powerful psychic ability and we assume humans don't have advanced technology in order to place a nano-chip in an unknowing victim. In the future, we may have either or both, of these abilities. We are all-too-anxious to make ourselves inferior to the aliens – something which is fool-hearty and perhaps just plain erroneous. We do not take our own human potential into consideration.

Here is a closer look at both natural psi ability (ESP, remote viewing, precognition), and high tech nanochips and nano-systems as related to Future Humans and their probable "psychic influence."

The ESP, Remote Viewing, Research at Sanford Research Institute:

Remote viewing is the practice of seeking impressions about a distant or unseen target, purportedly using extrasensory perception (ESP) or "sensing" with the mind.

In 1972, Russell Targ, a physicist who was already known for his work with lasers and laser applications, joined the Stanford Research Institute in Menlo Park, California, intent on researching ESP and its application of remote viewing. Hal Puthoff, also a respected physicist, joined Targ in this new research.

The remarkable, eye-opening film on Stanford research and the subsequent Stargate (CIA) phase of remote viewing research, is in a film called **Third Eye Spies** available on Amazon and You Tube. The film **Men Who Stare at Goats** is also about this topic.

In the first years of this research, the objective was to simply examine the remote viewing ability of an individual to "see" remotely; for instance, Russell Targ would travel to a spot in the San Francisco Bay area; meanwhile, back at Stanford, Puthoff would ask the remote viewer to sketch where Dr. Targ had gone.

There were many amazing successes. The researchers found several talented remote viewers. This would be news for all humankind, because all of us have psi (ESP, and other) ability to varying degrees; at last, we would be finding this out about ourselves with no hesitations on the part of science!

Yes, the researchers had amazing success with a series of gifted remote viewers; in fact, that's how the CIA joined up and ruined everything. They saw the opportunity for gifted individuals to use remote viewing to "view" thousands of miles away in Russia, and to go into secret rooms and vaults. The CIA felt that if remote viewing was real, this was a whole new spy vs. spy ballgame. Of course the problem was that Russia, which had ESP research better funded and many years ahead of the U.S, had gifted remote viewers "viewing" in the U.S.

Why would the CIA believe remote viewing could be done at will and render actuate results? This was simply because the results at SRI were so amazing and because the projects had been carefully administered and controlled.

Later on, it was said there was a lack of oversight as to how carefully experiments were done, but this may well have been an excuse to control it and then to "close it down" after 23 years (1972 – 1995). Many believe it simply went "underground" and became military controlled at that point.

Three of the best known remote viewers with whom Stanford researchers worked, Igo Swann, Pat Price, and Joseph McMoneagle. These men were from different walks of life; Igo Swann was an eccentric artist, Pat Price was a former police officer, and Joseph McMoneagle (now retired) was an Army Chief Warrant Officer. It is my theory that these talented remote viewers happened to have a more evolved gene (or genes) for this ability, than most of us.

Footnote 72: New Dualism.org, "CIA Initiated Remote Viewing at Stanford," by Hal Puthoff, Ph.D.

Footnote 73: Wikipedia, "Russell Targ SRI, Remote Viewing"

Just as someone has a gene which makes him a great pianist, there is a gene which make a few humans ESP-gifted. I also feel there is a continuum of ESP ability, with some humans having more than others – but we all have it to some degree, as do animals! As well, someone might have precognitive talent but not be great at remote viewing, and so forth.

That ESP gene is no doubt in the strands of DNA which deal with our pineal gland (third eye). Advanced genetic scientists can find that area in our genome.

Probably, if a gene or two were "tweaked" in the rest of us, we would have remote viewing capability which was dependable and amazing. This may be true of Future Humans; that third eye gene may have been enhanced.

Or, it is also possible that human psi ability will evolve as we change and evolve naturally. Evolution usually takes millions of years, and so we cannot really examine if we have more (or less) psi ability than, for example, the ancient Egyptians had 3,000 years ago. However, humans from, say, 100,000 years in the future, might have had natural evolutionary advancement psi abilities.

Another possibility: Our Future Human visitors' dependence on technology might lessen the development of their natural human psi ability. This night be true especially for Future Humans only 250 years ahead. Even today, older people feel that younger generations are losing contact with nature and with themselves, and that they are depending too much on fascinating technologies.

The fact is, we are already far up the path of becoming dependent on advanced tech running our lives. And, the Future Humans will be raised in an even more radically advanced technology environment.

I will stipulate here that I believe most visitors in our skies, whether alien or human, are ahead of us in technology but not by millions of years. I have no evidence on this, but I feel that if a group of humans is millions of years ahead of us, they would not bother playing **Top Gun** with our fighter jets, not bother abducting humans in what amounts to sometimes sloppy kidnapping, and not bother hanging around our nuclear installations. Where will we be in a million years? Will we even have physical bodies? We may simply be quantum particles of consciousness and information.

However, from what I have experienced and researched for over 40 years, I think we can get a rough picture of the level of technology of UFO occupants. I conclude they are 75 to 2,000 years ahead of us; there may be representatives from various times within that span and perhaps from beyond 2,000 years. Of course, once we escape time, we are of "all time" and perhaps "no time."

The Nanochip Aspect: It's interesting that natural telepathy is considered a gift. "I am telepathic!" is considered a positive. Even the ability to read someone's thoughts is usually alright if it happens naturally, "I just knew you were going to phone me!"

However, if someone has information that was given through a nanochip, it is considered a terrible violation by our current society. People fear they might be mind-controlled in everything they do, say, and believe. And yet, the result is the

same, whether sent by natural telepathy or nano-chip: Information arrives in your head, just as your own thoughts do.

Looking into the not-distant future, we could each have a nanochip which receives a system similar to WiFi. It might be like having your smartphone in your head with no hands involved. I realize this is not necessarily a good thing because we are already too enmeshed with smart phones and computers; certainly, the nano-system would have to be controlled by the individual so as to use it only when she wishes.

From "information," we can easily take the next step to hacking someone else's information-feed, which would cause that old spy-vs. spy battle to go into red alert.

I do know the fears, but it is up to us as a species to use advanced technology with intelligence and integrity. To say "No!" outright to all advanced technology doesn't seem to be the answer. If we stagnate, rejecting all advancing technology, evolution dictates that we will become extinct. The universe does not let you stand still.

Bits of Information: What Is a Nanochip? *A nanochip is an integrated circuit (IC) that is so small, in physical terms, that individual particles of matter play major roles. Miniaturization of electronic and computer components has always been a primary goal of engineers. Today, such a computer can be placed inside a microscopic capsule. Some nanochips are so small as to be called "nano-dust."*

A nanometre is one millionth of a millimetre. Your fingernail is about one millimetre thick. There are a lot of nano-materials making up your finger nail! Nanotechnology scientists move atoms and molecules around to make amazing new technologies.

Computer giant IBM announced that they had developed functional nanochips measuring just seven nanometres. In comparison, a strand of human DNA is about 2.5 nm and the diameter of a single red blood cell is approximately 7,500 nm.

The future of nanotechnology: *Nanotechnology is an emerging science which is expected to have rapid and strong future developments. The first generation is all about material science with enhancement of properties that are achieved by the incorporating "passive nanostructures."*

Footnote 74: Newsweek, World's Smallest Nanochip Will Double Processing Power of Smartphones, by Conor Gaffey, July 2015

"Not So Alien" Time Travelers: The assumption in 1947, that it was extraterrestrials in those flying saucers, created two distinct groups of those humans who became interested in the topic: Some people were anxious to have interactions with these strange beings from somewhere (or somewhen) in the mind-boggling, overwhelmingly vast universe. It was assumed that our minds could understand their incredible consciousness, which they sent to us telepathically. That was a big assumption.

The other group of humans did not welcome the ETs; this group felt great fear and foreboding, wondering about invasion, enslavement, horrific genetic experiments, and more. These were also huge assumptions. With both extremes, urban legends grew.

It may be that Future Humans as the source of UFOs, did not register in human minds because this concept does not impact that powerful good/evil (extreme) perception as significantly as bizarre aliens do. Human time travelers don't seem as magnificently god-like with promises such as, "ETs are coming to save us, to teach us how to be good, and they will bring me personally good fortune." Nor is the Future Human idea as horrifically horrible as, "Aliens are here to serve humans, but only as the main course of dinner."

We tend to think, "What? It turns out it is just some humans in UFOs. They must think they are better than us because they have all that technology. They won't personally help me because I know humans all too well!"

I believe the UFO occupants, whether ETs or FTs, have always been about our collective consciousness more than about individuals. Some people are more smitten with the idea of "contact from beyond" than other people are, but that is due to those human individuals, not the UFO occupants. If there is "choosing" to be done in the UFO phenomenon, we choose ourselves.

So, let's look at what might be available to help us if we do adopt nanotechnology because there is an amazingly positive side to all this!

***From researchers in 2014:** Tapping directly into someone's brain in order to share thoughts isn't just for Spock anymore. An international team of researchers were* able to replicate the Vulcan mind meld by creating a device that allows two people to share information through thought. The researchers tested the technology by separating the users over 8,000 km (5,000 mi) apart—with one user in France and the other in India.

"We wanted to find out if one could communicate directly between two people by reading out the brain activity from one person and injecting brain activity into the second person, and do so across great physical distances by leveraging existing communication pathways," co-author Alvaro Pascual-Leone said.

Through this method, users were able to exchange simple messages of "ciao" and "hola" to one another without the use of speech, writing, or body language. Though there were minor errors during the trials, the system was, on average, over 90% accurate. There are other methods that would likely be more accurate, but require being embedded into the users. This EEG method is noninvasive and is therefore the best choice at this stage.

"By using advanced precision neurotechnology including wireless EEG and robotized TMS, we were able to directly and noninvasively transmit a thought from one person to another, without them having to speak or write," Pascual-Leone continued. "This in itself is a remarkable step in human communication, but being able to do so across a distance of thousands of miles is a critically important proof-of-principle for the development of brain-to-brain communications. We believe these experiments represent an important first step in exploring the feasibility of complementing or bypassing traditional language-based or motor-based communication."

This is the first time that the technology has been used to connect two human brains directly.

EEG is already used by paralyzed people to direct their motorized wheelchairs with their minds. In the future, this technology could be used in a variety of positive ways to help communicate with patients who, following disease or injury, are still aware but unable to speak. Consider what this would mean to severely disabled people! No use to reject "nanochips" in a sweeping disavowal of all higher (artificial) technology!

Footnote 75: IFLScience!.com "Direct Brain to Brain Communication Used in Humans," August 2014

In future years, neuroscientists foresee a mind chips in each person's head. Of course, this has all sorts of nightmare scenarios shown to us in science fiction books, movies and television series. We assume a nanochip would dictate to us how to act and what to say, but what if a nanochip was there only to guarantee a long life with no threat of a stroke, seizure, cancer, mental illness, or other dreaded ailments? Nanochips have specific uses, we are wrong to mindlessly make them the general boogieman.

Another example of nanotechnology today which happens to echo **Original Series Star Trek;** Dr. McCoy has that nifty tool which looks like a salt shaker which heals flesh wounds very quickly. Here it comes in reality:

A new technique, called tissue nanotransfection, is based on a tiny device that sits on the surface of the skin of a living body. An intense, focused electric field is then applied across the device, allowing it to deliver genes to the skin cells beneath it – turning them into different types of cells.

That, according to the researchers, offers an exciting development when it comes to repairing damaged tissue, offering the possibility of turning a patient's own tissue into a "bioreactor" to produce cells to either repair nearby tissues. It allows new circulation in a limb which had been cut off from its blood flow, emaciated and dying. This tiny device renewed that limb which returned to normal use.

"By using our novel nanochip technology, injured or compromised organs can be replaced," said Chandan Sen, from the Ohio State University, who co-led the study. "We have shown that skin is a fertile land where we can grow the elements of any organ that is declining."

"With this technology, we can convert skin cells into elements of any organ with just one touch. This process only takes less than a second and is non-invasive, it could provide radical new treatment for heart attacks. This is difficult to imagine, but it is achievable, successfully working about 98 per cent of the time," said Dr. Sen.

"With this technology, we can convert skin cells into elements of any organ with just one touch. This process only takes less than a second and is non-invasive, and then you're off. The chip does not stay with you, and the reprogramming of the cell starts. The technology could see cells grown on a human patient's skin and then injected into their body to treat conditions such as Parkinson's disease, Alzheimer disease, nerve damage and strokes."

Footnote 76: The Guardian, "Nanochip Could Heal Injuries or Regrow Organs with One Touch"

I theorize that this is the kind of world in which children of the Future Humans grow up. So many of the problems, health conditions, worries, and threats which are accepted aspects of life in the 21st Century, will have disappeared, becoming simply not a part of reality.

However, I am sure new problems and threats develop and "children are not what they used to be." But then, our own children are not what our parents were, in both good and bad ways. This is social change. This is also evolution.

Nature is a concern, our exquisite planet is not only threatened environmentally but our grandchildren seem more removed from the joys of playing free and wild, in nature. Ironically, advanced science and technology may be the only hope nature has of surviving with diversity, quality, and quantity.

And, we are not sure the children of Future Humans do not love to play in nature, nor are we sure that due to advanced technology, cherishing nature is lost. Having had such a wounded planet as of the 20/21st Century, which the Future Humans will have inherited, they may love and protect the planet more than our generations did.

What I am baffled about, is that we don't perceive how amazing it is that Future Humans may be overhead, in our skies! Thus, yes, we survived 2020! Yes, we survived all the eons before 2020, come war, plague, starvation, slavery, and all the evils – our species survived!

I am disgruntled with "us" at present too, as so many people are. But it seems suicidal as a species not to believe we have great potential and thus keep hope and dreams alive; thus we keep our future alive and foresee a time when we can say, "Just look at us now!"

***

Chapter Eleven: Ancient Time Travelers

"The distinction between the past, present and future is only a stubbornly persistent illusion." – Albert Einstein

Note: The previous chapters in this book are based on solid evidence and speculation based in science and technology. However, when dealing with the ancient past, little real evidence is left, and the waters are murky regarding folklore accuracy. "Consciousness" which is the final chapter, is by definition an awesome if unknown phenomenon. And so, we take flight just a bit in the final three chapters, but our craft is still be balanced by a logical, if speculative thought process.

One day, we will advance science and technology enough to traverse from Now to Now – traveling to those other layers of time in the Eternal Now. "Time is simultaneous" and, "The only reason for time is so that everything doesn't happen at once," will become perceptible truth, not just the ranting of the genius, Albert Einstein.

Perhaps it is not ancient aliens who helped build ancient civilizations, but it is instead, "ancient" human time travelers from the future?

Did the early humans trudge and stumble forward over eons of time, and finally make it to the advanced science/technology level? Then, with the ability of spacetime travel, do these descendants of the first humans, travel back in time to the beginning?

Have we seeded ourselves, perhaps endlessly, throughout time?

Consider: Future Humans with the secret of time travel, can travel to any Moment they wish.

Why assume it was extraterrestrials who arrived as "sky people?" The cave dwellers were human or hominin. They weren't reptile or octopus-like; no, this is the beginning of the human race.

Ignoring hundreds of millions of years of natural evolution, it is said that the extraterrestrials must be human-like because they created us. Or alternatively, that

that ETs created hybrids of themselves and apes, who became what we know as human, through some amazing hocus pocus genetic engineering.

However, the least complicated explanation: The advanced beings who came back to begin the path of Homo sapiens, were advanced humans from Earth. Occam's razor strikes again, offering the answer with the least assumptions to be made.

Image from **2001: A Space Odyssey**

"Ouroboros" is an ancient mystical symbol; why does it possess such an important and profound role in human mythology? Ouroboros is "the snake eating its tail" as a symbol of infinity, wholeness, and of life and death.

Where did this symbol originate and what legend, myth, or historical truth was being remembered by embracing it?

Ouroboros was used as an ancient Egyptian motif in Tutankhamun's tomb and elsewhere in ancient Egyptian art. Egyptologists write that it symbolizes Osiris being born again as Ra. Possibly this connects to the reaching back of Future Humans to seed the beginning of humankind. It is only one possibility, but we have never considered Ouroboros in this light. And, this is just the beginning for the sacred symbol of Ouroboros in subsequent mystical and philosophical traditions.

Ouroboros entered the Greek tradition of alchemy and magic. The enlightened Gnostics and Hermetic religious, philosophical, and esoteric traditions both paid homage to the meaning of Ouroboros. An early alchemy text in the 10th century declared "all is one" as the mystical message of Ouroboros. There are possible connections to the Yin/Yang symbol and to the legend of the Philosopher's Stone. Ouroboros is arguably humankind's most identifying symbol.

Alchemist and physician Sir Thomas Browne, in his medical treatise full of case histories and witty speculations upon the human condition, wrote, *"...that the first day should make the last, that the Tail of the Snake should return to its Mouth precisely at that time, and they should wind up upon the day of their Nativity, is indeed a remarkable Coincidence..."*

Footnote 77: wikipedia.org, "Ouroboros"

This can relate to the concept of the individual dying and going to new life, whether through reincarnation, rebirth, or as a newly released quantum particle heading back into the universe, but it also can apply to the entire human race being seeded anew, by its children's children (human travelers back in time).

Ouroboros is then a perception of reincarnation not only for an individual, but for a sentient species. This entire scenario may be a part of the universal evolution of any sentient species. Once an advancing species can travel back in its own timeline, the sky is the limit; the number of possibilities is infinite. Suddenly that species perceives its own history differently and "must" travel back, to begin anew.

The same as the individual's consciousness (or soul) may have a long journey of reincarnation, renewal, transformation, or even ascension, so it may be with an entire species. This is usually perceived in a spiritual light, but spirit and science are two sides of the "coin of consciousness," so the process applies scientifically as well.

Of course, there are physics loops and paradoxes to ponder, but it might be "the way of the universe, a trick," as Jack Sarfatti says, not of physics this time, but of evolution. Evolution is a powerful force.

Perhaps this process is not a loop but a spiral, rising steadily upward upon completion of each loop. Perhaps most advanced races across the universe, once they find the key to time travel, enter into this cycle

Space Gods, Civilizations, and Monoliths: Whether a person believes there was no outside influence in humankind's development, or she believes ancient extraterrestrials seeded human civilization, or she feels that Future Humans, in their zero gravity bubble, traveled back in time, it is hard to find evidence for the preferred theory. It was long ago and the mythology of ancient civilizations, from Sumerian to pre-Mayan to Egyptian to pre-Celt, was sensationalized by oral storytellers and scribes who liked to tell and write, melodrama.

Many of us were at first impressed with the idea that ancient astronauts ("sky people") arrived on Earth and therefore, Ezekiel's wheel was really a UFO. Upon reflection, we realized this concept robs good old human beings of credit for building great civilizations and it is perhaps too literal an answer.

We do agree that ancient stone structures across the planet have similarity in the way they were astonishingly built with giant monoliths weighing many tons being elevated high and fit into place. There must have been a group of people or beings who traveled across the planet to at least influence the engineering of these structures.

One possibility: A group of humans managed to travel across the vast oceans thousands of years B.C., made friends with the natives, and then suggested what to build and how to build it, bringing their very advanced stone cutting machines (or near-magic technique) with them.

Structures in Peru, Egypt, Turkey, and other ancient sites across the planet, are almost identical in their seamless engineering of huge blocks of stone. The huge blocks in these structures must have been cut by advanced stone-cutting machines we don't have today; they fit together tightly and perfectly. They used no mortar.

Outside Cusco, Peru, lies the walled complex of Saksaywaman

There does seem to have been a race of very advanced humans until about the Year 12,000 B.C., who then, it is said, were wiped out. Their advanced stone cutting tools were somehow left behind as well as other aspects of civilization such as relics and even customs.

Theories go that an asteroid, tsunami, or nuclear war wiped out these advanced people; this might have included the legendary Atlantis.

How did this mysterious advanced race of humans in 12,000 B.C. become so advanced that even today, we have not invented their stone cutting machines? Perhaps Future Humans were involved. Instead of getting wiped out or going into hiding in a different dimension somewhere, they simply left for while via their low power warp drive bubble, returning to the "home point" in the future.

Perhaps they returned in time to help the Sumerians, Greeks, Egyptians, Mayans, and others, in the 2,000 to 5,000 B.C. era.

It has been assumed the "sky people" came from "somewhere else." Instead, what if they came from "some-when else? Again, we are confronted with the fact that the gods depicted in almost all ancient cultures, are human-like.

Picture: From Mayan culture, an astronaut or burial sarcophagus?

Taking credit away from the native human beings of the time for the actual building of civilization and its structures, is wrong. Probably neither Future Humans nor ETs levitated the pyramids into place and created other monuments and civilizations of their time. That was up to The People. I am suggesting that perhaps teams of Future Humans simply appeared at times to ignite the spark of civilization within their own species. They were "community organizers."

The time travelers may have been mistaken for space gods or more likely, they intentionally gave that impression, because there are indeed multiple "space god" and "sky people" legends throughout human history.

How can the time travelers break their Non-Interference Directive? I believe that the non-interference policy is a complicated one with many caveats and loopholes. I'm not saying this is a good thing, the rules simply may have a familiar degree of complexity which humans always create when we create doctrine and law (just look at the U.S. income tax code)! Then add the contradictions and convolutions of time travel to it, and the "Non-Interference Directive" must be a formidable document!

The rules and regulations of non-interference may change depending on the time period of human history. There is a policy of increased interference in the earlier years of our species, I believe, including the years when the ancient civilizations blossomed. There is still qualified interference in modern times, as with abductions.

Traveling back to the early human days may be a special branch of service, a time when there was more overt contact, more overt manipulation, by time travelers. It had to be done, because it had always been done.

I am not suggesting Future Humans were omniscient and wonderful gods. They may often have been wrong, lacking empathy for individuals, and ambivalent as to what was right in the first place. Of course, similar criticism can probably be offered regarding extraterrestrials.

Chicken and Egg Speculation: "Future Humans travel back to ancient times" is, of course, a chicken and egg scenario but so is the Big Bang. What was there that caused the Big Bang? In religions, we ask, "Who created God?"

What doesn't make as much sense, is that another chicken from a far distant planet, traveled to Earth to assist an egg which was not hers. The assumption that ancient astronauts were extraterrestrial, once again is not the least complicated answer. It is also not very logical.

Or, maybe this reaching back to ancient times by Future Humans happened only once; in that case, this *is* the Human Timeline, no second tries.

1947-2020 is a dark moment in human history, and so human time travelers focus on this moment as well as the ancient past, to observe and covertly nudge us forward or at least to try to protect their planet. They cannot change the future, but they must be here – trying – in order to keep a new dark alternate timeline from stabilizing in reality. This is, of course, speculation.

I believe there is evidence to indicate extraterrestrials were not the "ancient astronauts," but rather, it was us. It is us. It will be us.

These statues are renovated artwork originally from about 450 B.C., done while the Greek gods still flourished.

The Greek Gods: We are taught that the gods of ancient Greece were fictional. The strange thing is, in the art from ancient Greece, the gods are brilliantly lifelike in great detail; it would seem the common people actually saw or encountered the gods upon occasion. Some artwork of Jesus, for instance, is also very life-like, but he was probably a real man too. There is realism somehow permeating the ancient Greek artwork.

As well, the Greek gods had "real lives" about which the common people seemed to know details. All sorts of drama happened. The gods and goddesses had love affairs, cheated on their mates and sometimes, they cheated with common humans. Babies were begotten. The gods had feuds with each other. They were the entitled celebrities of the day who entertained the common working man and woman with their antics.

Were the gods only myths? No doubt stories developed around them as time went on which were gossip or exaggerated. But there seems to be at least equal evidence that the gods were, at one point, a band of twelve humans (there were twelve primary gods), with advanced technology, living a cloistered life on (or inside) Mount Olympus, but mingling with the Greek people too. This was probably to ignite the spark of civilization, culture and organization honed out of chaos. In

Greece's case, that spark included democracy in government, of, by, and for The People.

In general, the gods of many ancient civilizations were the force which bound a region of formerly chaotic, primitive humans into a cohesive tribe who worked together for specific goals of a society and government or higher power. With organizing efforts, the people had infrastructure, military protection and learned to be willing to pay taxes to the government. It is reasonable that Future Humans would work toward this kind of "coming together," to pave the way for the advanced world from which they came.

The Greek gods might have been real entities, community organizers of sorts, who announced they were gods and backed it up with advanced technology like "lightning" bolts of energy. It sounds like some clever Future Humans to me.

Reasons to Consider "Ancient Astronauts" to be Time Travelers

The Greek gods as opposed to other ancient gods, will be our examples here, but most of these reasons also apply to gods of most ancient cultures.

Reason One: Greek gods, were said to throw lightning bolts when angry. Might "lightning bolts" have been laser or even scalar technology?

If so, the gods can thank **James Clerk Maxwell,** a mathematical genius whose work led to the development of quantum physics. Maxwell is also famous for offering the concept of an imaginary creature opening a tiny door to the right or to the left, to contradict the second law of thermodynamics. This tiny imaginary creature became known as "Maxwell's demon." Maxwell explained "the demon haunted world" characterized sound, scientific thinking, but in the mid-1800s, the Church fathers exorcized him anyway. James Clerk Maxwell is a fascinating figure, far ahead of his time.

Maxwell was brilliant in his work with electromagnetism; his electromagnetic spectrum went higher than our 3D physical reality and traveled into hyperspace where the fine indiscernible scalar waves exist. Maxwell said they flowed in the ether (or hyperspace). Scalar waves are so fine that they are only one-hundred-millionth of a square centimeter in width, hence finer than X-rays and gamma rays. They can also be manipulated into various types of modes and frequencies.

When Maxwell died, his work was interpreted by **Nikola Tesla**, among others. Of course, Tesla has been the subject of much interest in the UFO and futuristic fields. Tesla's "free energy" would allow people to tap into the vacuum of pure energy (hyperspace) to get their own "free-energy" at no cost. Thomas Edison, who was Tesla's adversary, needed a plant ten stories high, taking up an entire city block to supply electricity to one square mile of customers.

Tesla experimented with violently erupting, direct current electrical discharges and discovered scalar energy, a new force, in the process. In 1904 Tesla announced he had completed his work using scalar waves to transmit energy without wires. Tesla claimed his "Death Rays"' had a range of hundreds of miles, which were useful against aircraft. He stated that entire cities could be devastated by explosive EM transmissions across intercontinental distances to anywhere on the planet. Today, this is one of many threats we face.

Footnote 78: bibliotecapleyades.net, "Scalar Weapons," by Christi Verismo

Most Greeks probably knew better than to believe a god was causing actual lightning, but they were unfamiliar with laser or scalar technology, so "lightning bolts" would be a convenient descriptive term. Granted, extraterrestrials probably know about laser and scalar technology, but "lightning bolts" might have been a way to keep the common people in line, whether by ETs or FTs.

We do know for certain that Future Humans have laser and scalar technologies, because, due to Maxwell and Tesla's work, we have these technologies already. In another 100 years, it boggles the mind to guess what advancements there will be. A time traveling "god" might well have a hand-held scalar weapon.

Reason Two: The Greek gods kept themselves separate from common people. They resided on or in Mount Olympus, a perfect base of operations.

Having a "verboten" and secretive headquarters adds to the mystique of divinity and power. If the Greek gods were only myth, the storytellers might give them such a home; but, just as likely, would be the practical necessity that real beings would need a reclusive home and headquarters away from the common people. Not interacting with the people unless by careful design, means less chance of making mistakes. We know that UFOs slip into mountains and oceans.

Again, we realize that epic wars and other grand tales emerged in Greek mythology which could not have happened, at least not as related. However, the twelve strangers said to be gods, may have inspired fanciful odysseys, but could have themselves been actual humans, with advanced technology to back up their pretense of godhood.

Few archeologists have ventured to excavate the higher reaches of Mount Olympus due to difficult terrain. It rises straight up from the Aegean Sea, 2,917 meters high (9,573 ft). On its lower slopes are dense, forested gorges with dramatic waterfalls and many caves. The lesser gods were said to live at this elevation. In fact, security and others involved in this ruse, would guard the main "community organizers" (gods) from an encampment on this "first level" of the mountain.

Mount Olympus has 52 separate peaks which are snow-capped eight months of the year and covered in clouds the rest of the time.

The mythology says that the gods looked down upon Earth every day to decide the fate of humanity. This "attitude," gives credence to the idea that the Future Humans established a position of power so that they could, perhaps, lead the common people and be able to change their ways.

The following description is interesting in light of "the gods" returning perhaps to a larger spacecraft, or returning to their own future time, on some occasions: *"The sacred mount was believed to have a temperate climate all year round, and mountain gorges lush with forests. The gods did not always reside in their paradise, however, and would depart or return from there via a gate of clouds guarded by the* Horae, *the goddesses of the seasons."*

And this: *"Authors claim the tables in Zeus' palace on Olympus were made of gold and were actually automatons, created by Hephaestus. They moved in and out of the rooms as required by the gods."*

Did the gods have automatrons? Robots? Androids? Artificial intelligence?

All twelve gods seemed to stick together: *"All 12 Olympian gods resided at Mount Olympus: Zeus and his wife Hera, Athena, Poseidon, Artemis, Apollo, Demeter, Hester, Aphrodite, Hermes, Hephaestus and Ares. Since Hades resided in the underworld, he was not considered an Olympian god and did not visit the great mount often."*

Footnote 79: mythology.net/"Mount Olympus"

How to explain Hades? I do not know. His name means "unseen one." Perhaps he maintained the underwater submerged craft in the Aegean Sea. We can guess at specifics and be wrong, but the possibility remains that possibly 12 (or 13) Future Humans helped civilization and even democracy become established in Greece. Then, the ancient Greeks gave this aspiration, this step forward, to the rest of us. I am sure there were many mistakes made also, because they were human.

Daedalyys is said to be the inventor in Greek mythology who, through his inventions, strived to bring humans to the level of the gods. Maybe Daedalyys' spirit of discovery is an example of the inspiration the gods hoped also to give.

Reason Three: The Greek gods abducted common people. If we take the abduction accounts in Greek mythology and other ancient mythologies seriously, they are horrific whether ETs or Future Humans, were responsible. However, most of them are impossible tales. For instance, Europa was the beautiful daughter of King Agenor, king of Phoenicia; they were humans of that time. She was abducted by Zeus when he approached her in the form of a white bull. He then regained his form as Zeus and mated with her under an evergreen tree.

Either Zeus was a shapeshifter, if those exist, or the tale is not true and this account got highly exaggerated as it was passed along orally by storytellers and written by scribes. I suspect it was highly exaggerated.

This brings us to today's conspiracy theories. The ancient Greek people did not have the Internet or television, but humankind always loves gossip. We create tales, we pass them along by word of mouth to everyone we can. And the tale changes and grows each time it is passed along. As well, Homer, Hesiod, Sophocles, and Euripedes among others, wrote down dramatic and melodramatic tales based on oral storytellers' accounts.

Here is an example of humankind's storytelling ability in the current day, augmented by the media and malicious foreign intervention: A well-known professional woman ran for president of the United States. She is like the rest of us, part good, part bad, and mostly in between. She has deserved to be criticized over the years, but she has also done good for the country. However, rumors popped up that she was running a child pornography ring out of a suburban pizza parlor. A man went there with a gun but was fortunately stopped before he shot up the pizza parlor. There was no child pornography ring.

We also gossiped about her failing health as that disinformation ("gossip") was spread around our communities, when in fact her health was fine for her age. Give this tall tale 2000 years and see where it goes! Therefore, Zeus might not have shown up to abduct Europa as a white bull!

The sad truth, Greek mythology is full of accounts of brutality toward women in particular, including many violent rapes. I have included the topic of abductions by those who said they were Greek gods, only because of the connection to abductions by UFO occupants. The truth about abductions by "the gods," is lost in the mists of time, but such tales are in Greek mythology. I can only say, bad behavior by a male dominated society as well as the power of gossip, is very human.

Reason Four: The Greek gods rode chariots across the sky. The Greek people must have witnessed these zero-gravity craft and explained them through their own cultural context. Of course, the "ancient astronaut" theory has always pointed this out, but not in the context of the Greek gods as being Future Humans.

Reason Five: Reports of gods mingling with humans run throughout Greek mythology; hybrid children were said to have resulted many times through these couplings.

Hybrid Herakles: Consider Herakles, whose father was the god Zeus and mother was the mortal, Alcmene. Many sculptures were created of Herakles at the time of the Greek gods and placed in or on amazing structures such as the Parthenon. These statues depict a physical human who looks like the same man in every sculpture available.

Herakles' conception may have happened because a (future) human father and (ancient Greek) human mother, conceived and gave birth to a living child. There is an entire echelon of Greek heroes who are "hybrids."

However, I believe Herakles and others were not extraterrestrial hybrids. Simply, it would never work; two very different species cannot mate.

Occasionally a god is shown with horns or some small detail which is not human but he or she still looks like a specimen of humanity. It is easy to put on a set of horns to impress the common people and keep the god mystique. The gods of Olympus could relate tales of their magnificent battles, all in keeping with the level of the people. Would advanced humans do this to ancient humans? Of course, we would. If we "should," is another thing.

"Hercules," sculpted by ancient Greeks looks 100% human

Reason Six: The Greek gods seemed to have advanced medicine for themselves and also, did not seem to age like common humans; they might have been immortal or close to it.

The gods were said to have "ichor" instead of blood. There is a myth about the goddess Aphrodite who was wounded on the wrist in battle causing the ichor to flow.

Aphrodite is said to have then borrowed the chariot of her brother Ares, the god of war, so she could hurry back to Olympus for medical treatment. There, her mother Dione ran something over her wrist and it soothed and cured the wound.

Sometimes it really sounds like the storytellers were basing their tales on something that really happened. If there is any truth in the reality of the Greek gods, they seemed to be thoroughly human, not from a far-distant planet.

Footnote 80: UFO Casebook, "Reasons the Greek Gods Were Possibly UFO Occupants," by Diane Tessman July 2014

UFOs Throughout Human History, Always Here

It seems that if the occupants in UFOs are from Earth, just as we are, but come from the future when the key to traveling back in time has been found, we would see UFO reports throughout human history. After all, the Future Humans are right here on top of us, on the same spot in space. Only "the moment" is different.

On the other hand, it is difficult to imagine extraterrestrials just hanging around Earth, a small rocky planet in the boondocks of the Milky Way, for millennia. Even if ETs were tampering with human progress for better or worse (as admittedly Future Humans might do as well), why become such a constant? If ETs had then invaded Earth, or otherwise taken it over, their presence would make sense

In fact, UFOs have appeared at every stage of humankind's development. Once again, it makes more sense if UFO occupants are humans who are right here to begin with, from a different moment of time.

The description of unidentified flying objects (UFOs) has remained constant throughout history, stretching back into antiquity. While many could be attributed to natural phenomena, an in-depth study by NASA's Richard Stothers says, "There nonetheless remains a small residue of puzzling accounts, and regardless of what interpretation one places on them, these constitute a phenomenon that spans centuries of time and widely different cultures."

UFO sightings in B.C. and early A.D.:

#1: Sightings During the Second Punic War in Rome:

Many sightings were recorded during and following the Second Punic War (218–201 B.C.). The lists were derived from the Annales Maximi, published by the Pontifex Maximus of Rome. This source is considered trustworthy and accurate because of the time-consuming and thorough procedure required by Roman authorities to investigate claims before they would be recorded.

In Rome, in the winter of 218 B.C., "A spectacle of ships gleamed in the sky."

In 217 B.C., "at Arpi, round shields were seen in the sky."

In 173 B.C., "at Lanuvium, a spectacle of a great fleet was said to have been seen in the sky."

It is not likely that suggestive cloud formations would have been mistaken for UFOs, Stothers says, since these formations had long been understood and were familiar features. These sightings are also not likely a mock sun, because mock suns are routinely described as "double suns" or "triple suns."

Account 2: Thousands of Roman Soldiers Witness UFO?

Plutarch wrote of a sighting witnessed by thousands. In 74 B.C., the Roman army was moving to engage the forces of King Mithridates VI in the area of modern-day Turkey.

"With no apparent change of weather, but all on a sudden, the sky burst asunder, and a huge, flame-like body was seen to fall between the two armies," he wrote. "In shape, it was most like a wine-jar (pithoi), and in color, like molten silver. Both sides were astonished at the sight, and separated. This marvel, as they say, occurred in Phrygia, at a place called Otryae."

Stothers points out that freshly fallen meteorites are black, not "molten silver" color, which suggests it was not a meteorite. Plutarch also made no mention of the impact.

Stothers writes: "The object must have measured much more than a meter across, since it was easily resolved at a distance greater than half the range of a bowshot. If it had remained on the ground, a meteorite of such size would doubtless have become a cult object in Phrygia, with its long tradition of meteorite worship, yet later historical records referring to Phrygian meteorites are silent about it."

Nonetheless, there is a chance the UFO was a bolide, a bright meteor that often explodes.

Account 3: Chariots in the Sky Witnessed by Many

Historian Josephus wrote around 65 A.D. about a fantastical sighting over Judea: "On the 21st of the month Artemisium, there appeared a miraculous phenomenon, passing belief. Indeed, what I am about to relate would, I imagine, have been deemed a fable, were it not for the narratives of eyewitnesses and the subsequent calamities which deserved to be so signalized. For, before sunset throughout all parts of the country, chariots were seen in the air. They came hurtling through the clouds over the cities."

Account 4: "Angel Hair" Glassy Fibers

Think of a cobweb: Its fibers are perhaps similar to the gossamer substance said to be left in the wake of a few UFOs.

In modern UFO reports, there are accounts of either glassy fibers or a chalky substance left behind by the UFO, known as angel hair. Ancient reports also include angel hair.

In 196 A.D., the historian Cassius Dio wrote: "A fine rain resembling silver descended from a clear sky upon the Forum of Augustus. I did not, it is true, see it as it was falling, but noticed it after it had fallen, and by means of it I plated some bronze coins with silver; they retained the same appearance for three days, but by the fourth day all the substance rubbed on them had disappeared."

Two other "rains of chalk" were reported in Cales 214 B.C. and in Rome 98 B.C.

Illustration of angel hair based on in Florence, Italy, 1954 accounts of angel hair covering a large area due to overhead UFOs

Account 5: UFO Inhabited: The brother of Pope Pius I was probably the only witness of this UFO sighting near Via Campana, Italy, around 150 A.D.: "On a sunny day, a 'beast' like a piece of pottery about 100 feet in size, multicolored on top and shooting out fiery rays, landed in a dust cloud accompanied by a 'maiden' clad in white.

Stothers concludes, "This collection of what might be termed ancient UFO reports has been culled from a much larger number of reports of aerial objects, most of whose identifications with known phenomena are either certain or at least probable. Embedded in the mass of relatively explicable ancient reports, however, is a small set of unexplained (or at least not wholly explained) reports from presumably credible witnesses."

"Any viable theory must reckon with the extraordinary persistence and consistency of the phenomena discussed here over many centuries."

Footnote 81: The Epoch Times, "NASA reports on Credible UFO Sightings in Ancient Times, by Tara Macisaac, May, 2014

Two Cases from the Middle Ages

The Middle Ages: In 1211, A.D., Gervase of Tilbury, an English chronicler of historical events, recorded this bizarre story:

"There happened in the borough of Cloera, one Sunday, while the people were at Mass, a marvel. In this town is a church dedicated to St. Kinarus. It befell that an anchor was dropped from the sky, with a rope attached to it, and one of the flukes caught in the arch above the church door. The people rushed out of the church and saw in the sky a ship with men on board, floating before the anchor cable, and they saw a man leap overboard and jump down to the anchor, as if to release it. He looked as if he were swimming in water. The folk rushed up and tried to seize him; but the Bishop forbade the people to hold the man, for it might kill him, he said. The man was freed, and hurried up to the ship, where the crew cut the rope and the ship sailed out of sight. But the anchor is in the church, and has been there ever since, as a testimony."

Note: The occupants of the ship are called "men." Possibly this account includes the concept of a rope and anchor because the 13th Century people could not fathom a craft hovering overhead with no anchor. The account is told in the perception of that moment in time.

It is also possible that a "landing party" of time travelers would have conspicuous "items of the time being visited" such as a rope and anchor in the report below; also, being dressed to match the time being visited, is an obvious precaution.

On my second encounter, the being I met on a UFO in my first encounter, came in the door of the Eagle Lake cabin, with jeans and a red checkered shirt. Several other people who have had encounters, have also seen entities in "street clothes." Jeans and a "working class shirt," seem to be a wise choice, perhaps made by the computer aboard the starship which dresses time travelers appropriately to the time being visited.

Account #2, Middle Ages: *In a 9th-century Latin manuscript, Liber contra insulam vulgi opinionem, the Archbishop of Lyons complained about the French peasantry's insistent belief in a 'certain region called Magonia from whence come ships in the clouds.' The occupants of these vessels "carry back to Magonia, those fruits of the Earth which are destroyed by hail and tempests; the sailors paying rewards to the storm wizards and themselves receiving corn and other produce." The archbishop said he had even witnessed the stoning to death of "three men and a woman who said they had fallen from these same ships."*

Jakob Grimm, a 19th-century folklorist, speculated, "'Magonia' takes us to some region where Latin was spoken, if we may rely on it referring to Magus, i.e., a magic land."

Footnote 82: Howstuffworks.com, "UFO History: Ancient and Medieval UFOs"

Jacques Vallee wrote **Passport to Magonia** in 1969, utilizing a concept similar to the "land of Oz" as the possible origin of UFOs and their occupants. In other words, he did not accept the common "Extraterrestrial Hypothesis" (ETH) and explained why. He still does not accept ETH and has qualified the possible source as "dimensional;" of course "time" is the 4th dimension.

Vallee's' "Why it is Not Extraterrestrials:"

1. Unexplained close encounters are far more numerous than required for any physical survey of Earth.

2. The humanoid body structure of the alleged "aliens" is not likely to have originated on another planet and is not biologically adapted to space travel.

3. The reported behavior in thousands of abduction reports contradicts the hypothesis of genetic or scientific experimentation on humans by an ET race.

4. The extension of the phenomenon throughout recorded human history, demonstrates that UFOs are not a contemporary phenomenon

5. The apparent ability of UFOs to manipulate time and space suggests radically different and richer alternatives.

The Renaissance and Onward, Nuremberg Uproar: A broadsheet (newspaper), written in German, describes a shocking event over Nuremberg, Germany on the morning of April 14, 1561:

"At daybreak, between 4 and 5 a.m., a dreadful apparition occurred on the sun, and then this was seen in Nuremberg in the city, before the gates and in the country – by many men and women. At first there appeared in the middle of the sun two blood-red semi-circular arcs, just like the moon in its last quarter. And in the sun, above and below and on both sides, the color was blood, there stood around ball of partly dull, partly black ferrous color. Likewise there stood on both sides and as a torus about the sun such blood-red ones and other balls in large number, about three in a line and four in a square, also some alone. In between these globes there were visible a few blood-red crosses, between which there were blood-red strips, becoming thicker to the rear and in the front malleable like the rods of reed-grass, which were intermingled, among them two big rods, one on the right, the other to the left, and within the small and big rods there were three, also four and more globes. These all started to fight among themselves, so that the globes, which were first in the sun, flew out to the ones standing on both sides, thereafter, the globes standing outside the sun, in the small and large rods, flew into the sun. Besides the globes flew back and forth among themselves and fought vehemently with each other for over an hour. And when the conflict in and again out of the sun was most intense, they became fatigued to such an extent that they all, as said above, fell from the sun down upon the earth 'as if they all burned' and they then wasted away on the earth with immense smoke. After all this there was *something like a black spear, very long and thick, sighted; the shaft pointed to the east, the point pointed west. Whatever such signs mean, God alone knows..."*

Debunking efforts have been made on this one and no one is sure what it was. The main debunking explanation centers around a sundog which is the sun shining on ice crystals in very cold climates. As the inhabitant of a very cold climate, I know it would be difficult to mistake a sundog for a UFO battle. I give the people credit for more intelligence than that.

Footnote 83: Astonishing Legends.com, Nuremberg, 1561, February 2019

Puritan Abduction? John Winthrop was a Puritan who in 1639, wrote of the many hardships of his fellow English Puritans in America. He was governor of the Massachusetts Bay Colony; he recounted an unusual event which was well known by the Puritan community.

He wrote that James Everell, "a sober, discreet man," and two others had been rowing a boat in the Muddy River, which flowed through swampland and emptied into a tidal basin in the Charles River, when they saw a great light in the night sky. "When it stood still, it flamed up, and was about three yards square," the governor reported, "when it ran, it was contracted into the figure of a swine."

Over the course of two to three hours, the men said that the mysterious light "ran as swift as an arrow" darting back and forth between them and the village of

Charlestown, two miles away. "Diverse other credible persons saw the same light, after, about the same place," Winthrop reported.

The governor wrote that when the strange apparition finally faded away, the three men in the boat were stunned to find themselves one mile upstream, "as if the light had transported them there." They had no memory of their rowing against the tide, although it's possible they could have been carried by the wind or a reverse tidal flow.

"The mysterious repositioning of the boat could suggest that they were unaware of part of their experience. Some researchers would interpret this as a possible alien abduction if it happened today," write Jacques Vallee and Chris Aubeck in **Wonders in the Sky: Unexplained Aerial Objects from Antiquity to Modern Times.**

Footnote 84: New England Today Living.com by Christopher Kleins, May 2019

Utsuro-Bune, Japanese Encounter:

There is an intriguing new book from **Flying Disk Press** by author Scoichi Kamon, which explores the Japanese legend of Utsuro-Bune. A round, hollow, boat washed up on the shore of eastern Japan in 1803 with a strange passenger. This strange event is documented in three Japanese texts.

A beautiful woman of unknown origin was aboard the boat;" she was not quite 5 feet tall, had long red hair and very pale skin. Her clothes were smooth and long, and she always kept close to her, a small quadratic box made of unknown material. She did not allow anyone to touch the box.

She began speaking but no one knew her language and although she was friendly, they felt her mysterious and "odd."

Inside the boat, the walls were covered with writing which no one could identify and have not identified to this day. The shape of the boat was described as an "incense burner" which is very similar in shape to a flying saucer

One of the possibilities which might explain Utsuro-Bune: She was a Future Human emerging from Future Human headquarters under the ocean, whose small craft, which was shaped like a flying saucer, malfunctioned.

The "perfect attractiveness" of the woman reminds me of the female humans Travis Walton saw onboard the UFO.

Footnote 85: Flying Disk Press, "The Mystery of Utsuro-Bune, Ancient UFO Encounter in Japan?" by Scoichi Kamon, September 2019

Account 3: The Airship Wave of 1886-1897: In 1886-1897, human occupants of phantom "airships" were viewed by observers on the ground in Northern California, Oregon, Washington, and British Columbia. Occasionally these human occupants landed their "airship" and seen up close, still appeared to be human although they had "unusual behavior, manners, and clothing." One crew claimed they were from Mars.

The airships began moving eastward across the United States in ships which were bigger, faster, and more robust than anything then produced. They seemed to fly enormous distances in relatively short amounts of time. The unidentified craft sometimes flashed red, green and white.

As the wave progressed, there were a few daytime sightings but most sightings were at night. The daytime sightings featured "cigar-shaped" and "sausage-shaped" craft, similar to a dirigible.

These airships were purported to be flown by alien visitors, enemy spies, or eccentric inventors. In fact, Thomas Edison had to issue a public statement denying responsibility.

Footnote 86: Wikipedia.org, "Mystery Airships 1886-1897"

An account from Aurora, Texas, April 1897, in the **Dallas Morning News** reported that an airship had smashed into a windmill, later determined to be a sump pump -- belonging to Judge Proctor, then crashed. The occupant was dead and mangled, but the story reported that presumed pilot was clearly "not an inhabitant of this world." Strange "hieroglyphic" figures were seen on the wreckage, which resembled a mixture of aluminum and silver, "It must have weighed several tons.""

(In the 20th Century, unusual metallic material recovered from the presumed UFO crash site was shown to contain a percentage of aluminum and iron, mixed together).

The story ended by noting that the pilot was given a "Christian burial" in the town cemetery. In 1973, MUFON investigators discovered the alleged stone marker used in this burial. Their metal detectors indicated a quantity of foreign material might remain buried there. However, they were not permitted to exhume, and when they returned several years later, the headstone -- and whatever metallic material had lay beneath it -- was gone.

Footnote 87: Crystalinks.com, "Mystery Airships"

The pilot of the airship which crashed hitting a sump pump, was said to be "not of this world," but it also says he or she was "mangled," and with excitement at fever pitch, it is hard to tell if the citizens of Aurora described the body accurately.

There is something strange about the entire airship phenomenon – slightly different than most UFO flaps which always have a strangeness factor. In the 1890s, automobiles were poised to change city streets forever. Ferdinand von Zeppelin was earning patents on his "rigid airship," and the Wright Brothers and others were racing to build a functional fixed-wing airplane, culminating in the Wright Brothers iconic powered, controlled flight of 1903.

Futuristic flying machines and "The Future" itself, were entering into the collective human consciousness. Things were changing drastically, never to be the same again. Then, only about five years ahead of the coming revolutionary developments, these airship UFOs showed up and made themselves known across the United States and the world.

One final account from the early 1900s:

August, 1914, Lake Ontario, Georgia Bay, Canada: "Here are the answers of Mr. Kiehl of Georgia Bay, about the small men he witnessed, 'They appeared to be four feet tall or under, were dressed in tight fitting suits which revealed their human form, and which appeared iridescent, for they were green or purpose as they moved about in the late afternoon sun. Each of the men wore a box-shaped or square yellow headpiece.' "

I cannot find a source for this report, it accompanied a sketch of a UFO occupant, obviously from a later date. I include it because it is somehow clear and seemingly honest.

Today, a leap is made in computer technology and before you know it, your computer from 2019 is way out of date, still in 2019, and an antique by 2020. Even going to war is on a speeded-up schedule; we as a species can annihilate most higher life on the planet in perhaps 30 minutes, whereas men used to march to war, taking weeks to arrive across the ocean and reach the place where the enemy was to be confronted.

Maybe the Future Humans have different criteria for different eras of past time. It is often said that we are an adolescent species, our brains not fully developed, we are headstrong, self-centered, and emotional. Maybe back in the 1200's when the UFO occupants were said to have a rope and anchor with them, the occupants thought of people of that time as toddlers. But today, we can't afford to be toddlers and in fact, we have grown to the more dangerous stages of adolescence. The Future Humans know their own evolutionary development and so show up accordingly.

This is pure speculation. We have looked at the evidence, we have profiled the UFO occupants from many angles, and it seems likely that time travelers are the visitors in our (and their) skies, at least to a large degree. Perhaps they (we) warp to far distant planets too or perhaps they (we) don't, for some reason.

As I said when I began, perhaps extraterrestrials visit also, but the staying power of the phenomenon, over millennia, is part of the evidence that in the future, we have indeed discovered and developed the ability to travel back in time. All beings with human DNA are in the same spot in the universe: Earth.

Time is simultaneous; The Eternal Now has many faces.

***

Chapter Twelve: That's Just Us

Think for yourself and let others enjoy the privilege of doing so too. – Voltaire

This will be the briefest of my chapters. Before the final chapter of this book, I have a few words from my soul.

Many people know me for my spiritual writing. If you are one of these, I hope you do not think I have gone all "nuts and bolts," indicating there is nothing and no one else, in the universe but "nuts and bolts" Future Humans.

It seems to me, there has always been a fundamental, unanswered contradiction among all of us who are fascinated by UFOs and their occupants. Do we think it is a nuts and bolts phenomenon or do we think it is, above all, spiritual contact?

There are sub-divisions in our choices; for the nuts and bolts folk, do ETs seem non-threatening and we'd like to meet them or (the negative choice), are they planning to invade or do something dire with our DNA?

For the spiritual folk, are they wonderful transcended masters or are they demonic?

The nuts and bolts folk usually have no time for the subjective spiritual fool and the spiritual folk feel that nuts and bolts stuffed heads ignore the heart of the matter.

I have, from the beginning, seen both sides. I'm not tooting my horn because I have plenty of failings, but on this topic, it is simply how I am. I am ambidextrous, maybe that has something to do with it – brain wiring? And, I am sure there are many others who feel as I do.

After 38 years of spiritual writing, and 40 years of objective UFO research and investigations (looking at life from both sides), I needed to write this book and it had to be on the objective end of the continuum with some subjectivism included.

Why did I need to write this book? It is because I perceive a gaping hole in the objective view that "of course" UFO occupants are extraterrestrials. Back in the late 1970s, I wrote on the same premise in the MUFON Journal. This is nothing new, it began with me when I was 4 years old. "We are from your future," said he who abducted me.

I didn't take his word for it. I have researched and researched until I am now 72 years old. It is a fascinating objective/subjective lifelong endeavor and quest. I feel no contradiction between the two approaches.

I also think there is a gaping hole in the subjective view of spiritual folk.

The subjective spiritual hole: The nature of our species is ignored by the spiritual folk. Evolution is ignored.

Can humankind leap from being an adolescent species into a sparkling cosmic cloud of highly advanced spiritual particles? Can and should humankind sit at the feet of ascended masters and be told what we are "lacking"?

We are lacking nothing. But we are hare-brained adolescents who keep crashing the car. Can we climb out of the wreckage and advance millions or billions of years in one electrifying moment of consciousness, to become wise beings who have developed over billions of years?

Yes, we are changing. These times are so insane that there may well be a huge point (or moment) of change in our consciousness. The Renaissance popped up after a time of darkness and so did the 1960s, that brief Age of Aquarius.

However, we have very far to go; those two times of great change were only a drop in the bucket. And of course, we insist on going two steps forward and one step backwards, that's just us.

The objective hole: The nuts and bolts people ignore the nature of our species. They ignore evolution.

Wait, both objective and subjective groups have the same problem?

In focusing on extraterrestrial fly-overs of nuclear sites, harassment of our military, alien abductions and much more, investigators have not taken into account that humankind will evolve. They look for ET evidence in the trees and miss the Future Forest.

If we as a species have a future, it is full of incredible technology; we have our failings, but we do have a huge sense of curiosity and exploration. We can rest assured that when "low power warp" is ready to be tested, there will be some damn fool-crazy, test pilot/astronaut who will climb aboard, happily. In fact, there will be intense competition to have the honor of achieving this next feat. That's just us.

We must begin thinking and perceiving as a species, not locked in our own individual prison of an opinion. This is the first of many evolutionary steps we need to take, I believe.

It is time we figured out this UFO puzzle together. I suspect when we do, universal doors will open to us as we finally reach our early 20s as a species and leave our adolescence full of pimples and catastrophes, behind. Disclosure or bust!

Finally, as I stated in the first sentence of this book, do not think I am discounting the reality nor the presence of extraterrestrials. I have many friends who *know* it is ETs as much as I *know* it is time traveling humans. It almost certainly is both and they may well work together.

However, that is a subjective statement. Here's another: I suspect that future humans have the right to lead the way in Earth matters, whether objectively patrolling the skies or subjectively nudging the adolescent humans along by putting weird messages in our heads. It is our descendants who have the vested interest in Earth and her life-forms, not ETs.

Maybe in the far-distant future, no species has the right to any planet, it is all communal and unconditionally loving. Even the Future Humans have a long, long way to go in evolution before having this particular opinion. I feel they love and covet Earth.

The readers of my own publications know that I've said all this for nearly 38 years, so I hope this book is not a nuts and bolts shock for you. This book is for my "star friends" who have supported my work and loved me all these years.

"A garden to walk in and immensity to dream in--what more could he ask? A few flowers at his feet and above him the stars."
   — *Victor Hugo*

***

Chapter Thirteen: Consciousness Voyage

All I ask is a tall ship and a star to steer her by...

--John Masefield

There is a lot of evidence pointing to Future Humans as being the answer to the UFO phenomenon. However, we are missing the driving component of this entire human saga over multiple millennia; this main ingredient is *consciousness*.

I would love to see humans warping out into the galaxy as a respected, peaceful young species and it would be fine with me if our starship crewmembers mingled with a variety of consenting adult aliens. I do not stress the "human to human" idea as a human chauvinist or because of a philosophy that humans must stick to humans. My view is quite the contrary. However, to go out into the galaxy successfully, we would need a strong sense of who we are on the human starship: Our strengths, our nobilities, our limitations, our warts.

Being a member of a sentient species is a weighty burden from which we can't escape. It is how we behave, how we think, how we feel. If you were from Proxima Centauri B, you would be bound through consciousness to other Proxima Centaurians B, regardless of what moment of time you lived. Time becomes very relative when compared to the enormity of consciousness.

Many people are interested in finding their genealogical information; in a sense, this curiosity is an example of the consciousness of your ancestors reaching out to you, so that you know more about them and more about yourself. You might hear of your great, great grandmother from Ireland who survived the Irish Potato Famine and immigrated to America, being held at Ellis Island and finally finding her safe but meager home in the Land of the Free and the Home of the Brave.

Or you might find through genealogical research, that your great, great grandfather came over to America as an African slave, that he was involved in a daring slave rebellion and in his older years, was active in establishing libraries for black children. You are bound to your ancestors through DNA but there is something more, too; they reach out to you through consciousness.

Human travelers who come back through time, must feel a connection to us whether we are in 2,000 B.C., 1897 A.D., or 2020 A.D. I believe this is one of the two reasons which keeps them coming back, keeps them checking the nuclear installations, the rainforests, and the oceans. The second reason is no doubt some benefit to their collective future selves. These two reasons are why the UFO phenomenon exists.

This connection to us, typical of human dealings, is not as simple as just checking things. They obviously have all sorts of reasons, precedents, loopholes, and policies, for everything from abductions to staying hidden or semi-hidden. There certainly were past days, such as their possible Greek god personae, in which more interference was allowed for better or worse.

It is my basic argument that extraterrestrials simply would not have a powerful "consciousness connection" to Earth and Earthers. Of course, they have it with their own "people back home."

Whoever this is up there, keeps coming back and coming back *to us*.

On top of this, any ETs worth their salt, would know they had no right to interfere with a planet which has an advanced group of its own entities, protecting and working with the planet (assuming Future Humans actually patrol Earth skies). To say the extraterrestrials care about Earth and help us, but future humans do not care or help (or that there are no future humans), assumes that we are a failed, hapless species. I reject that assumption!

Yes, this could all be the makings of a science fiction story, except, that most of us do think there is plentiful evidence to show UFOs do exist; I believe this plentiful evidence points strongly not to ETs, but to time travelers from Earth. We haven't looked at the evidence in this light; we have simply accepted that our visitors are ETs and continued from there.

The fact that UFOs exist and are an "unknown" has just been confirmed and updated by Dr. Michio Kaku. In September 2019, Professor Kaku of the City College of New York, the astrophysicist physicist who appears so often in the media and is respected by many, spoke at the Ufology World Congress in Spain. He addressed the question of the recent Navy videos and what implications they might have for us. For years Kaku has considered the UFO topic to be a fanciful one but he has reached a "turning point" and has had a big change of heart.

Dr. Kaku stated as of September 14, 2019, *"Even if not smoking-gun proof, the declassified videos — bolstered by confirmation of multiple sightings of unexplained aerial vehicles during 2014 and 2015, including at least one near-collision — are giving ufology new weight.* **We've reached a turning point**.*"* (Bold font is the author's).

It used to be that believers had to prove that these objects were from an intelligent race in outer space. Now the burden of proof is on the government to prove they're not from intelligent beings in outer space."

"The possibility that they are vehicles from other planetary civilizations, now has to be put on the table."

Footnote 88: HotAir.com, "Michio Kaku: We've Reached a Turning Point on UFOs," by Jazz Shaw, September 14, 2019

What difference does it really make if the source of our visitors is a planet out in distant space or if they are fellow humans who come from "time"?

It makes a difference, a huge difference, for us of the 21st Century, especially. It is more important for us than for those of the future, in fact.

Many people these days are disgusted with their own human race. Many look to extraterrestrials as having the motivation and methods to help, while others feel there is no help and that we probably deserve to go extinct. Some days, I can't argue with them.

However, have we been brainwashed or "dumbed down" so as to have little or no confidence in our own species? Have we buckled because we have experienced an onslaught of "let us dominate you," psychology from huge corporations? Almost every advertisement is for something we are supposed to have wrong with us, from cancer to toenail fungus, to the fact our tennis shoes are not trendy enough, to the fact we must now buy a new expensive smartphone because it has a slow motion feature. In politics, a segment of the population seems to prefer a dictatorship which relieves them (The People) of their power. Have we really failed as a self-determining, boldly-going, species?

And, is there a possible malicious and malignant disinformation scheme, with theories pushed on us about ETs, while any mention of time travelers is marginalized and negated as "impossible!" As "shallow, happy consumers" we are supposed to live for today only as a stupid consumer, having not even a concept of The Future in which our progeny will live; if we dream at all, it is to be of a cute ET, a wise, omniscient ET, or an evil ET, but—no time-traveling humans need apply because "they are not real."

Most of us are of good intent but we are simply fatigued, we work hard but find ourselves losing out financially. We seem to be taking two steps back for every step forward, both regarding Earth's environment and our human society. Partially, this is a result of having been robbed of our ability to conceive of our species' future and to care about it.

We haven't failed as a species yet, but, we are in a really hard patch of the 21st Century! Yes, governments and corporations do try to dumb us down but with some of us, the more you try to dumb us down, the more we rebel and the more we fight back. The more we are taught to hate, the more we love. (We do have our mutants).

As they prepare for time travel, our great, great grandchildren will feel our DNA and thus our consciousness in them. The spirit of exploration and discovery still lives in them (and us).

In a moment, you may wonder if this has turned into a book about **Star Trek**. There are several methods in my madness: This book has stuck to evidence and mostly the iconic well-proven UFO cases, to present the argument that humans traveling back in time account for all or many of UFO occupants in our skies.

However, since 1947, the extraterrestrials have received most of the subjective credit (and discredit), for creating a cultural phenomenon and seeming to reach many individual humans' minds and hearts. I wish to offer the cultural phenomenon of the Future Human presence, as well; why should Future Humans be relegated to "just the evidence, mam and no dreaming allowed!"

The UFO phenomenon *is* more than just facts or lack thereof, there is a huge subjective, cultural aspect to it. As the Jacques Vallee character played by Francois Truffaut, exclaims in **Close Encounters of the Third Kind,** "This is a phenomenon sociologic!"

The UFO phenomenon is also an evolutionary scream on our part, that we want to move forward but we are prisoners, stuck in the muck of corrupt politicians, a planet-wide climate crisis, the everyday stress of trying to earn a living as it becomes more and more difficult to do so, and finding ourselves locked out of one of our basic human directives: curiosity! We *need* to explore and discover!

Yet, some people have disavowed NASA's reality, even, declaring it all a fake. This is sad, and it is symptomatic of what's been done to us.

Close Encounters of the Third Kind: Were those extraterrestrials or evolved little humans who deplaned from the mothership? Steven Spielberg used children to play the roles of many of the UFO occupants. When he made the film **ET,** he created the character of ET, who was *more alien,* but the occupants of **CE3K** welcomed Roy Neary aboard like long-lost relatives. The occupants were what we imagine a physically evolved or changed, future human form might be.

You may think I am creating something that "wasn't." Is there no chance that the enduring love of the film **CE3K** can involve Future Humans? No chance that Spielberg intended this possibility?

It is known that Steven Spielberg visited a famous (or infamous) channeling group of well-known individuals, some in the CIA, others in show business, others in powerful positions, back in the early 1970s. It was called The Council of Nine and its conclusion (reports of their conclusions do vary), is said to have been that the contact which the group felt from "beyond," was with humans of the future. However, these entities were from so far in the future that they were "particles" (sheer consciousness) and thus non-corporeal, although they also seemed to have a physical manifestation.

Close Encounters of the Third Kind was made in 1977. Perhaps Spielberg did create the CE3K extraterrestrials to be quite human-like following his experience in channeling of the Council of Nine.

It is easy to see how film makers made the decision to tell us stories of ETs instead of Future Humans, it was thought to be bigger box office. There are films on time machines and time travelers, but **Original Star Trek** remains by far the biggest (and one of the only) media productions to seriously combine UFOs/starships with humans inside, warping through space.

Gene Roddenberry, who created **Star Trek,** was also a member of the Council of Nine. Members of the Stanford Research Institute, of remote viewing fame (which we covered in Chapter Eight), were also involved with the mysterious Council of Nine as well as Timothy Leary, Jon Povil, Uri Geller (also a remote viewer), Andrijah Puharich, and others who still try to keep their names out of it.

It is important to note that Gene Roddenberry created **Original Series Star Trek** in 1965 before his involvement with the Council of Nine. The inspiration for **Star Trek** came to Roddenberry directly. But obviously, the future human concept called to him.

The lack of consideration for Future Humans being the possible answer to the UFO puzzle has been a personal frustration for me for over 40 years. My research, intuition, and curiosity have always included the possibility that it is Future Humans. The psi contact I have felt (telepathic, ESP, whatever to call it), has been with Future Humans.

We do know 100% that **Star Trek** or **CE3K** are science fiction; yes, these are simplified, overly optimistic (about the future) Hollywood productions. Just as UFO researchers usually don't wear tin foil hats and have no problem being objective and scientific when investigating an actual UFO case, so it is with us. We can love **Star Trek** in our spare time and not be a nerdy "Trekkie" as the media paints us to be (and what's wrong with nerds!). We simply find enjoyment and inspiration in these fictional productions.

But we *know* there is truth in the premise that humans are out there in the galaxy; we are a species with integrity and intelligence even if not as evolved as those "particles of consciousness" who have evolved beyond the beyonds. Perhaps I should say, "Humans *will be out there*," but having the secret to time travel puts us *out there now*!

This chapter is not only about the influence of Future Humans on our culture, it is about giving them *credit* for influencing our culture, or at least considering doing so. It is interesting that when we list individuals who state they have been influenced by **Star Trek;** they are mostly the scientists who take us forward.

A Small Sampling of Accomplished People Who Find *Star Trek* Inspiring:

Marc Rayman is the Chief Propulsion Engineer at NASA's Jet propulsion Laboratory (JPL), and was the head of NASA's Deep Space One mission which was the first NASA craft to use ion power. Its mission was a flyby of an asteroid and a comet. The mission was extended, a great success.

Dr. Rayman was also director and chief engineer for NASA's Dawn mission, which was launched in 2007 on a mission to orbit the two most massive bodies in the main asteroid belt between Mars and Jupiter, named Vesta and Ceres. That mission too was a great success.

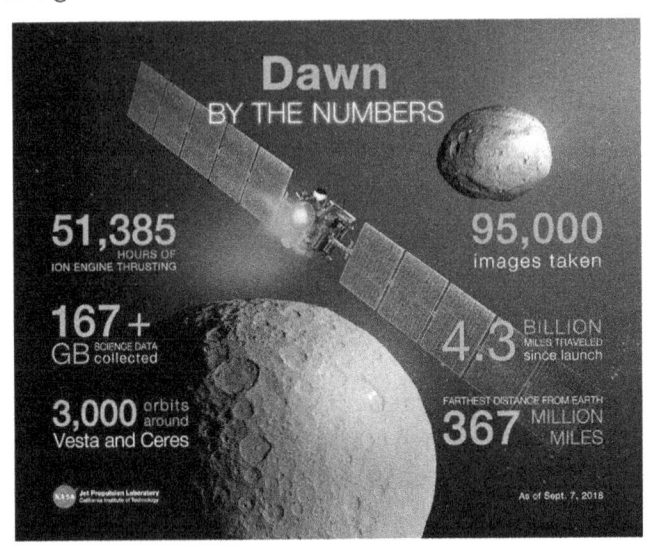

Dawn BY THE NUMBERS

- 51,385 HOURS OF ION ENGINE THRUSTING
- 95,000 images taken
- 167+ GB SCIENCE DATA collected
- 4.3 BILLION MILES TRAVELED since launch
- 3,000 orbits around Vesta and Ceres
- 367 MILLION MILES FARTHEST DISTANCE FROM EARTH

As of Sept. 7, 2018
Jet Propulsion Laboratory, California Institute of Technology

Footnote 89: dawn.jpl.nasa.gov, "Dawn Journal," Dr. Marc Rayman

Dr. Rayman exclaims, "I was fortunate enough to be involved in all the technical aspects of the operation of the Dawn mission to dwarf planets Ceres and Vesta. Our Dawn craft had three ion engines. I first heard of ion power in the episode called "Spock's Brain" filmed in 1967 on **Star Trek.**"

"My older brother introduced me to **Star Trek** and I sat spellbound in front of a black and white television set and watched every episode of **Original Star Trek.** He exclaims, "I was captivated by the future which **Star Trek** showed me and as I grew up, I found another medium into which to guide my **Star Trek** passion. I must tell you of the time I could either go to my Friday advanced physics class or go to the latest **Star Trek** movie premiere. Which do you think I did? I went to the **Star Trek** movie, of course!"

These are the words on Marc's umbrella, "Where No Man Has Gone Before," and his work as chief engineer at California's Jet Prolusion Laboratory is the backbone of America's deep space program. From the Voyager Probe, which is now flying through interstellar space, to all the Mars probes which seem to be telling us convincingly that the red planet is not a dead planet, to the Dawn mission, just completed, Trekker Marc Rayman has guided and lead the JPL program. His main control room at JPL looks astonishingly like Engineer Scott's control room. Marc is part of the team which works on creating ion power.

Martin Cooper invented the cell phone. In an interview, he states that he loved **Star Trek** and especially their communicators. He grew up with that treasured inspiration and though it was called an "impossible dream," he invented the cell phone.

Martin Cooper holds **Star Trek** communicator and his first cell phone invention

Dr. Lawrence Krauss from Case Western Reserve University and of the Institute for Advanced Technology (think tank of geniuses), has written the book, "**The Physics of Star Trek.**" Lawrence is works on how we can use wormholes to get from here to there – in reality.

Seth Shostak states that science fiction and especially **Star Trek** changed his life when he was a boy; he and his brother cuddled into bed and watched **Trek** on black and white television. "It has an emotional appeal, it told us extraterrestrials do exist, they manifest and most can be reasonable if you find the key, and it speaks to the best in all of us." Seth went on to become Senior Astronomer of the **SETI** program (The Search for Extraterrestrial Life).

Professor John Adler states that **Star Trek** changed the world with its imagination, inventiveness, and vision of a positive future. He is professor at Stanford University and concludes that **Trek's** concept of "sickbay" revolutionized the medical field. Adler has led the way in this revolution. Now there are medical scanners, almost identical to those shown in **Trek**, and if you have a brain tumor, today they can find it as easily as Doctor McCoy would have. However, when they filmed **Trek** in 1966, real medicine was still nearly barbaric. Finding a brain tumor, for example, was hit and miss. Professor Adler saw **Trek** as a boy and said, "Why not?"

Mae Jemison is the first African-American female astronaut. In 1992, she went to space in Space Shuttle Endeavor. She says, "I opened every day's transmission to

NASA with, "Hailing frequencies open." Mae tells us how inspired she was by Lt. Uhura, played by Nichelle Nichols, and because of this science fiction show, she saw as a little girl that she, too, could live her dreams and go to space.

Footnote 90: UFO Digest: "Trail Blazing Science Fiction Creates Our Future in the Galaxy," by Diane Tessman, July 2012

Maybe people like Mae Jemison and Marc Rayman (and others), go into science careers, especially space-science careers, because they *do* perceive that we as a species have such a bright future in space and time – if only we can evolve just one-more-step. Advancements in the science world, nudge our evolution along! The rest of that "one step" is *within us*.

To Boldly Theorize on Future Humans

My friend of many years and many adventures, Della van Hise, wrote the **Star Trek** paperback, **Killing Time,** and has specialized in Carlos Castaneda and shamanistic philosophy in recent years. Her books include "**Quantum Shaman,**" "**Into the Infinite,**" and "**Scrawls on the Walls of the Soul.**"

Della and I have chased UFOs and consequently shared a few remarkable UFO sightings; we have tried remote viewing, we have defiantly ridden horses through a top secret facility, and we have generally theorized on the possibility that there exists a future out there, in which humans travel time and space. We have enjoyed a strange but wonderful friendship for over 40 years, and the saga continues.

Here are her thoughts on loops and glitches in time, reverse engineering of crashed UFOs, possible motives of the time travelers, and more!

Della Van Hise: Ask the Next Question!

To Boldly Loop Time: In the original Star Trek series there was an episode entitled *Tomorrow is Yesterday* that has always played with my head. The premise was that the *Enterprise* is accidentally thrown back in time to late 1960s Earth and finds itself under attack by a young fighter pilot named Captain John Christopher. When the pilot's plane is unintentionally crushed by the *Enterprise's* tractor beam and Christopher is brought on board, he has then seen too much of the future to be returned to his own timeline - the argument being that he could manipulate key stocks and industries or even influence political climates to such an extent that - should it be his intent or those to whom he might reveal what he had seen - the world Kirk and Spock know, the world of the future, might not exist at all. Captain Christopher, in the end, is returned to a point in time just moments *before* he spotted the *Enterprise* in a low orbit - and so even if he had wanted to tell anyone, there was nothing to tell because, theoretically, *it never happened.*

This, of course, brings up the subject of consciousness, and maybe even the question of morals and ethics. As a writer of both science fiction and books on the evolution of consciousness, I've always toyed with the idea of how Captain Christopher's encounter with the *Enterprise* affected the rest of his life. Did he have vague hints of memory that *something* had happened? Was he troubled by disturbing dreams, as many abductees are? Or was it all a blank and he simply returned to his human life on Earth, fathering a child and flying fighter jets? What did he *feel* after this, and how did it shape his awareness, let alone his mental/emotional stability? Is it possible to experience something "outside of time" and be caused to forget it entirely - whether through technological means such as so-called "amnesia drugs", or through being returned to one's own time a moment before one would have been abducted?

And how does this affect the time travelers themselves? They would retain linear memory or else the encounter itself would be in vain. *This* seems to indicate that there are at least two "timelines" - and probably an infinite amount - but for the moment, I'll focus on just the two: the one in which the time travelers are clearly *outside* the flow of linear time; and the one wherein the time travelers step *into* the linear flow of time in order to interact with their human contacts.

The Hologram: If the universe is holographic as has been speculated, perhaps the easiest way to visualize it is to see it as a sphere containing everything that has ever happened or ever will. The hologram contains the experience of the universe in its entirety, in other words. Within it is the moment you were born, the moment you will die, and everything in between. To someone on the *inside* of the hologram, it's only possible to experience time as a linear phenomenon - things appear to have a beginning, middle and end. But how would it appear to someone *outside* the hologram? It's impossible to speculate what kind of technology or expansion of consciousness would allow someone to step outside of the hologram and view it from an objective perspective, but supposing for a moment that such ability does exist, it would certainly explain how the visitors are seemingly able to visit Earth in the now or thousands of years in the past, and probably deep into the future as well.

If the visitors can gaze into the hologram like looking into a digital book, for example, they can easily target precisely where they would want to project, based on whatever agenda they might have. They could visit an abductee as a child, again in their teen years, multiple times during their adult life, and even into old age - and each encounter could be intricately determined in the same way we are able to pinpoint precise locations with GPS technology, or even an old style map (remember those?).

Reverse Engineering But, From What Source? Prominent UFO researcher Jacques Vallee has speculated that perhaps some UFOs have influenced Earth technology just by their existence, by virtue of being *seen*. When UFOs looked like dirigibles, for example, was during a time when humans were on the cusp of developing dirigibles in the here and now. As the UFO technology seemingly advanced, so did Earth technology. Is it a case of monkey-see, monkey do, or a case of reverse engineering? And if it is reverse engineering, is the technology itself coming from crash retrieval sites such a Roswell, or is it being covertly given to us?

And, in fact, one must ask if some of these "crashes" are engineered as a means to "accidentally" provide humanity with the technology we will need to create the future in the first place. Such deliberate "crashes" would seemingly avoid direct repercussions from whatever non-interference directive might exist, in the sense that the captain who ordered that unmanned shuttlecraft down to Earth could always claim the craft malfunctioned or was shot down. Either way... "Ooops, it was an accident!" But... was it? As for any seeming "lifeforms" on board, were they ever lifeforms at all, or some cleverly crafted biological "doll" that was never alive to begin with?

In many ways, the idea of reverse engineering gives too much credit to humans. While we are a clever and imitative species by nature, we probably don't have access to a lot of the things that would power a UFO from hundreds of years in the future or especially if the vehicles themselves are from some far distant planet or even another galaxy. We might be able to figure out the wires and gizmos, but how to manipulate the heart of the engine which moves the craft from point A to point B... let alone from the year 2525 A.D. to the year 2000 B.C.? Of course, there are infinite possibilities, and I mention these few only as an example of some of the potential challenges to the idea of reverse engineering.

Subliminal Memories: Is it possible that some UFO abductions are such that the abductees have only subliminal "memories" of the events that occurred because they are being returned to their (our) timeline just *before* they were abducted in the first place? I've talked to a few abductees where this certainly seems it might be the case. In particular, some report what amounts to quasi-memories of things they were shown or told by the visitors, yet they couldn't tell you the design of the ship, or whether it was powered by dilithium crystals or cow manure, so while they might be able to speak of messages they were given - usually warnings that humanity needs to change direction "before it's too late" - they have absolutely *no* practical knowledge that could be used to influence human technology.

Motives of Time Travelers: If not to influence Earth technology or raise human consciousness, what is being gained by centuries-long intervention in human affairs, even if only involving a relatively small number of individuals? Are they simply tourists who occasionally dabble in human affairs just for the fun of it? Or perhaps likened to anthropologists who go into primitive societies and inadvertently influence that society just by virtue of their presence? In that scenario, I'm reminded of an incident that occurred during WWII, when cargo planes delivered supplies to Vanuatu, an isolated chain of islands in the South Pacific. The inhabitants developed a religion around the incident, believing the planes to be delivering items from "the messiah."

The parallels between this and certain factions of "true believers" can't be denied. What humans don't immediately understand, they often turn into a religion - and the UFO phenomenon is no exception. That doesn't diminish its authenticity as a phenomenon, but it does raise caution flags with regard to the great need to know the difference between actual events and false conclusions based on the events themselves. Just one more ingredient in the strange stew of the visitors and what it *might* all ultimately mean.

Deciphering Languages: Our current state of technological advancement *does* seem to indicate that we had some help along the way. Most reports about the crashed saucer at Roswell, for example, indicate that the writing on the instruments and throughout the vessel was a very strange-looking language that matches nothing on Earth.

Just because *we* can't make sense of something doesn't automatically mean it isn't of Terran origins - whether from the far-distant ancient times of the past, or the far-flung worlds of the future. Language changes and evolves, and I dare say many current day humans can barely read their own native tongue, let alone would they be able to decipher Old English or Middle English. It's a matter of perspective as to what we perceive as alien or human or somewhere in between.

Predictions and Prophecies: Some abductees are shown images (whether telepathic or technology-generated) of mass destruction on Earth. Some have said this is the result of a "great war" while others have conjectured that it is the result of massive environmental collapse. In either case (or perhaps it might be a bit of both that leads to the final chapter of humanity) the end result is that there are few if any survivors, virtually no technology left in existence, and humanity is reduced to primitive subsistence.

Alleged future time travelers may appear to warn us that we are approaching the crossroads of a cataclysm, and if we *don't* do something sooner rather than later, we will not only face our own annihilation, but ironically we will be the direct *cause* of it through nothing more than our apathy, our indulgence in distraction, and our tolerance of a political climate that has become far more insane than any science fiction horror story ever written about the prospect of what happens when madmen rule the world.

Edith Keeler Must Die: To use **Star Trek** as an example - how prophetic *is* that old show? - there is an episode called *City on the Edge of Forever*. Another of their time travel episodes, this one involving Kirk and Spock having to step back in time in an attempt to locate and rescue a deranged Dr. McCoy who had accidentally shot himself up with some mind-altering substance and subsequently leapt through a time portal which landed him on Earth in the year 1930.

In the context of the episode, the dilemma is raised wherein if one human woman, Edith Keeler, is allowed to live, it will mean the Nazis have time to finish their heavy water experiments, develop nuclear capability, and as a result they will win World War II, rise to power globally, and the future as it *must* exist will no longer exist at all. In the original timeline reality, Edith Keeler dies in a traffic accident. In the potentially altered reality, Dr. McCoy does something that prevents her from dying (a pure and noble act on his part), but results in a complete alteration of the future, and to such an extent that he and everyone else he knows would simply cease to exist.

A right nasty dilemma, to be sure - but one about which time travelers would have to be ever-vigilant. Even knowing the future intricately might not always give them the ability to avoid accidents or discovery. What if the Roswell crash had accidentally fallen into a populated area and killed Stephen Hawking while he was still a young boy?

The Revolutionary 1960's: Whether anyone likes or dislikes **Star Trek**, we can't deny that it played a role in shaping our future, maybe even have been a pivotal crossroads in our history. Having been a young girl of 11 when the series' first aired in 1966, I remember the strife and conflict faced by the world at that time. The Vietnam War. The struggle for the raising of consciousness itself. The Bay of Pigs was barely in the rearview mirror. Duck and cover under school desk to avoid radiation. These things were real. And it is happening again. And the *only* ones who can do anything about it are you and me... and it might already be too late, but we have-to-believe it isn't.

During that tumultuous time when **Star Trek** came along with its messages of peace, cooperation not only on a global scale, but a galactic one, racial equality, gender equality, and a future for humanity that allowed us to go the stars. We were perhaps covertly shown incredible technology that is now an everyday reality - flip phones, computers that fit in the palm of our hands, computers that talk (claimed to be impossible at the time **Star Trek** aired), and on down the long list. Today, what was science fiction is now reality. The only thing about **Star Trek** that we (seemingly) haven't developed is faster-than-light travel, but who's to say what *really* goes on behind the closed gates at Area 51 and other such facilities around the globe?

Why would future time travelers come back at all? If they exist, then surely we (humanity) *must* have turned the corner from imminent extinction to at least a somewhat longer term survival, so did they come back to insure we *do* make that turn - i.e., did they influence things such as **Star Trek** and the '60s peace movement, by perhaps having some manner of contact with individuals such as Gene Roddenberry, George Lucas, Steven Spielberg, and others? Many abductees have reported having "unusual dreams" throughout their life, and many have become writers or artists who attempt to share those visions with the outside world.

How *would* the world be different today if **Star Trek** never existed? In the same way, to what extent have the visitors guided our development through covert intervention in the expansion and evolution of human consciousness? This would begin at first with one or two individuals, then gradually spreading to global proportions as the technology itself improved from rabbit ears and tin foil "signal boosters" attached to lumbering antennae on the rooftops of isolated farmhouses, to instantaneous global availability of pretty much all information directly through the internet?

Who is calling the shots? Is the choice up to humans as a species, or to the very few in power, or to the future humans themselves?

Free Will vs. the Self-Consistency Loop: How would the presence of future time travelers affect free will? If they are coming back in time to influence us toward our own survival, do they have the power/ability to simply "Make it so" or is there some offshoot of a prime directive that might allow them to provide us with certain technology, but forbids them from outright landing on the White House lawn and installing a more benevolent government that would move in the direction of humanity's survival rather than personal and corporate greed?

But back to **Star Trek**: Can even the future time travelers have any certainty of what will happen to themselves if the past is altered even in a minor way? What of the future from which they come? Is it a dystopian, post-apocalyptic or post-environmental-collapse civilization, or is it more of a paradise of sorts, or somewhere in between? What is motivating their visits? Is it simply a matter of *their* own survival, or is it remotely possible there is a more sinister angle to it?

Are they seeking to move us in the direction of a peaceful and benevolent planet worthy of inclusion in what some might call "The Galactic Federation" or are they manipulating certain industries and individuals, as a means to guarantee their own success? I personally do not believe the visitors are here with a sinister intent, but that doesn't mean that those with whom the visitors come into contact are necessarily as benevolent. Give one man a spear and he will use it to hunt to feed his family. Give a different man a spear and he will use it to kill his brother to insure *he* is the only one with the spear or the ability to hunt.

It might not be as much about the visitors as it's about *us* as a species with undeniable self-destructive and violent tendencies inherent in our genes. We might want to believe that the visitors would know the difference between the one man and the other - and perhaps they actually do - but putting a weapon in someone's hand (whether a physical spear or a weapon of knowledge) can change that person down to their core and in ways that could never be predicted.

Can a Paradox Be Simultaneous? From a somewhat different perspective, is it possible future time travelers are survivors or descendants of survivors who are coming back strictly to save *themselves* - to warn themselves, in other words - so that a few *will* survive to change a future that might otherwise not exist at all? This is paradoxical but maybe worth a sideways glance, since time travel itself *is* a paradox just by virtue of time's simultaneous existence and the fact that it doesn't *really* exist at all. It wouldn't necessarily be any great noble effort on the part of some future galactic federation, but perhaps the desperate attempt of a few individuals who might possess the technology to make such a journey into the past to save themselves *from* themselves.

But then arises the paradox again. If the future time traveler exists, it seems to indicate that his past *did* survive, or he wouldn't exist to be hopping into his Superfly-Time-Machine to come back and influence Great Grandpa to build that ark (and this time don't leave the unicorns and dragons behind).

To Go Where Some Have Clearly Gone – Before: The questions are many and the answers are few. But the important thing is to keep asking the questions even when it might appear to be an exercise in futility. As a fiction writer, I used to engage in a lot of speculation-on-paper - having characters go through a plethora of unpredictable experiences and eventually come to conclusions as to what it all means and how it will determine the outcome of their lives. I'm tempted to do that here, of course - to state definitively that the future time travelers are here to show us the error of our ways, to provide us with a road map to the future that is both physical and *meta*physical, both practical and spiritual. But that would only be my own conclusions as a character in the play, rather than a time traveler looking down at the hologram from *outside* of time.

It's my hope to one day *be* such a traveler - to boldly go where some have clearly gone before - but until that day comes, I can only look up at the starry sky and gaze in wonder at the night that never ends.

My books are widely available on Amazon or through the Quantum Shaman™ website at www.quantumshaman.com

To Boldly Theorize (Part Two)

Marc Cushman is the author of ***Star Trek*, Season One**, a 580-page detailed history covering the first season of Gene Roddenberry's ***Star Trek*: The Original Series.** This book is wildly popular with ***Star Trek*** fans, and so there is also **These are the Voyages, Season Two,** and **These Are the Voyages, Season Three.** These three books are cherished because they have immortalized the day to day creative process on this iconic series; as Marc says, a bit of magic was involved or it never would have happened.

Marc has written a number of other fascinating books, among them, **Long Distance Voyagers, Part One and Two of the Story of the Moody Blues.**

Interview with March Cushman

Diane: How did you come to know Gene Roddenberry who created ***Star Trek*** and subsequently document and delight ***Star Trek*** fans with the details of how all three seasons came to be?

Marc Cushman: *My first connection with Gene Roddenberry was in 1982. I was in my early twenties and working for a production company in Los Angeles as a writer. They wanted to do a one-hour TV special on the Star Trek phenomenon,* and, when they heard I liked the show and knew a fair amount about it -- having read a couple of books that were out at that time, as well as magazine articles, as well as having seen the entire series -- they assigned me to the project. A meeting was set up for me to interview Gene Roddenberry at Paramount.

This was around the time "Wrath of Khan" was being prepared for release. And this was my first interview with him. Gene had Susan Sackett, his personal assistant, pull all the scripts from Star Trek and loan them to me so I could make copies. I was also given access to memos and other materials from the original series. This began a 30 year research and writing project which became the first three These Are the Voyages books, one volume for each season of the original Star Trek.

Throughout that time, I interviewed close to 100 people associated with the series, from the stars, to the producers, directors, writings, production crew members, and guest stars. And I continued to collect material, with the other producers sharing more documents form the series, until I had well over a few thousand documents.

Gene and the other producers had given me permission to use the memos and other production material in the books, and use them I did! I wove the memos together to form a dialogue between Gene, his producers Gene L. Coon, Robert H. Justman, John D.F. Back, John Meredyth Lucas, and Fred Freiberger, along with story editor D.C. Fontana, and NBC production manager Stan Robertson. We hear their conversation, from those memos, regarding not only the two Star Trek pilot films, but every single episode produced for the series, and dozens of scripts that were written but not produced, either because of budget considerations or subject matter which NBC found unsuitable. Every episode gets its own chapter, and the reader not only gets a detailed look at Star Trek, but an inside look at the thinking and efforts that went into the writing and making of every episode, and even the many episodes-that-never-were (those unprocessed stories and scripts).

Two of the things that come out of these memos, consistently, was, one, Roddenberry's determination that the series be believable from a scientific level, which resulted in him connecting with scientists from JPL and NASA to consult with him and review the scripts, and, two, his insistence that every episode have *a strong central theme -- meaning, that it be about something; every episodes stimulated thought. These things, among many others, set Star Trek apart from other science-fiction series and, I believe, account for its ongoing phenomenal popularity.*

September 17, 1976, The Rollout of the real Space Shuttle Enterprise in Palmdale, CA, with Gene Roddenberry and the crew of the science fiction Enterprise,

Diane: Are you a UFO believer, skeptic, or how do you feel about UFOs?

Marc Cushman: *I believe in UFOs. By saying this, I mean that I believe there is intelligent life beyond Earth and that we have been visited. In the Star Trek bible which Roddenberry wrote, there is a mathematical formula of how many solar systems there are in the universe, and how many planets circling each of those stars, which comes to billions, and how, if only 1% of those planets contain animal life, and if only 1% of them contain intelligent animal life, then there would still be over a million possibilities for evolved intelligent lifeforms out there.*

The numbers are in Roddenberry's presentation, and in the first volume of my books, and this information came from NASA back in the mid-1960s. Millions of possibilities! It is not hard for me to believe in the existence of intelligent alien life. To the contrary, it would be hard for me to not believe in their existence.

Diane: #3. Have you wondered about humans traveling back in time as opposed to UFOs being all-ETs?

Marc: *I keep an open mind to all possibilities, when it comes to UFOs and where they come from. Space travel is one possibility, time travel is another, and inter-dimensional travel is a third. And I imagine there could be a fourth and a fifth and a sixth that my mind is not capable of imagining or comprehending. Look how human science and technology has grown in the last century, and, more so, the last couple of decades, and more so, just the last several years. It is staggering. Could anyone have ever imagined something like the internet 50 years ago? Could anyone have imagined something like television a hundred years ago, or radio two hundred years ago? Or Star Trek? I expect there are things going on all around us that we cannot see, hear, feel, or understand.*

Diane: Did you/do you think it possible that **Original** *Star Trek* was a somewhat inexplicable production (low budget, often chaotic with changes in the middle of production week, done almost intuitively in order to complete episodes), which was inspired or driven by something "bigger" than those involved? Was it a stream of consciousness from the future, channeled from someone or something intentionally? Why does *Star Trek* feel so real to so many?

Marc Cushman: *For lack of a better word, I consider Star Trek to be the work of 'magic.' It has grown so much, and accomplished so much, that it has eclipsed anything that a mere TV series, on a restrictive budget and schedule, should be able to do. Now, whether that magic is just the manipulation of some unseen force to bring so many talented people together, or something beyond that, I can't say.*

But think about it. Remove writer producer Gene Coon from the equation, or writer and story editor D.C. Fontana, or William Shatner, or Leonard Nimoy, or so many others who made significant contributions, and it wouldn't have become what it has.

Sometimes there is something else at play when amazing things come about. Call it fate, or divine intervention, or alien intervention, or anything you like, but the one thing I can't call it is 'coincidence.' The power that comes out of the combination of the right people doing the right thing at precisely the right time is too great to be left to mere coincidence.

I've seen the transcripts of the channeling session, where Gene Roddenberry was able to talk to alien intelligence, in the Council of Nine. It's eerie, to say the least. And, to my thinking, it's absolutely believable.

Gene never had another success like Star Trek. Did he have help that even he was not aware of, in creating Star Trek? I think it is possible. But I will tell you that I have lived in his memos, and he was truly a brilliant and gifted writer. He thought in realms beyond most television writers. Now, you combine this with him connecting to a group of other very talented writers, and actors, and directors, and technicians, and it is completely possible that Star Trek happened on its own.

If you read enough of the memos, both his and those of his collaborators -- and I have read thousands -- then you can see how Star Trek may have come about without alien contribution. But you also see the possibility of that, when you consider how Gene was so much more 'on his game' when doing Star Trek, and, as I mentioned before, him meeting all of these talented collaborators at the right time and right place, it becomes easy to believe that there was some form of alien or future human intervention, manipulation, contribution; you pick.

Diane: Comment on the lasting power, the icon status, of **Star Trek** for over 50 years. Many movies and series have been spawned from it but in my opinion, the *magic* is in the original television series of the 1960s.

Marc Cushman: *I believe Star Trek impacted society as strongly as it did, from the very beginning, raising the level of people's thinking, open their minds to all sorts of possibilities, and inspiring the invention of the technological things that now dominate our lives, because Star Trek is a result of positive thought. It spoke to us, and continues to speak to us. It teaches us tolerance, and empathy, and inventiveness, and fills us with positive belief. This is not monster-of-the-week science fiction TV.*

Star Trek used, and still uses, science-fiction to its true and best potential, to open minds, and to allow us to examine ourselves through other words and dimensions. These things didn't happen by chance. There was a driving force which pushed their efforts into new frontiers of social awareness and response.

Diane: Is there any actual strangeness connected to **Star Trek** for you personally? I will tell you honestly, Marc, I have had many paranormal experiences connected in one way or the other, to **Star Trek**.

Marc: *I do feel like Gene Roddenberry has been looking over my shoulder as I wrote and continue to write these books. Gene was a hands-on collaborator, as a producer, a writer, you name it. He stayed involved. And Gene made it possible for me to begin the project that evolved into the These Are the Voyages books. So, after he passed, and as I wrote the books, I did feel that his spirit was guiding me.*

And I still feel that way, as I continue writing about his life and the life-force that is Star Trek, with the subsequent volumes that now cover the events of the 1970s and the rebirth of Star Trek. I have conversations with Gene about it, and I do not believe they are one-sided. I speak to him, and I believe he hears, because, after I ask questions, I'll wake up the next morning with the answers in my mind. And these answers are almost always in the form of how I already have the answers, there in those memos, in those interviews, in those scripts and treatments.

There are so many documents, it is impossible for me to remember them all, to know right where to go to find the answer to a particular question. And I'll search and search and not find it. Then, the next morning, I wake up and find it, often with very little effort. Now, some could say that the information is filed in my subconscious, and it comes forward while I sleep. But I don't believe that. I know me. I know what I am capable of and what I am not capable of. And during the years, when working on these books, I often manage to do things that I truly believe I am <u>not</u> capable of. Something nudged me, something guides me, something helps me. I can't explain it, and I can't get anyone who isn't open to this sort of thinking to believe it. But I believe it.

The thing is, I never had an agenda to believe or not believe in this sort of thing. I'm the type person who keeps an open mind, but is not going to believe anything until I've seen it. So, show it to me. And, guess what, things are shown to us all the time. Answers are all around us. We just have to be open to them. We just have to be willing to accept a gentle push from invisible hands that direct us toward what we are supposed to see and do. I would never have said anything like this ten years ago. I wasn't one of those people who would tell ghost stories, except when I was being paid to do so, writing scripts for shows like Beyond Belief: Fact or Fiction. I was open, but not convinced.

Now, as a result of writing these books, and sensing what I have been sensing about Gene's presence, I lean very much toward believing. And I worry all the time that I may be getting something wrong, misinterpreting a memo or other piece of information, or coming to a wrong conclusion, and I have said out loud on many occasions, "Gene, if I'm getting this wrong, please let me know -- however you can do it, let me know." And, every time, after saying that, I wake up the next morning and realize that I did get something wrong, and I go back to that section of pages and reconsider what I'd written. I'll sometimes modify it, sometimes delete it all together.

Of course, as a writer, I do this all the time, based on experience and the instincts one develops over the years. But not always in this case, with these books. There are things that become known to me, documents that I suddenly find, understandings that I suddenly feel, that are not instinctive in me, or known in me. I don't know how to better explain it, and I don't know if I have explained it. But I feel it.

Diane: I know you have written on Gene Roddenberry in the 1970s, as well. I found one quote which says the Council of Nine thought they were communicating with a "mind" or "minds" from the future (not ETs). Can you tell us more about Roddenberry and the Council of Nine?

Marc: *This would be Volume 5 of These Are the Voyages, the second and concluding volume that covers the 1970s, which goes into that. I don't consider myself an expert on that particular topic; it's one chapter. But I can say that I was greatly impressed by the transcripts form the channeling session that* *involved Gene, and the other documents, and the interviews I conducted. I believe it is real.*

I did not enter the room, so to speak, expecting to come out of it a believer. And the thing I now believe is the Council of Nine chose Gene Roddenberry, and Steven Spielberg, who was there prior to making Close Encounters of the Third Kind, and probably others we don't know about -- people of position, who would be able to get the word out in one form or another; people with the sort of minds that could accept and communicate what they had experienced.

Gene did not seek out the Council of Nine; they sought him. (By "Council of Nine," we mean the entities who channeled to the humans in the group). Gene declined at first; he felt he wasn't ready. Then, when he was ready, he went in. What he experienced, has been getting around, because it was/is Gene Roddenberry. The questions he asked the entities which channeled through to the group, were excellent, most people wouldn't have thought to ask them. So, the Council of Nine (entities) were right in choosing him for that reason if no other. But there was another reason - he was and is Star Trek.

I can't imagine how we track time is how they track time. But I can imagine that something will grow from these seeds. It will happen when it is supposed to happen, and not one day before.

Diane: Marc, thanks for this fascinating interview! (End Interview)

I heard Gene Roddenberry speak on three different occasions in school gymnasiums in the mid-1970s. He was trying to keep the **Star Trek** phenomenon alive, and he succeeded. He always told about his childhood as an autistic child. "People – my parents – felt sorry for me because they thought I was having another seizure. In fact, I was spinning around from the bullets fired at me in my other dimension, a wonderful game of cowboy and Indian."

Gene emerged from autism and was a soldier, a commercial pilot, and a policeman as well as a writer and tv producer, but his view of autism sheds new light on the autistic state. It seems in some cases, other dimensions become real, at least for the moment rather like a vivid dream. I have wondered if he got a glimpse of the Future Humans' positive world(s) which later became **Star Trek.**

The other input Gene offered which has always stayed with me. He said, "We humans are light years ahead of our petty governments."

So, the answers to the questions he asked about the future, time travel, the universe, space, and where humans fit in, are taking root even today. More people are awakening.

The Council of Nine chose well in seeking-out Gene and Steven Spielberg. In contacting these people, seeds were planted to open doors. Was the Council of Nine real? Who among us can say? Who even knows how to define reality?

Time for New Thinking: The Power of the Future, Calling!

Whether it is "merely" the force of scientific/technological progress, or there is a "psi/subjective/sociological" aspect to it as well, there is great power behind the idea that the UFO occupants are humans from the future.

I have spotlighted **Star Trek** as representative of that *power of the future*. Of course there is much more to it than **Star Trek**: Jacques Vallee, Jack Sarfatti, Marc Rayman, Martin Cooper, Dr. Lawrence Krauss, Seth Shostak, Mae Jamison, and Professor John Adler, have felt that power from the future, too. No doubt there are thousands, even millions, of others in science/technology, and in every walk of life, inspired to be a part of creating the future, in an idealistic yet tangible sense. Most of us might hesitate to say this "power of the future" comes in direct psychic in-put but whether it does or not, is irrelevant in the big picture.

The strictest of ufology's nuts and bolts **researchers** may still dismiss anything "psi" but most of us have come to accept that gifted sensitives such as Mary Rodwell and Suzy Hansen do have psi contact and messages to/from extraterrestrials. I would not question their knowledge of their source and say that they too hear from Future Humans. I know that many people who are "in contact" are correct in defining their source as extraterrestrial. They know it to be true.

An observation is that most people who do feel the power of Future Human contact, tend to become scientists or to stress a scientific approach. Gene Roddenberry "only" worked in television but as Marc Cushman says, Roddenberry insisted that **Star Trek** always have an accurate scientific aspect and Gene consulted with the **Jet Propulsion Laboratory (JPL)** and **NASA.** He went by a galactic map of star systems, based on his scientific consultations. The planets mentioned in **Star Trek** are the names of real stars. Thus Deneb 4 is the fourth planet orbiting the (real) Deneb star, in the Alpha Cygni Star System.

There must be scientists out there who feel the consciousness-power of the ETs telling them (for instance), to work with **NASA** or to delve into post-quantum physics and discover "low power warp" as Jack Sarfatti is doing. So far, I have not found those scientists who feel ET contact. A connection to the future seems to be the preference of scientists, but of course some of them search for ET life.

The messages I have received from Future Humans for 38 years, usually speak to the entire human species and to our collective consciousness. I have readers who have stayed with me for 38 years in my own publications, **The Star Network Heartline** and **The Change Times Quarterly**, so we must offer something to individuals even though it is through the prism of collective consciousness. Of course, the progress and welfare of Earth and all of her species, should be of concern to every individual.

Note: I have purposely left out my own subjective channeling work from this book, until this brief mention in the final chapter. I have done this in order to try to present a speculative but scientific, objective argument, based in established evidence.

Receiving contact and messages from Future Humans seems to be a bridge too far in some ufology circles, while messages and channeling from extraterrestrials, abound. We seem to find it less interesting to hear from "ourselves," and opt for an ET to tell us about our individual dream or experience.

Of course, it is not hearing from ourselves in 2020, it is hearing from, well, who knows?! Who knows what year? 2350 or 80,003? Both? It is The Future with a capital "F!" The snapshots we receive of our Future Humans are dynamic, intelligent, daring, and mind boggling. (No, we still are not angels).

We as a species have never been truly free to pursue our full potential in our thousands and thousands of years on Earth. Religions, tyrants, political systems, corporations, the money system, war, the aftermath of war, and much more, have thwarted us. Today's world is so crazy that we might feel we have lost that connection to our amazing potential; do we even care anymore that we may not have a future? We need to wake up, we need to care. In doing so, our human spirit will reawaken.

It seems the fate of our exquisite planet which abounds with an infinite diversity of life, is bound together with the fate of the human species. We have more than ourselves to save! I believe we can. We have indeed dug ourselves a hole environmentally, politically, and more; but, our present hole is not a permanent grave for our species – it is up to us.

"The great power of the future" lies in the human psyche. We cannot shape-shift into ETs. We are human. We have a future. Or we don't.

We as a collective planetary people did care in the 1960s when **NASA's** Apollo astronauts trained to go to the moon. Everyone was fascinated, "Would we really set foot the moon?" Incidentally, the astronauts stopped training to watch the latest episode of **Star Trek** each week, as did their mission organizer, Wernher von Braun. This information comes from a close friend who worked for NASA in the 1960s and 1970s.

We as the human species stopped what we were doing all across our planet, and watched as Neil Armstrong and Buzz Aldrin make those giant steps on the moon. The future of our species should be the greatest of our unifiers and our greatest of inspirations.

It is indisputable that we have contact with Future Humans through our DNA and our history. Our descendants, our progeny, our children's, children's children: There is a powerful bridge between us and them; there is consciousness itself!

In this book we have examined the most credible UFO cases which have stood the test of time, from UFO harassment of nuclear missile sites to iconic abduction cases. We have confronted the possibility of artificial intelligence, looked at the direction which physical human evolution is taking, and even offered a possible answer to how traveling back in time is accomplished.

Finally, we have looked at the power of consciousness and its bridge from present to future, grandparent to grandchildren. Can we say there is a definite bridge to any tribe of ET consciousness? Have we assumed UFO occupants are extraterrestrials when the source of UFO occupants should have been analyzed more thoroughly and openly?

Are Future Humans the answer to our UFO puzzle? Only one assumption is necessary; that assumption is that traveling back in time is possible. Anyone want to bet it isn't? It is time for new thinking.

***

FURTHER READING FROM FLYING DISK PRESS
www.flyingdiskpress.com

Made in the USA
Monee, IL
09 May 2020